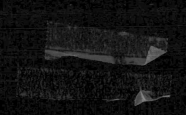

Green Lantern

RAGE OF THE RED LANTERNS

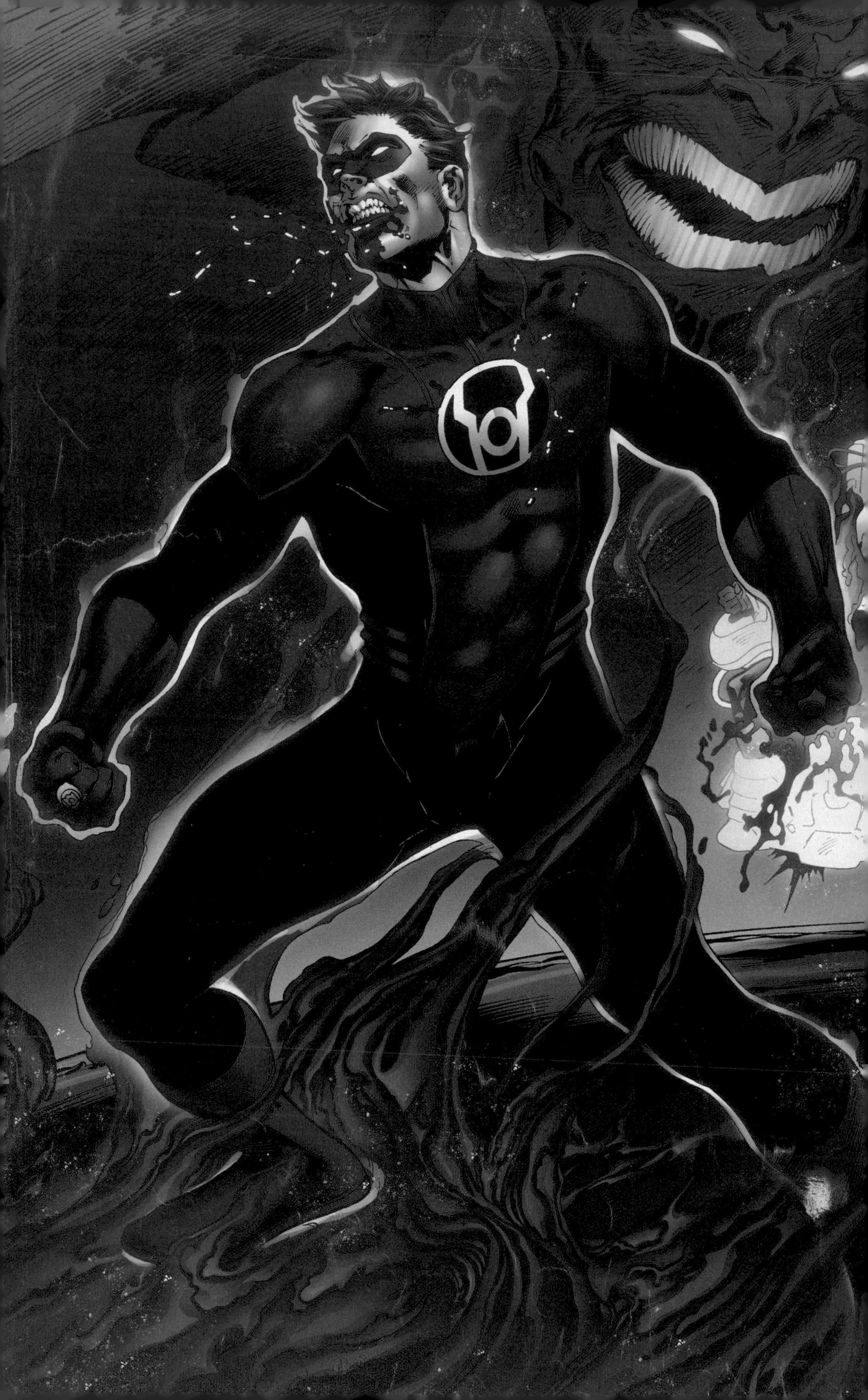

RAGE OF THE RED LANTERNS

Geoff Johns
Writer

Mike McKone   **Shane Davis**   **Ivan Reis**
Pencillers

Andy Lanning   **Marlo Alquiza**   **Cam Smith**
Mark Farmer   **Norm Rapmund**   **Sandra Hope**
Oclair Albert   **Julio Ferreira**
Inkers

JD Smith   **Nei Ruffino**
Colors

Rob Leigh   **Steve Wands**
Letters

DC COMICS

Dan DiDio Senior VP-Executive Editor
Eddie Berganza Editor-original series
Adam Schlagman Associate Editor-original series
Sean Mackiewicz Editor-collected edition
Robbin Brosterman Senior Art Director
Paul Levitz President & Publisher
Georg Brewer VP-Design & DC Direct Creative
Richard Bruning Senior VP-Creative Director
Patrick Caldon Executive VP-Finance & Operations
Chris Caramalis VP-Finance
John Cunningham VP-Marketing
Terri Cunningham VP-Managing Editor
Amy Genkins Senior VP-Business & Legal Affairs
Alison Gill VP-Manufacturing
David Hyde VP-Publicity
Hank Kanalz VP-General Manager, WildStorm
Jim Lee Editorial Director-WildStorm
Gregory Noveck Senior VP-Creative Affairs
Sue Pohja VP-Book Trade Sales
Steve Rotterdam Senior VP-Sales & Marketing
Cheryl Rubin Senior VP-Brand Management
Alysse Soll VP-Advertising & Custom Publishing
Jeff Trojan VP-Business Development, DC Direct
Bob Wayne VP-Sales

Cover by Shane Davis, Sandra Hope and Nei Ruffino

**GREEN LANTERN: RAGE OF THE
RED LANTERNS**

Published by DC Comics. Cover, text and compilation
Copyright © 2009 DC Comics. All Rights Reserved.

Originally published in single magazine form in
GREEN LANTERN 26-28, 36-38, FINAL CRISIS:
RAGE OF THE RED LANTERNS 1. Copyright © 2008,
2009 DC Comics. All Rights Reserved. All characters,
their distinctive likenesses and related elements featured
in this publication are trademarks of DC Comics.
The stories, characters and incidents featured in this
publication are entirely fictional. DC Comics does not
read or accept unsolicited submissions of ideas,
stories or artwork.

DC Comics, 1700 Broadway, New York, NY 10019
A Warner Bros. Entertainment Company
Printed in the USA. First Printing.

ISBN: 978-1-4012-2301-4
SC ISBN: 978-1-4012-2302-1

GREEN LANTERN 26 Cover by Mike McKone, Andy Lanning and Moose Baumann

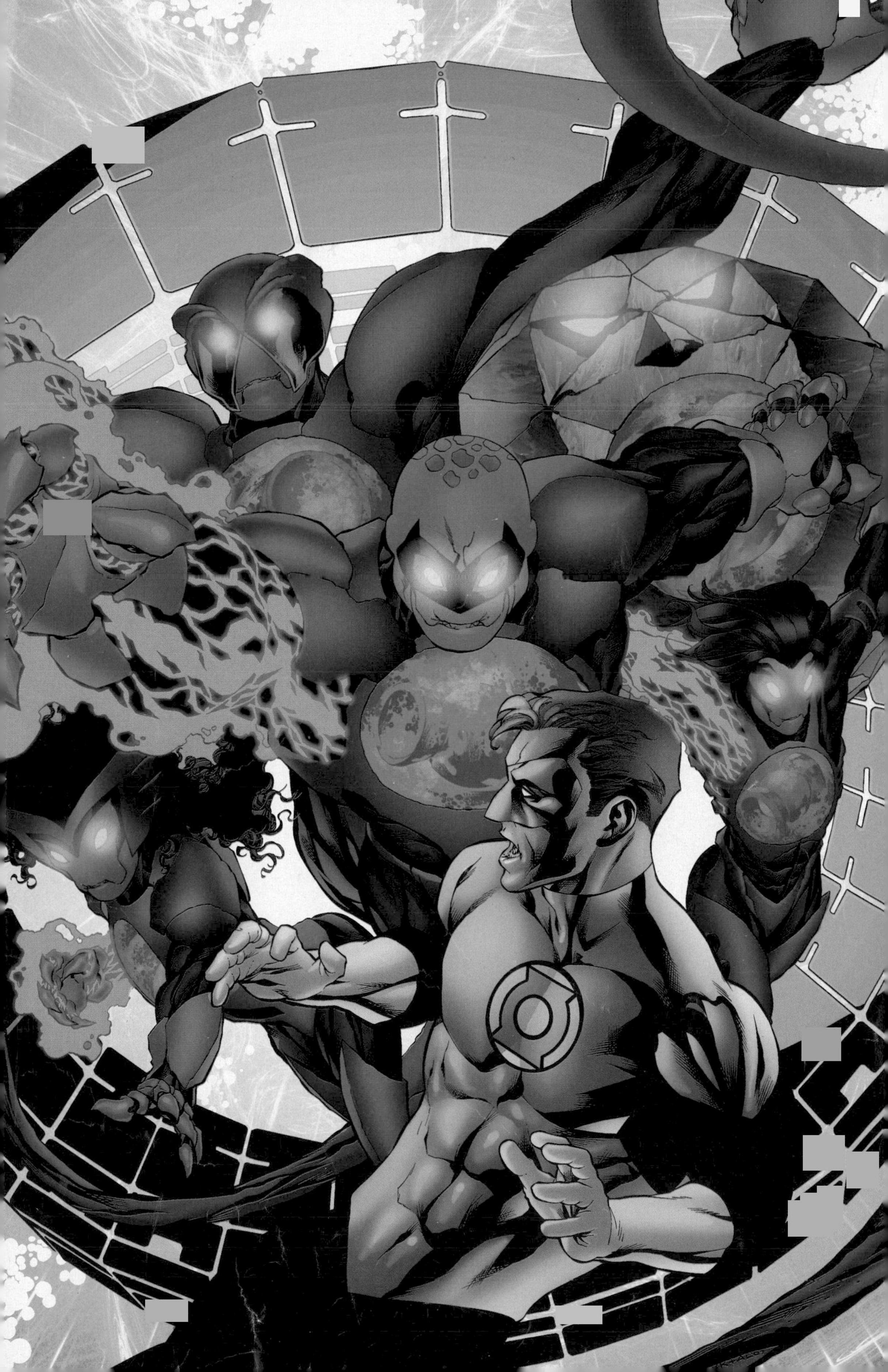

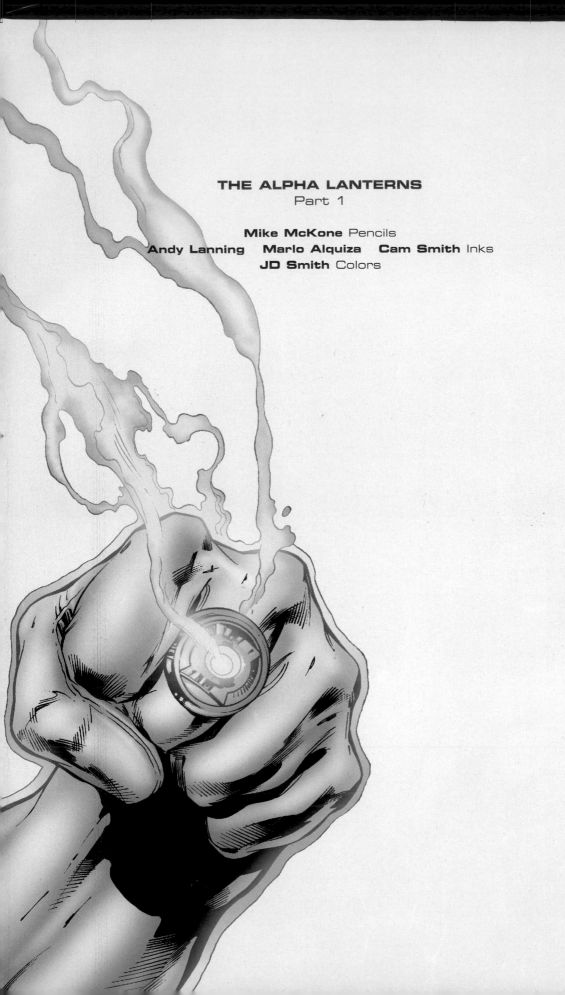

THE ALPHA LANTERNS
Part 1

Mike McKone Pencils
Andy Lanning   **Marlo Alquiza**   **Cam Smith** Inks
JD Smith Colors

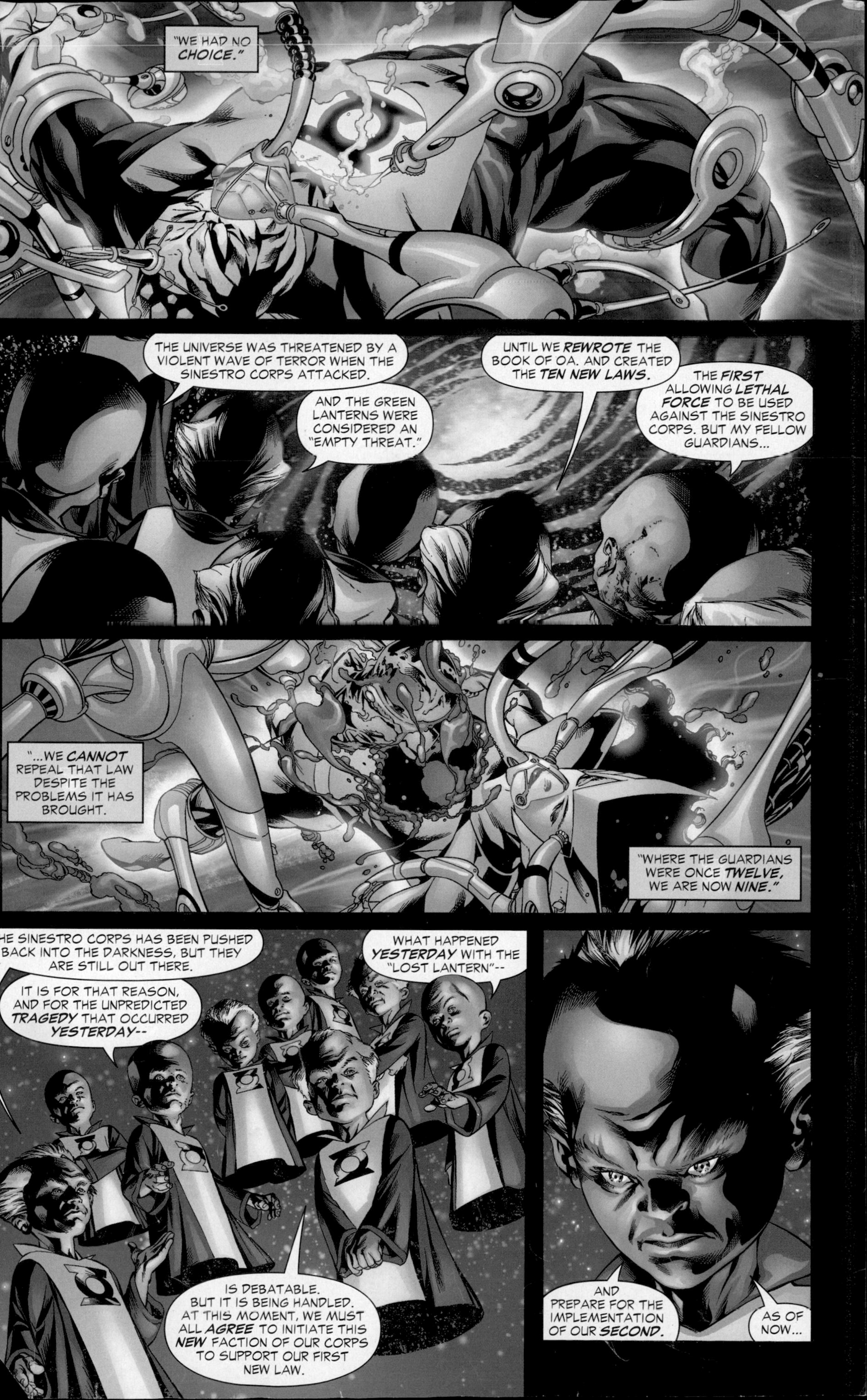
"WE HAD NO CHOICE."
THE UNIVERSE WAS THREATENED BY A VIOLENT WAVE OF TERROR WHEN THE SINESTRO CORPS ATTACKED.
AND THE GREEN LANTERNS WERE CONSIDERED AN "EMPTY THREAT."
UNTIL WE REWROTE THE BOOK OF OA. AND CREATED THE TEN NEW LAWS.
THE FIRST ALLOWING LETHAL FORCE TO BE USED AGAINST THE SINESTRO CORPS. BUT MY FELLOW GUARDIANS...
"...WE CANNOT REPEAL THAT LAW DESPITE THE PROBLEMS IT HAS BROUGHT.
"WHERE THE GUARDIANS WERE ONCE TWELVE, WE ARE NOW NINE."
HE SINESTRO CORPS HAS BEEN PUSHED BACK INTO THE DARKNESS, BUT THEY ARE STILL OUT THERE.
IT IS FOR THAT REASON, AND FOR THE UNPREDICTED TRAGEDY THAT OCCURRED YESTERDAY--
WHAT HAPPENED YESTERDAY WITH THE "LOST LANTERN"--
IS DEBATABLE. BUT IT IS BEING HANDLED. AT THIS MOMENT, WE MUST ALL AGREE TO INITIATE THIS NEW FACTION OF OUR CORPS TO SUPPORT OUR FIRST NEW LAW.
AND PREPARE FOR THE IMPLEMENTATION OF OUR SECOND.
AS OF NOW...

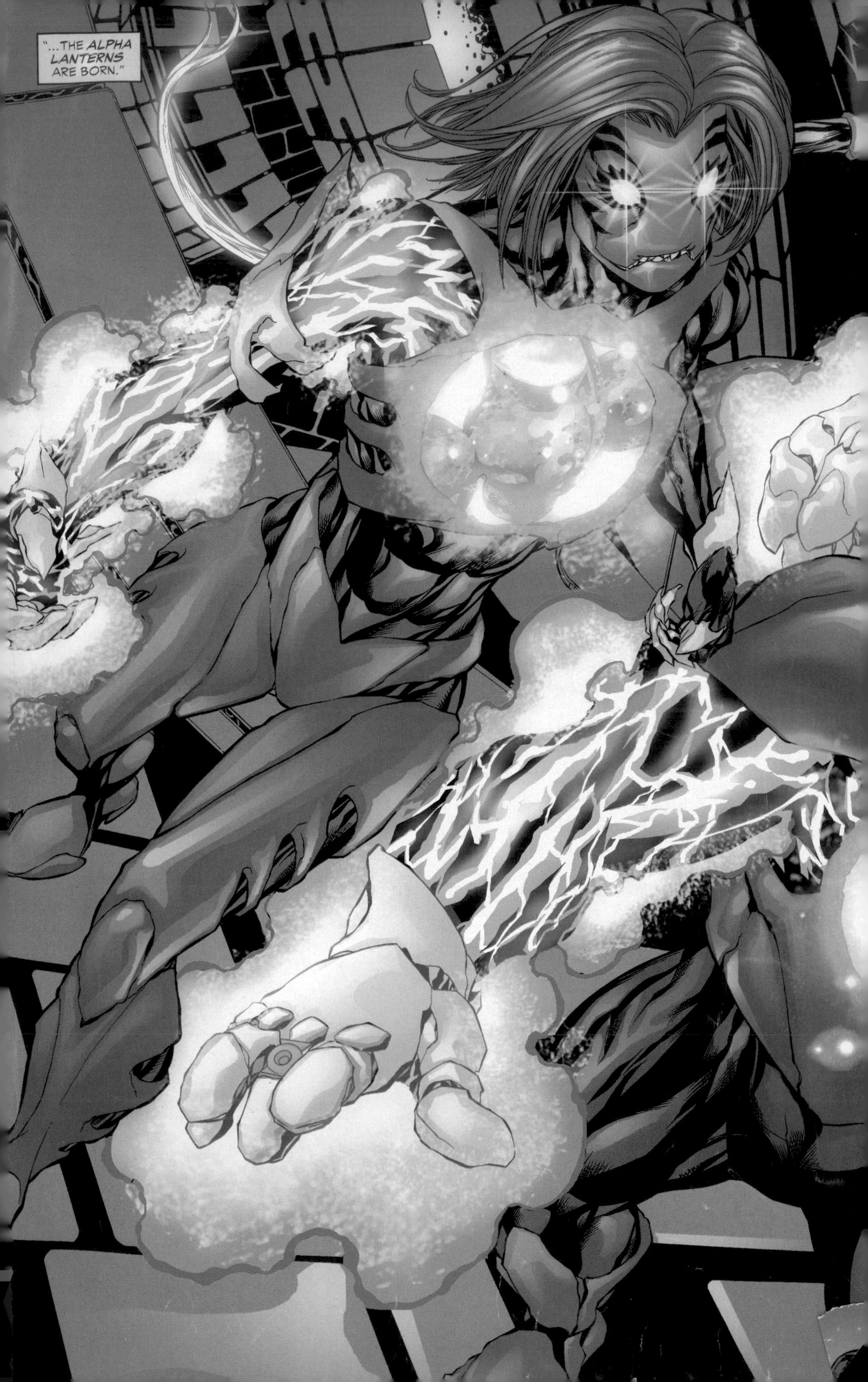
"...THE *ALPHA LANTERNS* ARE BORN."

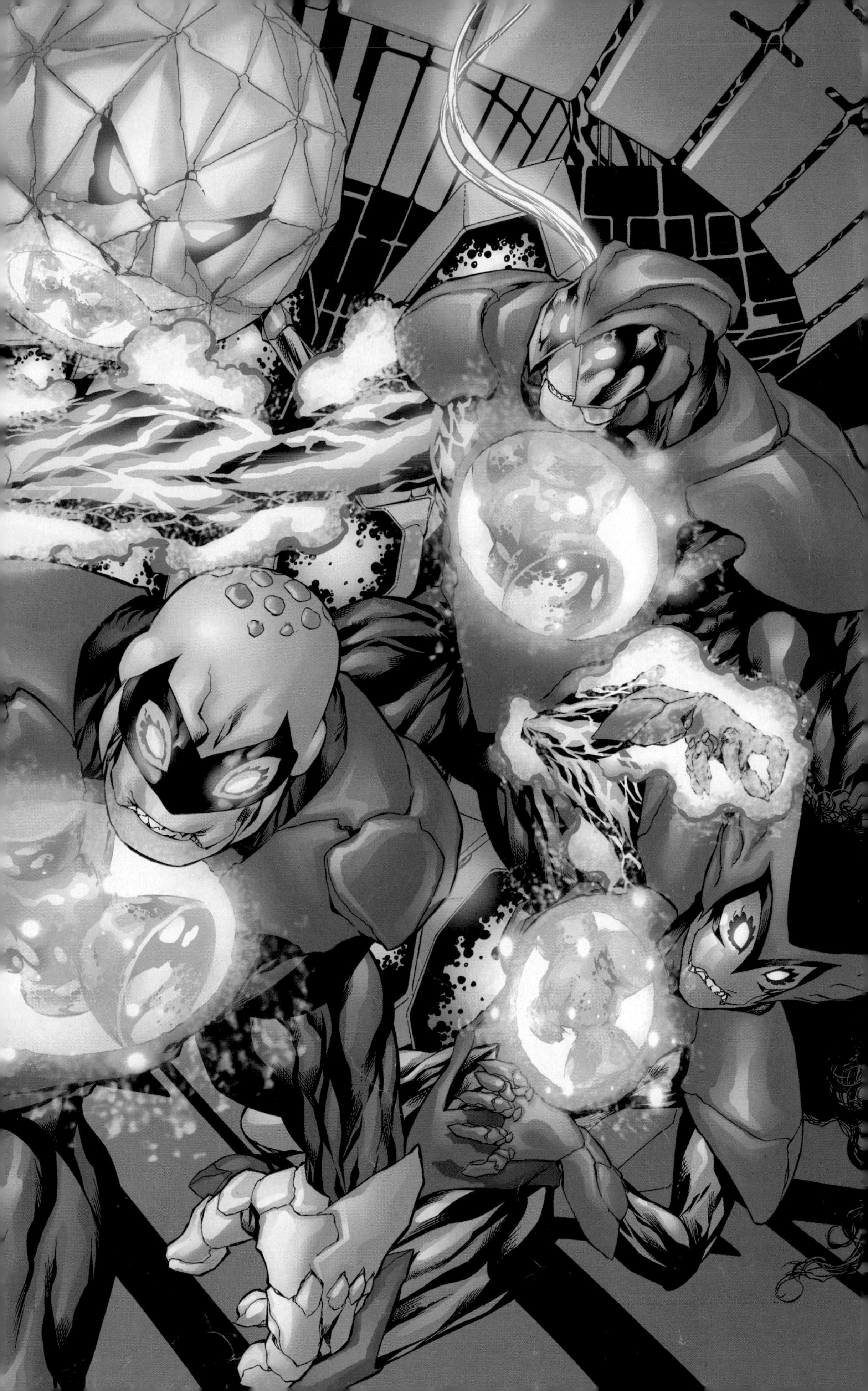

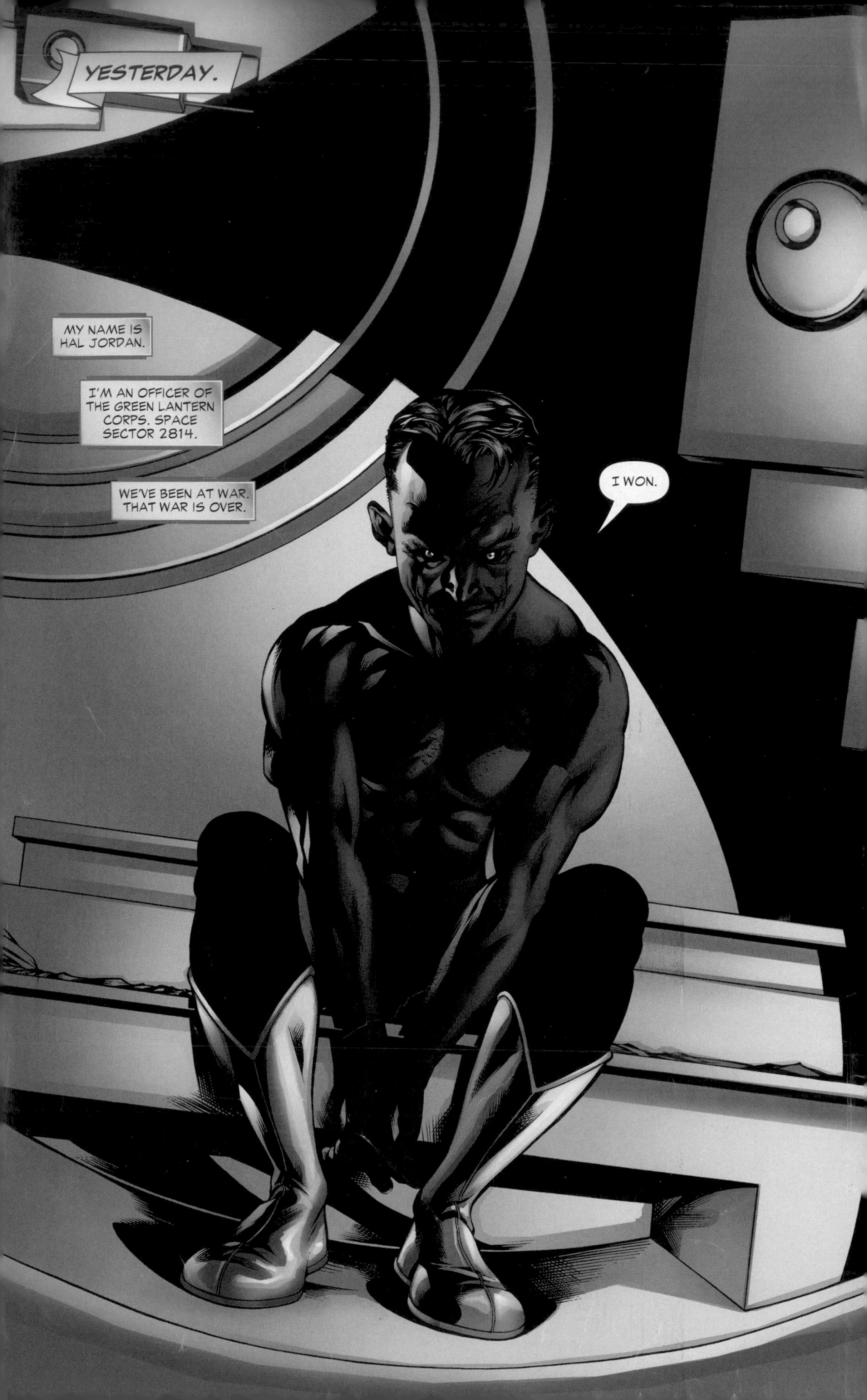
YESTERDAY.
MY NAME IS HAL JORDAN.
I'M AN OFFICER OF THE GREEN LANTERN CORPS. SPACE SECTOR 2814.
WE'VE BEEN AT WAR. THAT WAR IS OVER.
I WON.

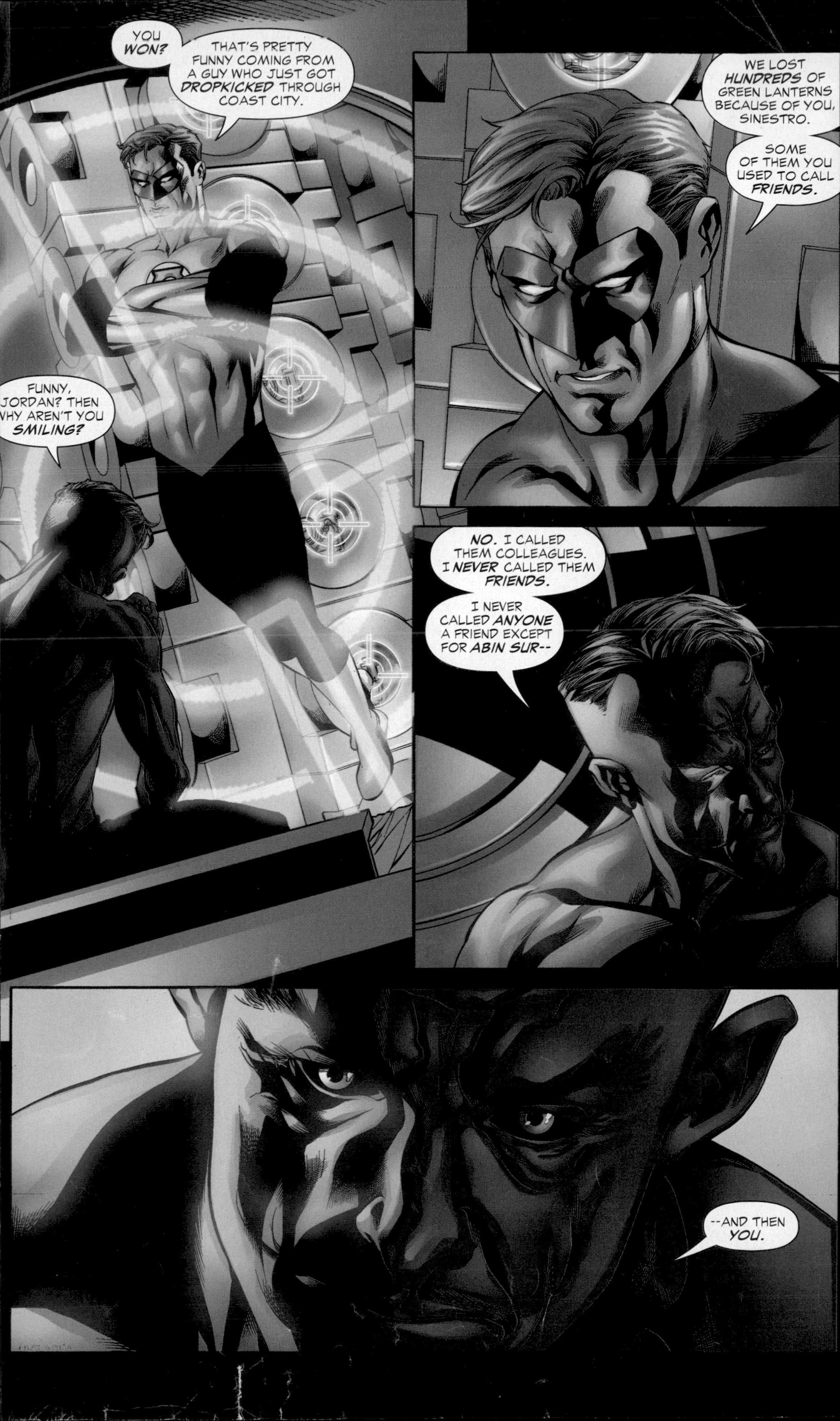
YOU WON?
THAT'S PRETTY FUNNY COMING FROM A GUY WHO JUST GOT DROPKICKED THROUGH COAST CITY.
FUNNY, JORDAN? THEN WHY AREN'T YOU SMILING?
WE LOST HUNDREDS OF GREEN LANTERNS BECAUSE OF YOU, SINESTRO.
SOME OF THEM YOU USED TO CALL FRIENDS.
NO. I CALLED THEM COLLEAGUES. I NEVER CALLED THEM FRIENDS.
I NEVER CALLED ANYONE A FRIEND EXCEPT FOR ABIN SUR--
--AND THEN YOU.

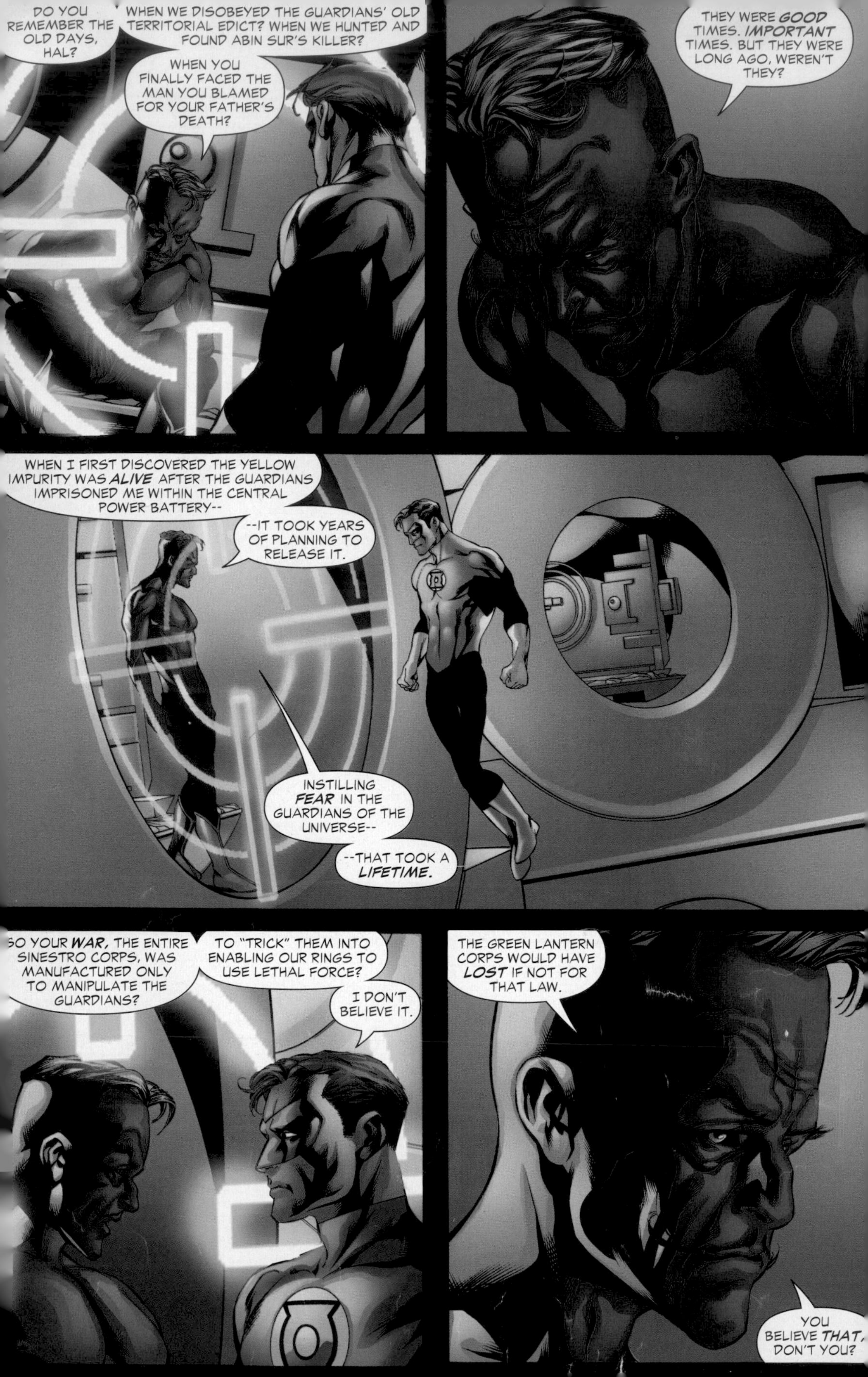
DO YOU REMEMBER THE OLD DAYS, HAL?
WHEN WE DISOBEYED THE GUARDIANS' OLD TERRITORIAL EDICT? WHEN WE HUNTED AND FOUND ABIN SUR'S KILLER?
WHEN YOU FINALLY FACED THE MAN YOU BLAMED FOR YOUR FATHER'S DEATH?
THEY WERE **GOOD** TIMES. **IMPORTANT** TIMES. BUT THEY WERE LONG AGO, WEREN'T THEY?
WHEN I FIRST DISCOVERED THE YELLOW IMPURITY WAS **ALIVE** AFTER THE GUARDIANS IMPRISONED ME WITHIN THE CENTRAL POWER BATTERY--
--IT TOOK YEARS OF PLANNING TO RELEASE IT.
INSTILLING **FEAR** IN THE GUARDIANS OF THE UNIVERSE--
--THAT TOOK A **LIFETIME.**
SO YOUR **WAR,** THE ENTIRE SINESTRO CORPS, WAS MANUFACTURED ONLY TO MANIPULATE THE GUARDIANS?
TO "TRICK" THEM INTO ENABLING OUR RINGS TO USE LETHAL FORCE?
I DON'T BELIEVE IT.
THE GREEN LANTERN CORPS WOULD HAVE **LOST** IF NOT FOR THAT LAW.
YOU BELIEVE **THAT,** DON'T YOU?

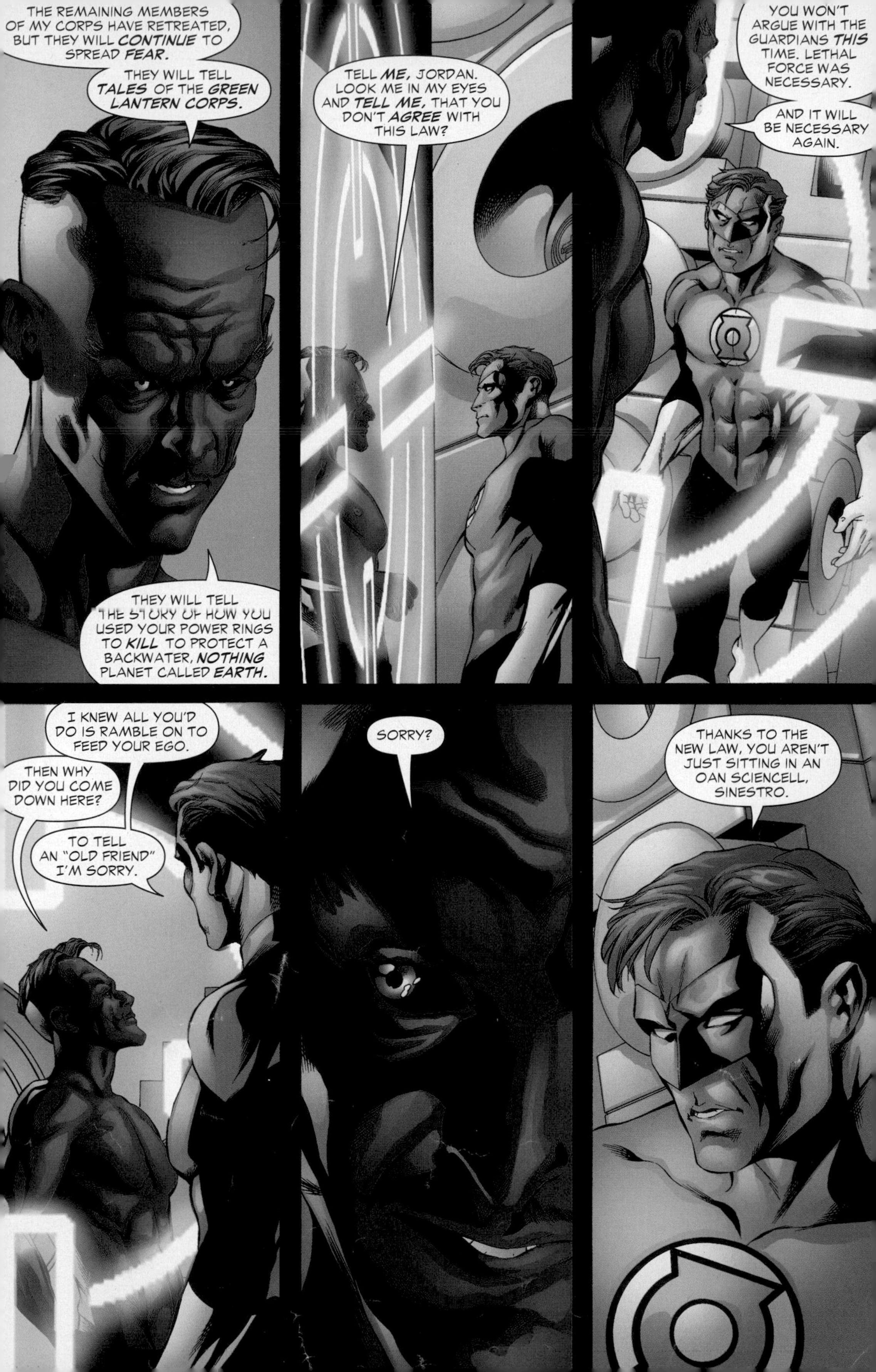
THE REMAINING MEMBERS OF MY CORPS HAVE RETREATED, BUT THEY WILL CONTINUE TO SPREAD FEAR.
THEY WILL TELL TALES OF THE GREEN LANTERN CORPS.
THEY WILL TELL THE STORY OF HOW YOU USED YOUR POWER RINGS TO KILL TO PROTECT A BACKWATER, NOTHING PLANET CALLED EARTH.
TELL ME, JORDAN. LOOK ME IN MY EYES AND TELL ME, THAT YOU DON'T AGREE WITH THIS LAW?
YOU WON'T ARGUE WITH THE GUARDIANS THIS TIME. LETHAL FORCE WAS NECESSARY.
AND IT WILL BE NECESSARY AGAIN.
I KNEW ALL YOU'D DO IS RAMBLE ON TO FEED YOUR EGO.
THEN WHY DID YOU COME DOWN HERE?
TO TELL AN "OLD FRIEND" I'M SORRY.
SORRY?
THANKS TO THE NEW LAW, YOU AREN'T JUST SITTING IN AN OAN SCIENCELL, SINESTRO.

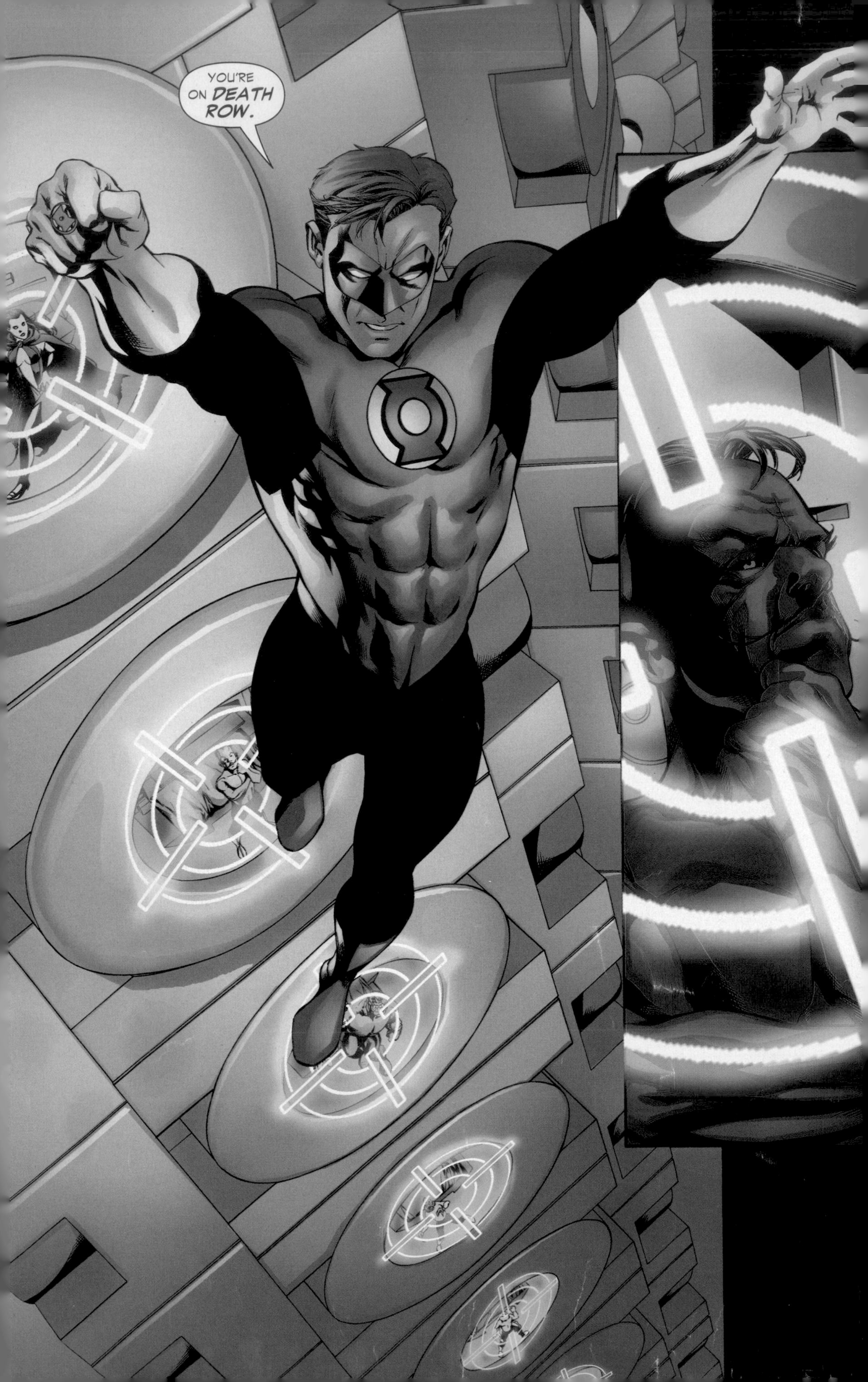
YOU'RE ON DEATH ROW.

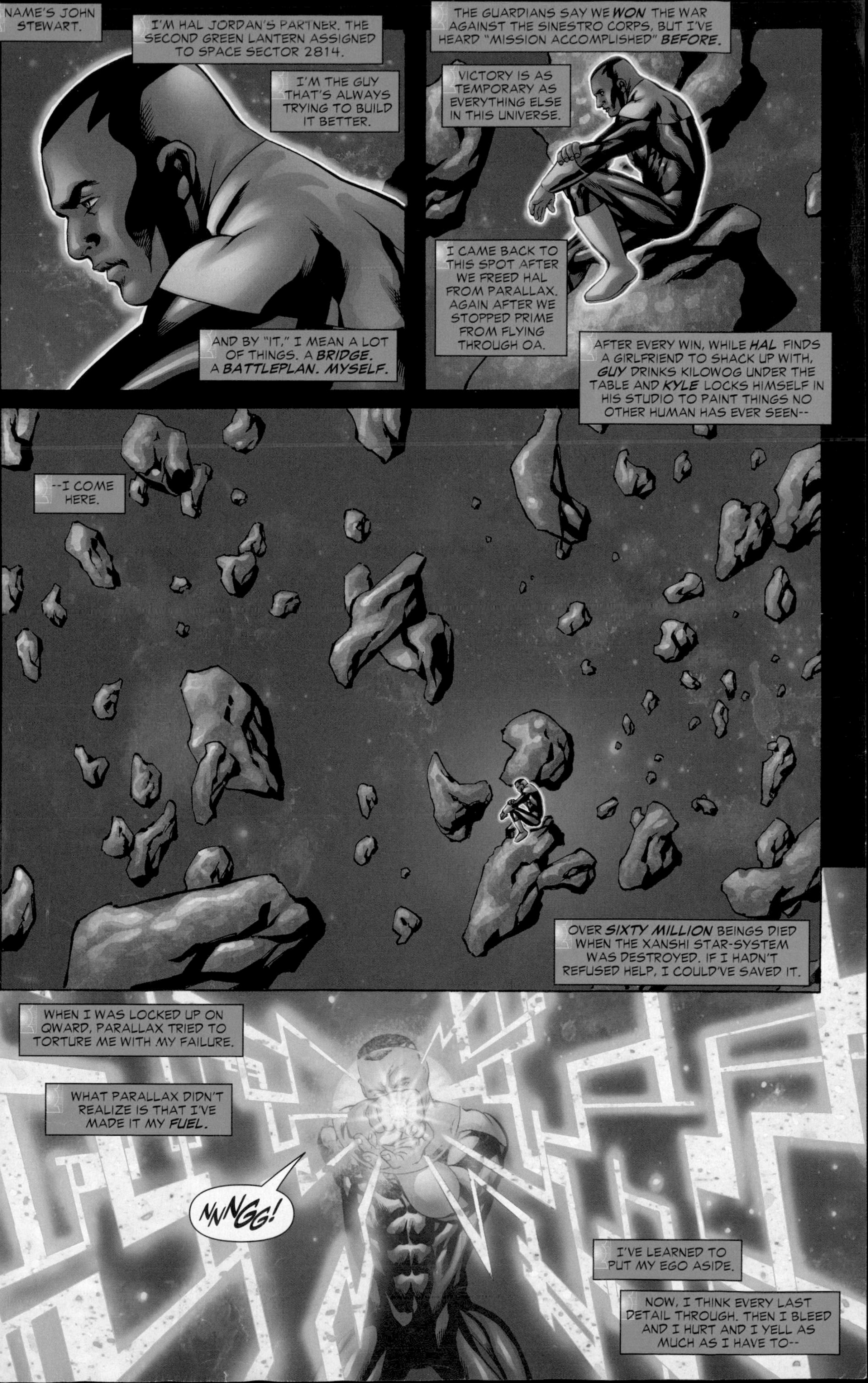
NAME'S JOHN STEWART.
I'M HAL JORDAN'S PARTNER. THE SECOND GREEN LANTERN ASSIGNED TO SPACE SECTOR 2814.
I'M THE GUY THAT'S ALWAYS TRYING TO BUILD IT BETTER.
AND BY "IT," I MEAN A LOT OF THINGS. A BRIDGE. A BATTLEPLAN. MYSELF.
THE GUARDIANS SAY WE WON THE WAR AGAINST THE SINESTRO CORPS, BUT I'VE HEARD "MISSION ACCOMPLISHED" BEFORE.
VICTORY IS AS TEMPORARY AS EVERYTHING ELSE IN THIS UNIVERSE.
I CAME BACK TO THIS SPOT AFTER WE FREED HAL FROM PARALLAX. AGAIN AFTER WE STOPPED PRIME FROM FLYING THROUGH OA.
AFTER EVERY WIN, WHILE HAL FINDS A GIRLFRIEND TO SHACK UP WITH, GUY DRINKS KILOWOG UNDER THE TABLE AND KYLE LOCKS HIMSELF IN HIS STUDIO TO PAINT THINGS NO OTHER HUMAN HAS EVER SEEN--
--I COME HERE.
OVER SIXTY MILLION BEINGS DIED WHEN THE XANSHI STAR-SYSTEM WAS DESTROYED. IF I HADN'T REFUSED HELP, I COULD'VE SAVED IT.
WHEN I WAS LOCKED UP ON QWARD, PARALLAX TRIED TO TORTURE ME WITH MY FAILURE.
WHAT PARALLAX DIDN'T REALIZE IS THAT I'VE MADE IT MY FUEL.
NNNGG!
I'VE LEARNED TO PUT MY EGO ASIDE.
NOW, I THINK EVERY LAST DETAIL THROUGH. THEN I BLEED AND I HURT AND I YELL AS MUCH AS I HAVE TO--

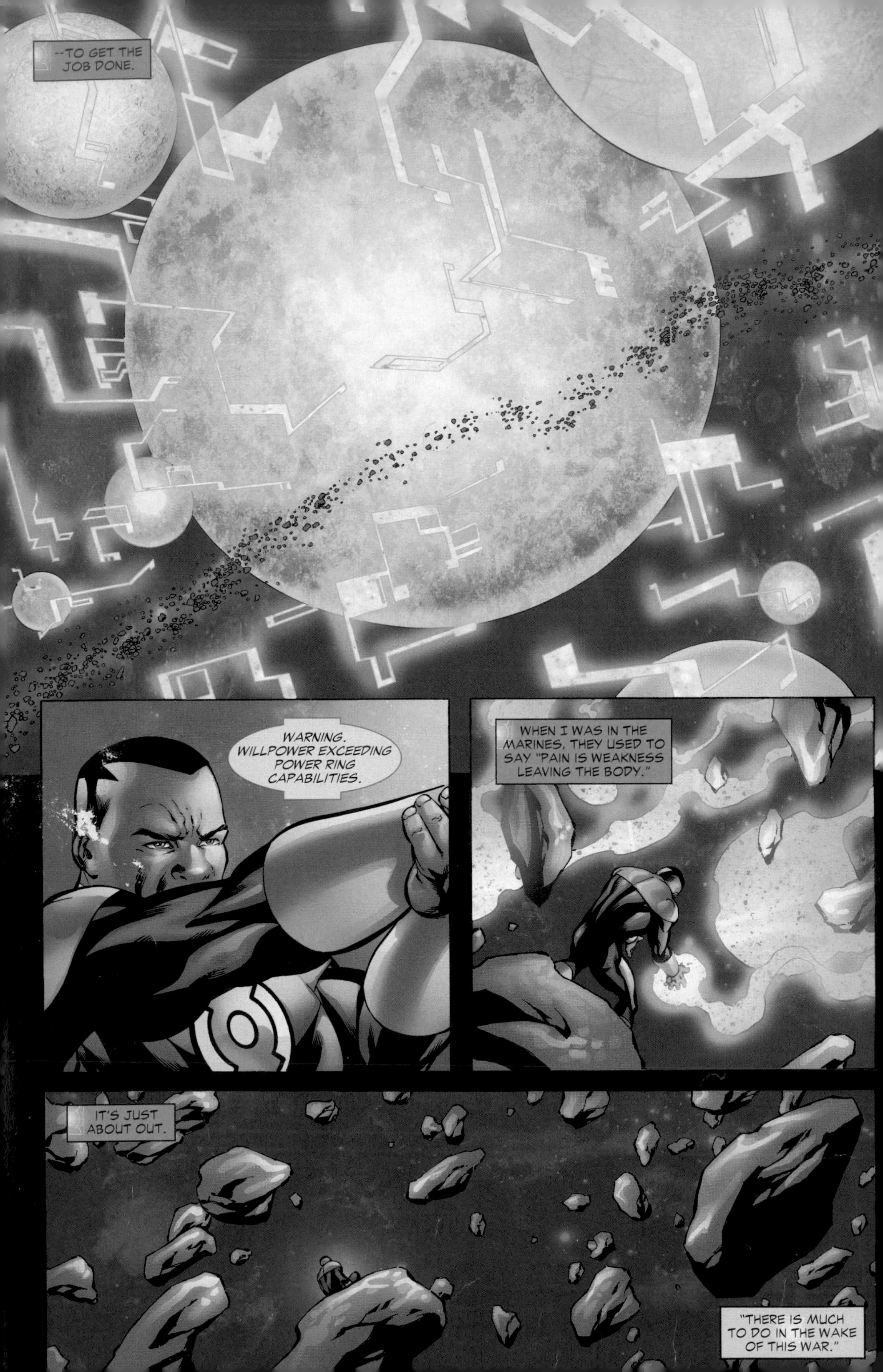
--TO GET THE JOB DONE.
WARNING. WILLPOWER EXCEEDING POWER RING CAPABILITIES.
WHEN I WAS IN THE MARINES, THEY USED TO SAY "PAIN IS WEAKNESS LEAVING THE BODY."
IT'S JUST ABOUT OUT.
"THERE IS MUCH TO DO IN THE WAKE OF THIS WAR."

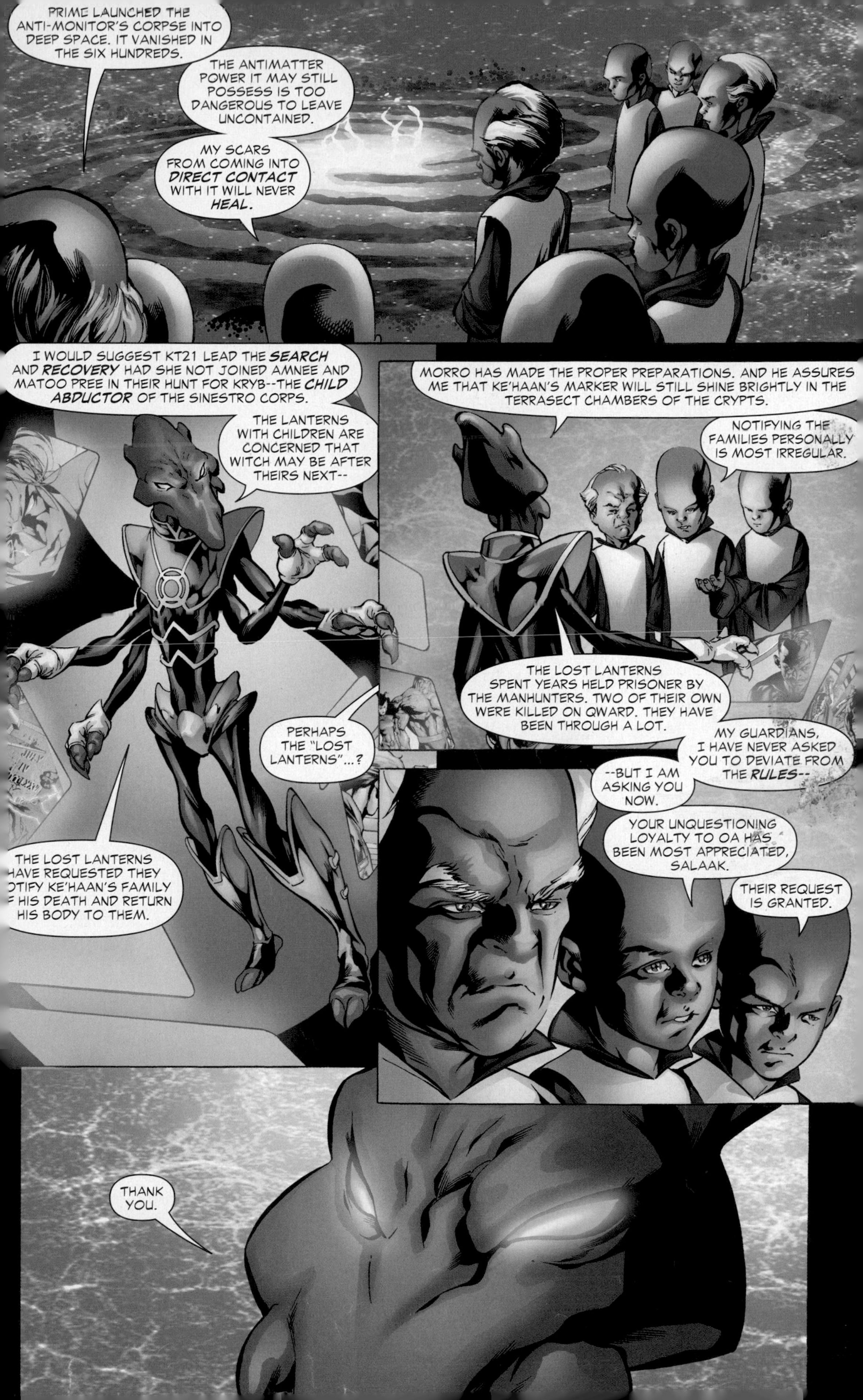
PRIME LAUNCHED THE ANTI-MONITOR'S CORPSE INTO DEEP SPACE. IT VANISHED IN THE SIX HUNDREDS.
THE ANTIMATTER POWER IT MAY STILL POSSESS IS TOO DANGEROUS TO LEAVE UNCONTAINED.
MY SCARS FROM COMING INTO DIRECT CONTACT WITH IT WILL NEVER HEAL.
I WOULD SUGGEST KT21 LEAD THE SEARCH AND RECOVERY HAD SHE NOT JOINED AMNEE AND MATOO PREE IN THEIR HUNT FOR KRYB--THE CHILD ABDUCTOR OF THE SINESTRO CORPS.
THE LANTERNS WITH CHILDREN ARE CONCERNED THAT WITCH MAY BE AFTER THEIRS NEXT--
PERHAPS THE "LOST LANTERNS"...?
THE LOST LANTERNS HAVE REQUESTED THEY NOTIFY KE'HAAN'S FAMILY OF HIS DEATH AND RETURN HIS BODY TO THEM.
MORRO HAS MADE THE PROPER PREPARATIONS. AND HE ASSURES ME THAT KE'HAAN'S MARKER WILL STILL SHINE BRIGHTLY IN THE TERRASECT CHAMBERS OF THE CRYPTS.
NOTIFYING THE FAMILIES PERSONALLY IS MOST IRREGULAR.
THE LOST LANTERNS SPENT YEARS HELD PRISONER BY THE MANHUNTERS. TWO OF THEIR OWN WERE KILLED ON QWARD. THEY HAVE BEEN THROUGH A LOT.
MY GUARDIANS, I HAVE NEVER ASKED YOU TO DEVIATE FROM THE RULES--
--BUT I AM ASKING YOU NOW.
YOUR UNQUESTIONING LOYALTY TO OA HAS BEEN MOST APPRECIATED, SALAAK.
THEIR REQUEST IS GRANTED.
THANK YOU.

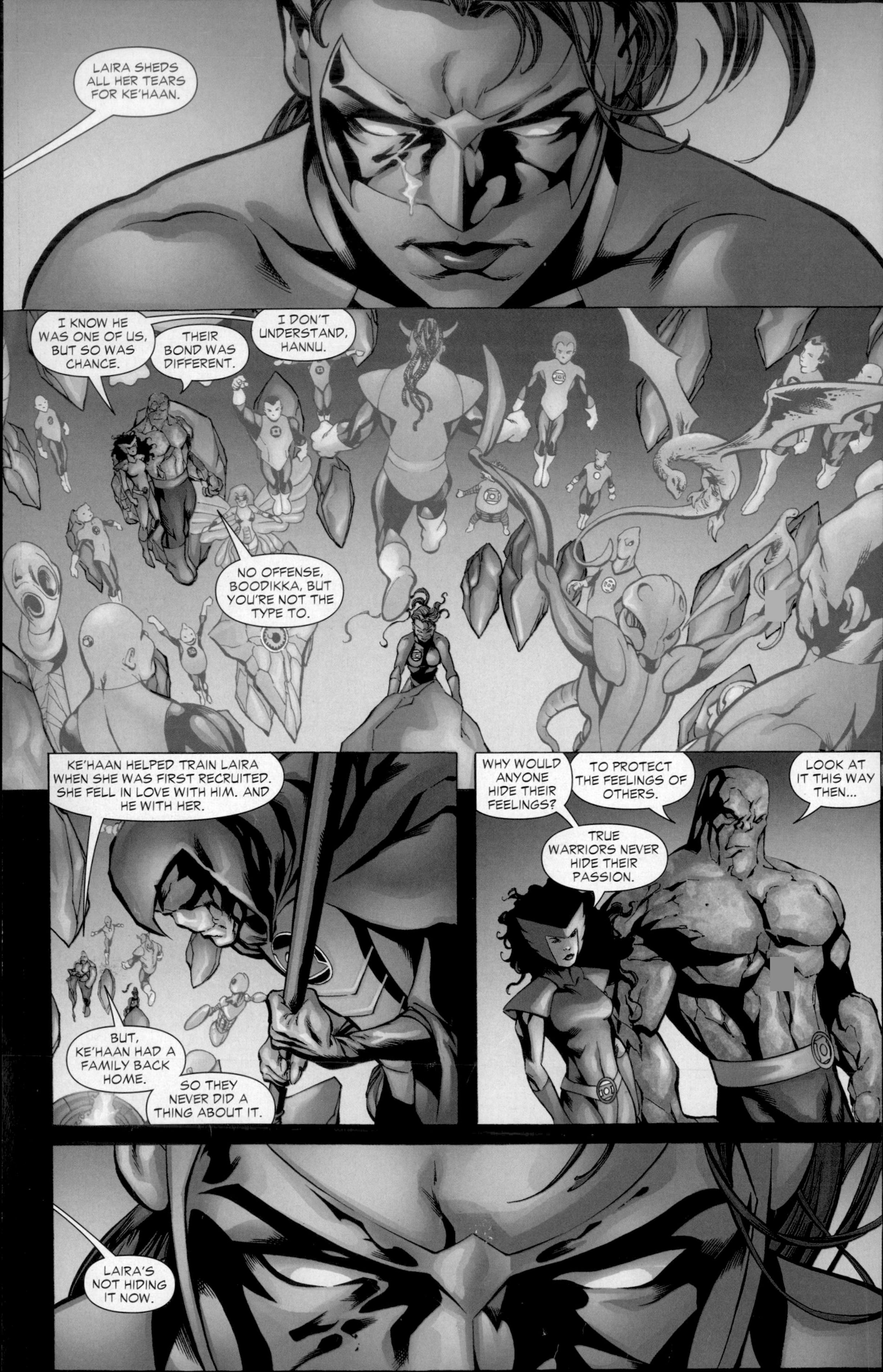
LAIRA SHEDS ALL HER TEARS FOR KE'HAAN.
I KNOW HE WAS ONE OF US, BUT SO WAS CHANCE.
THEIR BOND WAS DIFFERENT.
I DON'T UNDERSTAND, HANNU.
NO OFFENSE, BOODIKKA, BUT YOU'RE NOT THE TYPE TO.
KE'HAAN HELPED TRAIN LAIRA WHEN SHE WAS FIRST RECRUITED. SHE FELL IN LOVE WITH HIM. AND HE WITH HER.
BUT, KE'HAAN HAD A FAMILY BACK HOME.
SO THEY NEVER DID A THING ABOUT IT.
WHY WOULD ANYONE HIDE THEIR FEELINGS?
TO PROTECT THE FEELINGS OF OTHERS.
TRUE WARRIORS NEVER HIDE THEIR PASSION.
LOOK AT IT THIS WAY THEN...
LAIRA'S NOT HIDING IT NOW.

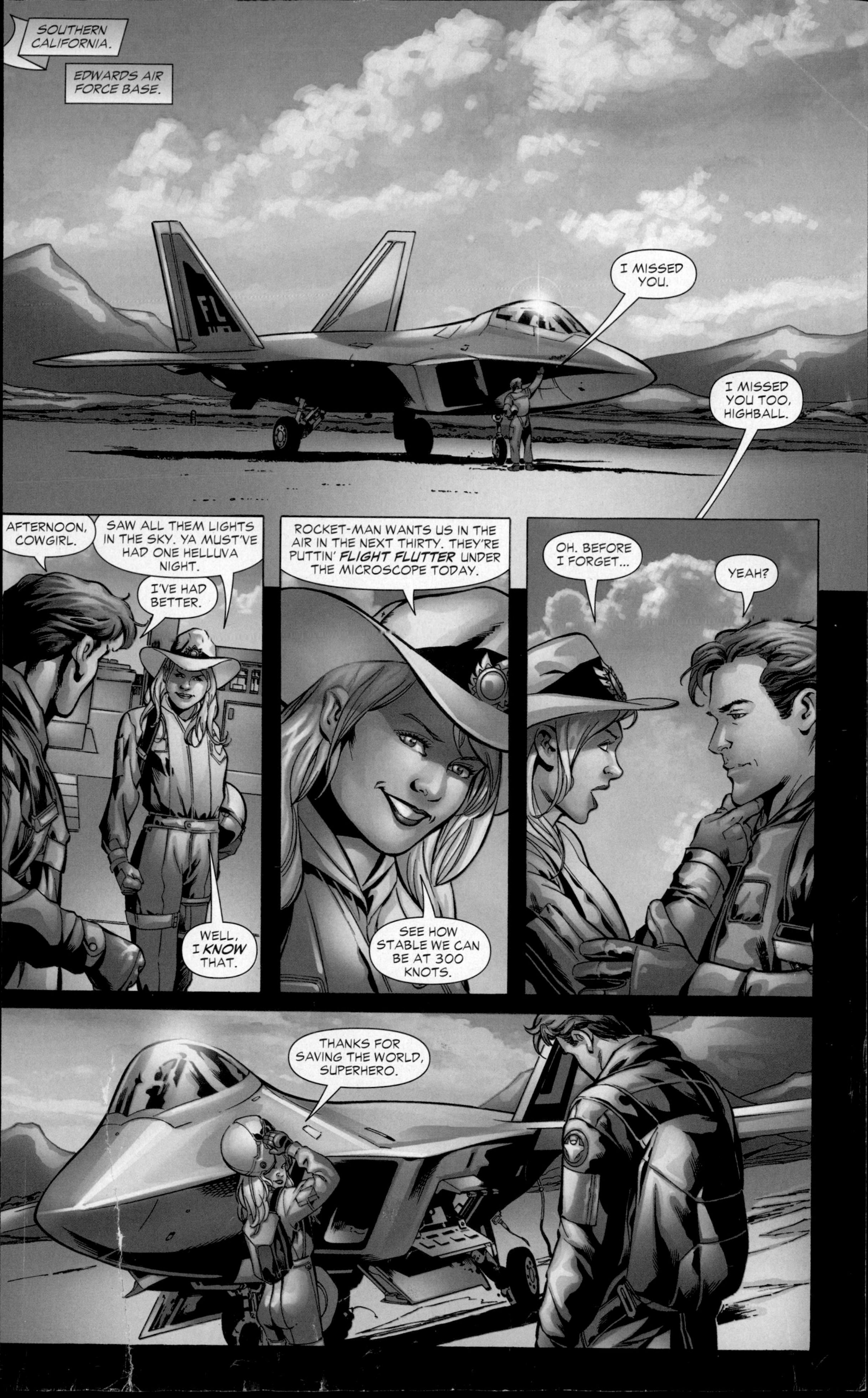
SOUTHERN CALIFORNIA.
EDWARDS AIR FORCE BASE.
I MISSED YOU.
I MISSED YOU TOO, HIGHBALL.
AFTERNOON, COWGIRL.
SAW ALL THEM LIGHTS IN THE SKY. YA MUST'VE HAD ONE HELLUVA NIGHT.
I'VE HAD BETTER.
WELL, I KNOW THAT.
ROCKET-MAN WANTS US IN THE AIR IN THE NEXT THIRTY. THEY'RE PUTTIN' FLIGHT FLUTTER UNDER THE MICROSCOPE TODAY.
SEE HOW STABLE WE CAN BE AT 300 KNOTS.
OH. BEFORE I FORGET...
YEAH?
THANKS FOR SAVING THE WORLD, SUPERHERO.

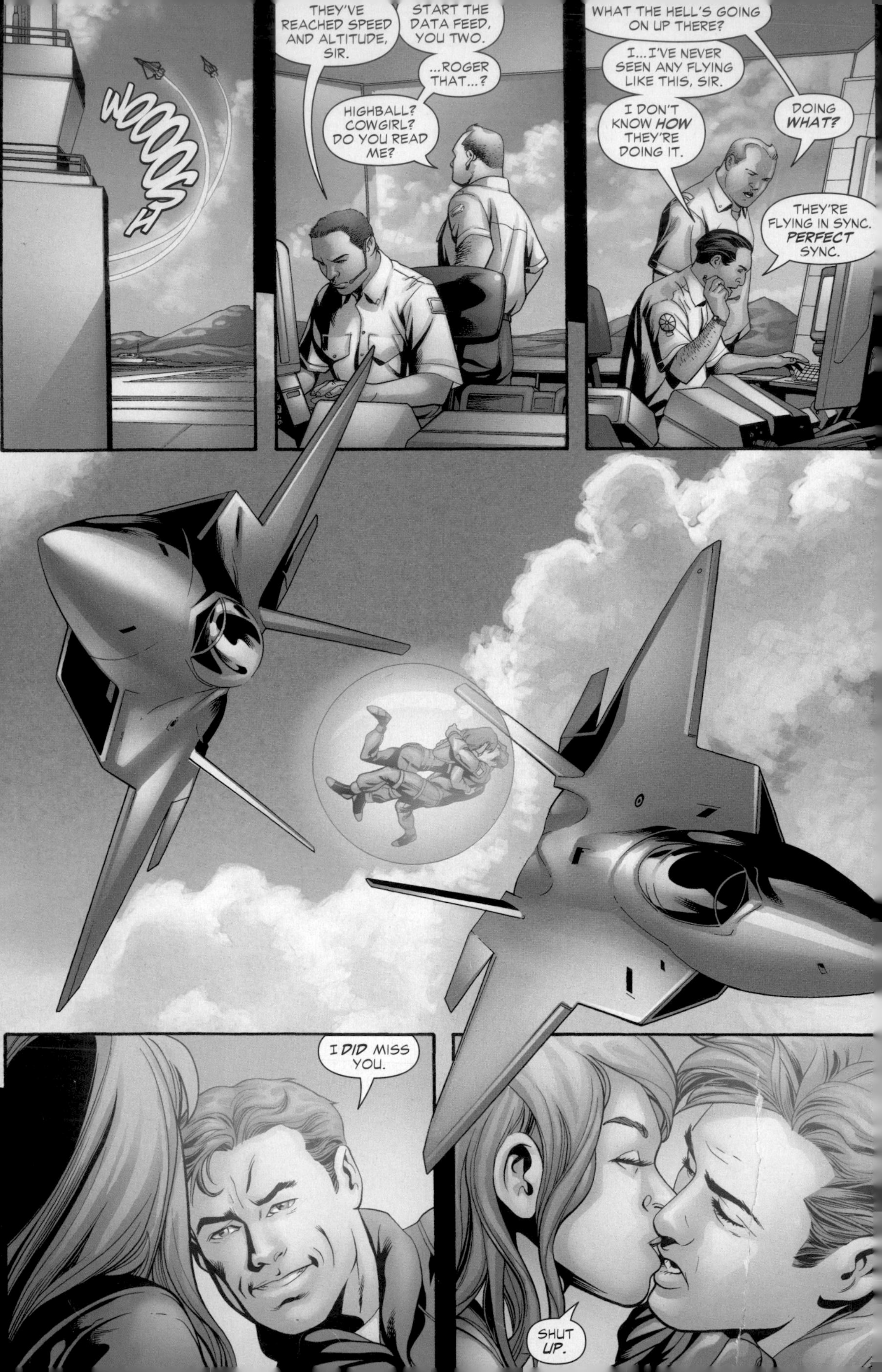
WOOOOSH
THEY'VE REACHED SPEED AND ALTITUDE, SIR.
START THE DATA FEED, YOU TWO.
...ROGER THAT...?
HIGHBALL? COWGIRL? DO YOU READ ME?
WHAT THE HELL'S GOING ON UP THERE?
I...I'VE NEVER SEEN ANY FLYING LIKE THIS, SIR.
DOING WHAT?
I DON'T KNOW HOW THEY'RE DOING IT.
THEY'RE FLYING IN SYNC. PERFECT SYNC.
I DID MISS YOU.
SHUT UP.

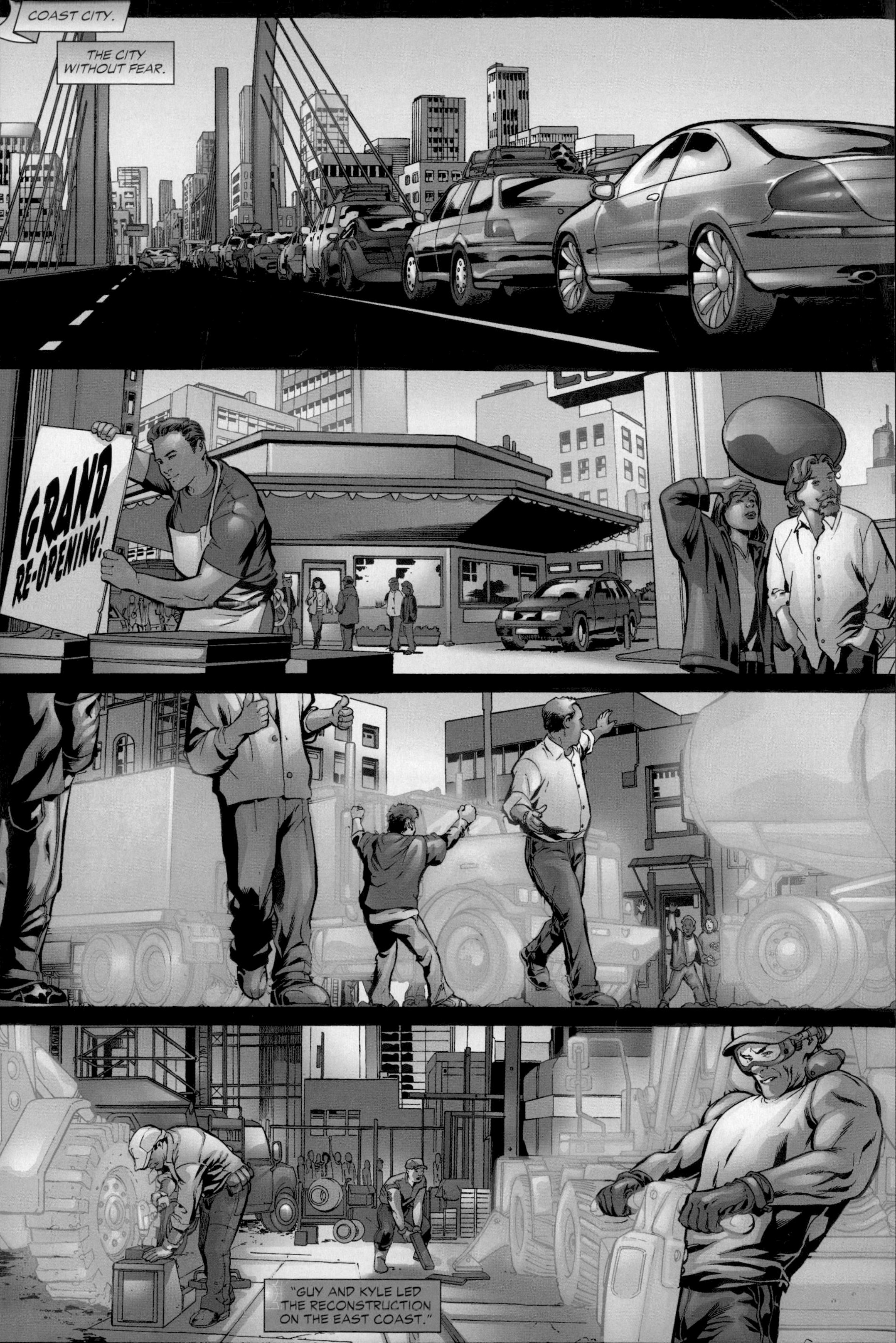
COAST CITY.
THE CITY WITHOUT FEAR.
GRAND RE-OPENING!
"GUY AND KYLE LED THE RECONSTRUCTION ON THE EAST COAST."

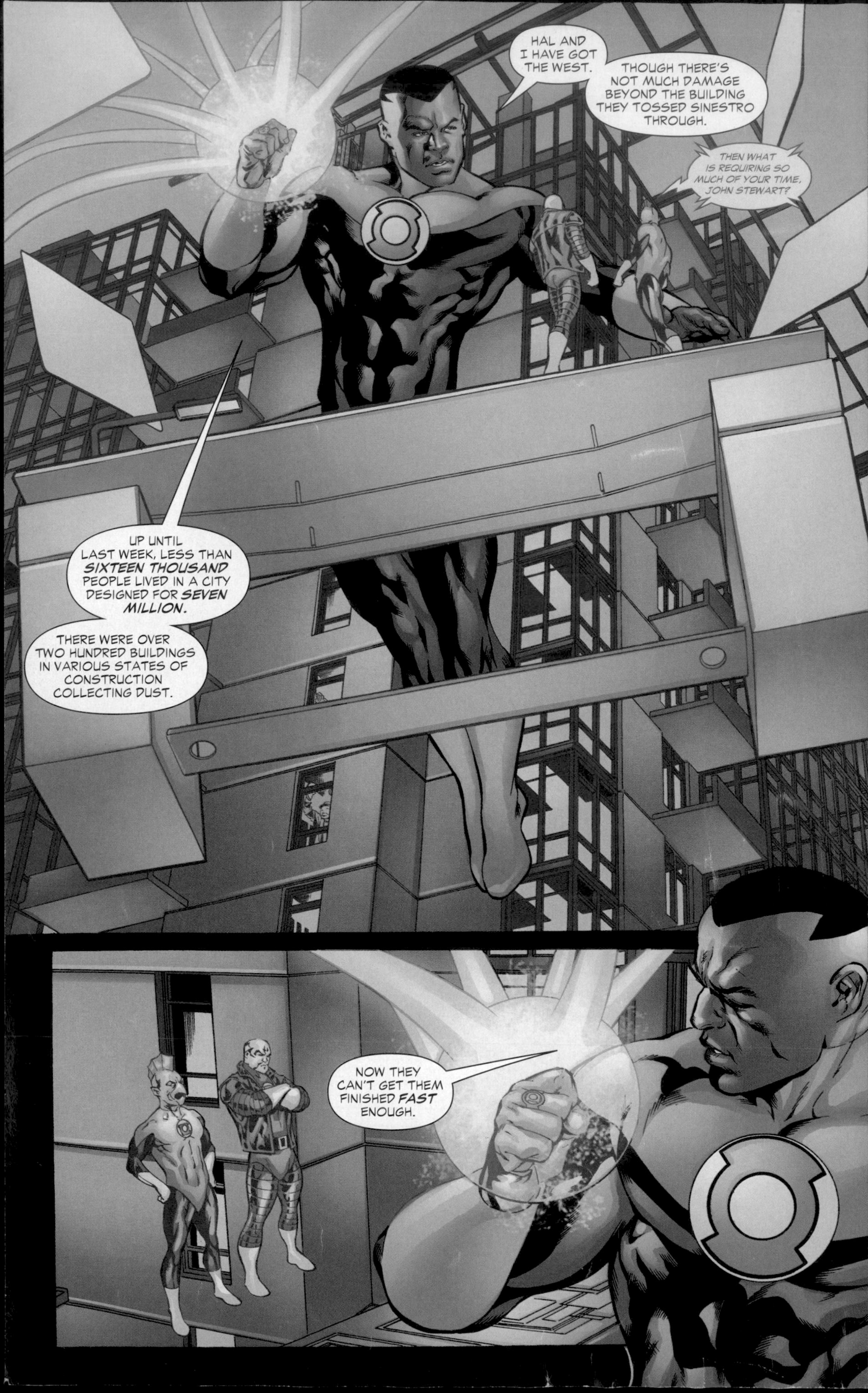
HAL AND I HAVE GOT THE WEST.
THOUGH THERE'S NOT MUCH DAMAGE BEYOND THE BUILDING THEY TOSSED SINESTRO THROUGH.
THEN WHAT IS REQUIRING SO MUCH OF YOUR TIME, JOHN STEWART?
UP UNTIL LAST WEEK, LESS THAN SIXTEEN THOUSAND PEOPLE LIVED IN A CITY DESIGNED FOR SEVEN MILLION.
THERE WERE OVER TWO HUNDRED BUILDINGS IN VARIOUS STATES OF CONSTRUCTION COLLECTING DUST.
NOW THEY CAN'T GET THEM FINISHED FAST ENOUGH.

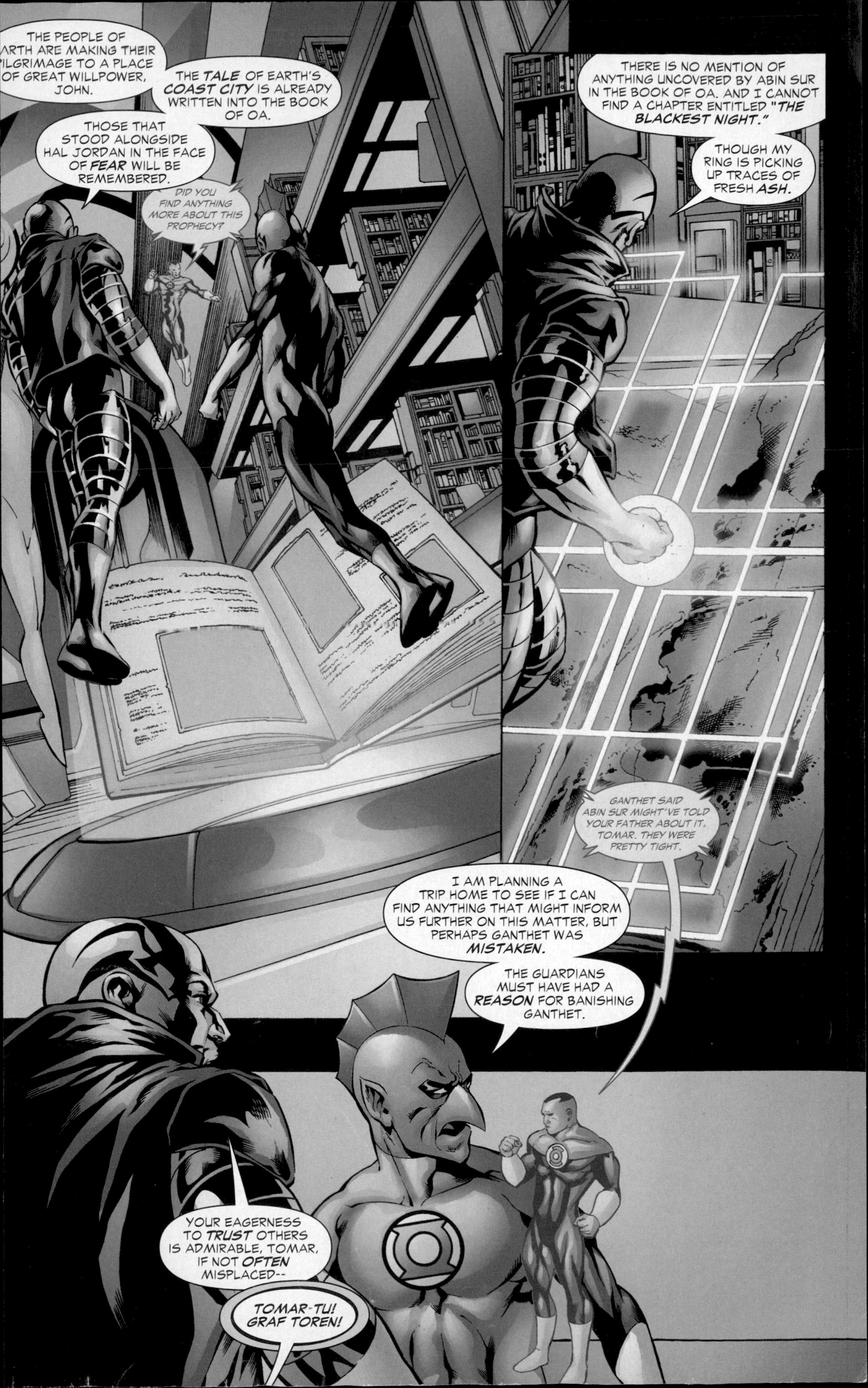

THE PEOPLE OF EARTH ARE MAKING THEIR PILGRIMAGE TO A PLACE OF GREAT WILLPOWER, JOHN.
THE TALE OF EARTH'S COAST CITY IS ALREADY WRITTEN INTO THE BOOK OF OA.
THOSE THAT STOOD ALONGSIDE HAL JORDAN IN THE FACE OF FEAR WILL BE REMEMBERED.
DID YOU FIND ANYTHING MORE ABOUT THIS PROPHECY?
THERE IS NO MENTION OF ANYTHING UNCOVERED BY ABIN SUR IN THE BOOK OF OA. AND I CANNOT FIND A CHAPTER ENTITLED "THE BLACKEST NIGHT."
THOUGH MY RING IS PICKING UP TRACES OF FRESH ASH.
GANTHET SAID ABIN SUR MIGHT'VE TOLD YOUR FATHER ABOUT IT, TOMAR. THEY WERE PRETTY TIGHT.
I AM PLANNING A TRIP HOME TO SEE IF I CAN FIND ANYTHING THAT MIGHT INFORM US FURTHER ON THIS MATTER, BUT PERHAPS GANTHET WAS MISTAKEN.
THE GUARDIANS MUST HAVE HAD A REASON FOR BANISHING GANTHET.
YOUR EAGERNESS TO TRUST OTHERS IS ADMIRABLE, TOMAR, IF NOT OFTEN MISPLACED--
TOMAR-TU! GRAF TOREN!

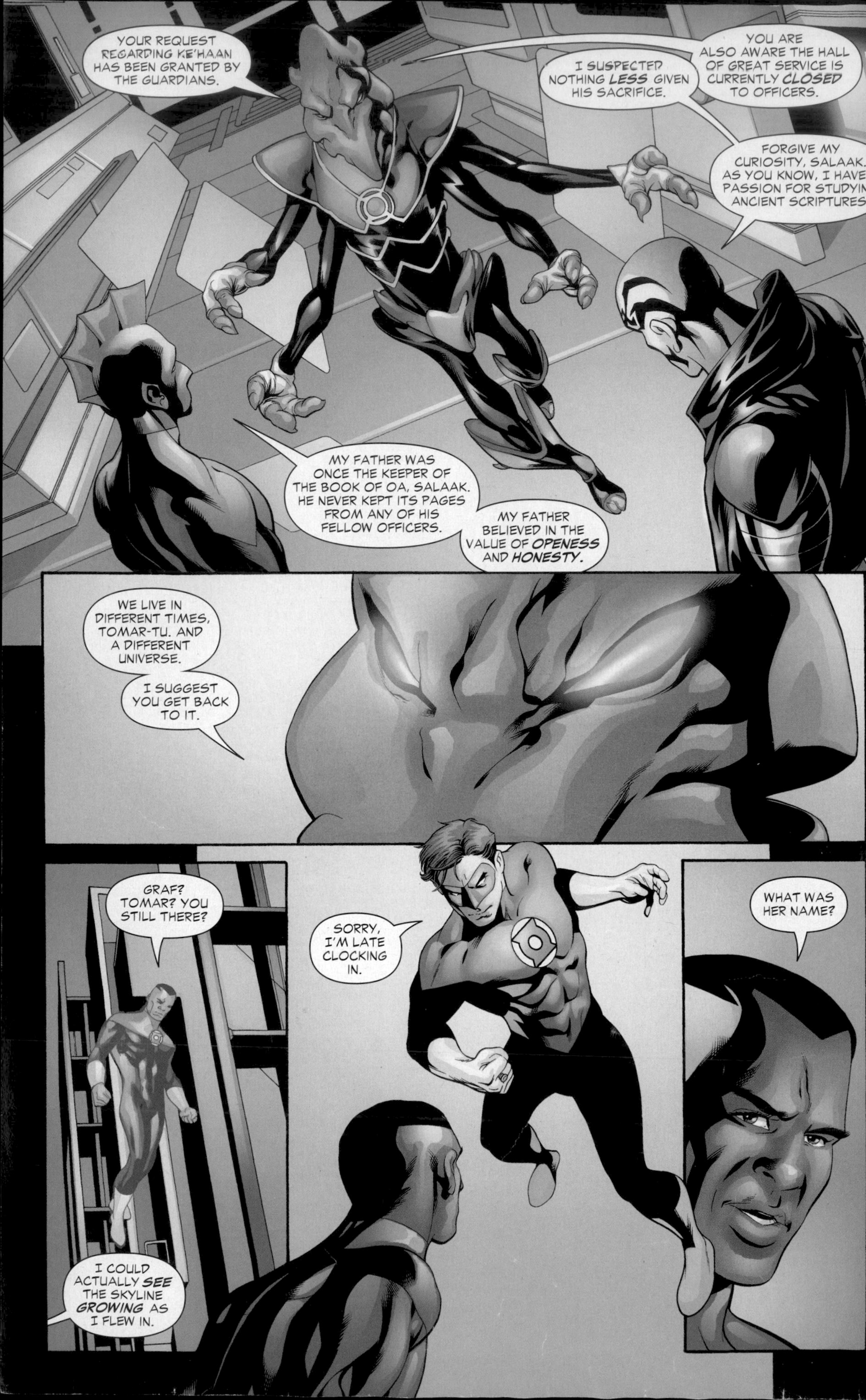
YOUR REQUEST REGARDING KE'HAAN HAS BEEN GRANTED BY THE GUARDIANS.
I SUSPECTED NOTHING LESS GIVEN HIS SACRIFICE.
YOU ARE ALSO AWARE THE HALL OF GREAT SERVICE IS CURRENTLY CLOSED TO OFFICERS.
FORGIVE MY CURIOSITY, SALAAK. AS YOU KNOW, I HAVE PASSION FOR STUDYIN ANCIENT SCRIPTURES
MY FATHER WAS ONCE THE KEEPER OF THE BOOK OF OA, SALAAK. HE NEVER KEPT ITS PAGES FROM ANY OF HIS FELLOW OFFICERS.
MY FATHER BELIEVED IN THE VALUE OF OPENESS AND HONESTY.
WE LIVE IN DIFFERENT TIMES, TOMAR-TU. AND A DIFFERENT UNIVERSE.
I SUGGEST YOU GET BACK TO IT.
GRAF? TOMAR? YOU STILL THERE?
I COULD ACTUALLY SEE THE SKYLINE GROWING AS I FLEW IN.
SORRY, I'M LATE CLOCKING IN.
WHAT WAS HER NAME?

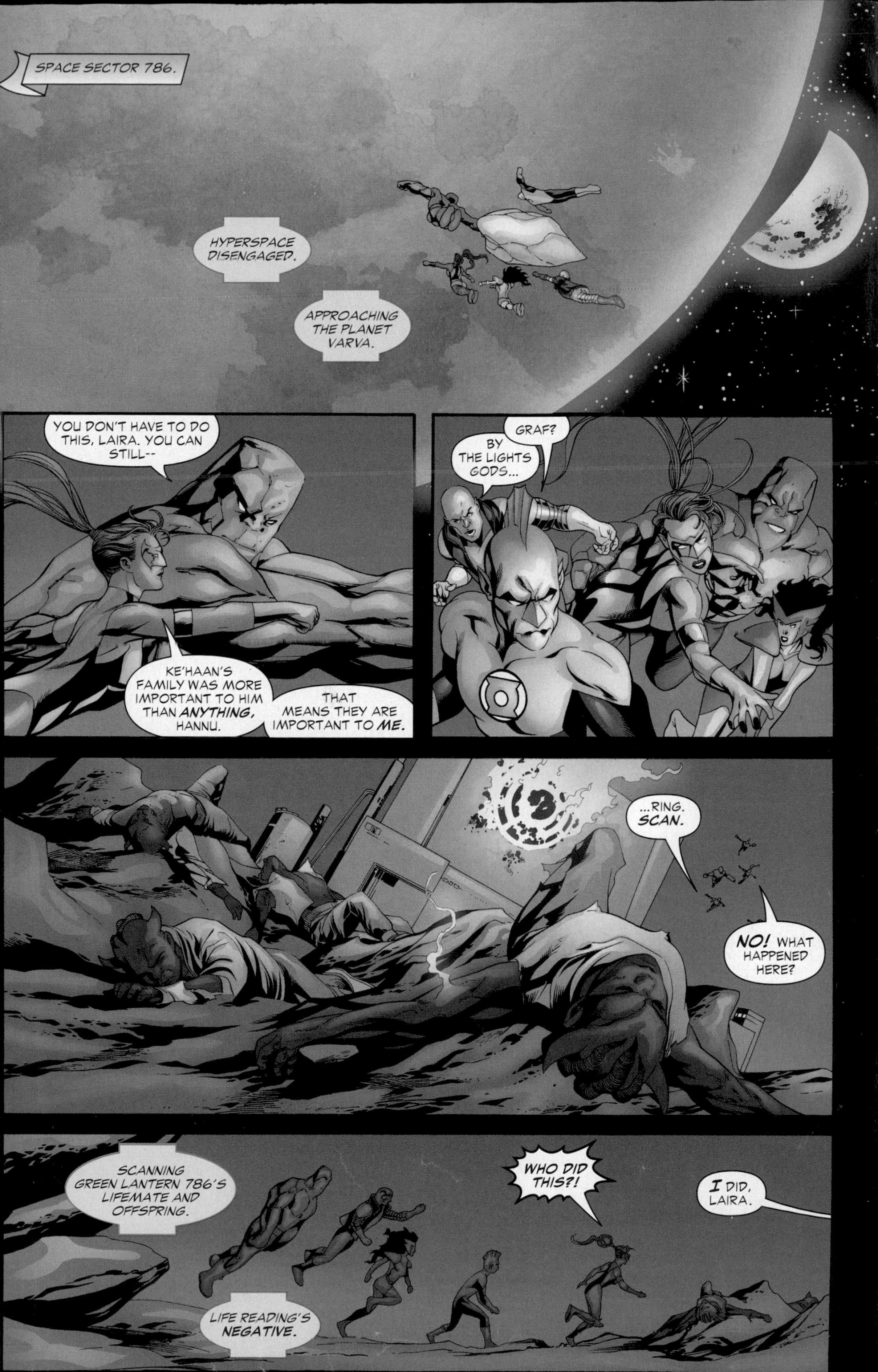
SPACE SECTOR 786.
HYPERSPACE DISENGAGED.
APPROACHING THE PLANET VARVA.
YOU DON'T HAVE TO DO THIS, LAIRA. YOU CAN STILL--
KE'HAAN'S FAMILY WAS MORE IMPORTANT TO HIM THAN ANYTHING, HANNU.
THAT MEANS THEY ARE IMPORTANT TO ME.
GRAF?
BY THE LIGHTS GODS...
...RING. SCAN.
NO! WHAT HAPPENED HERE?
SCANNING GREEN LANTERN 786'S LIFEMATE AND OFFSPRING.
LIFE READING'S NEGATIVE.
WHO DID THIS?!
I DID, LAIRA.

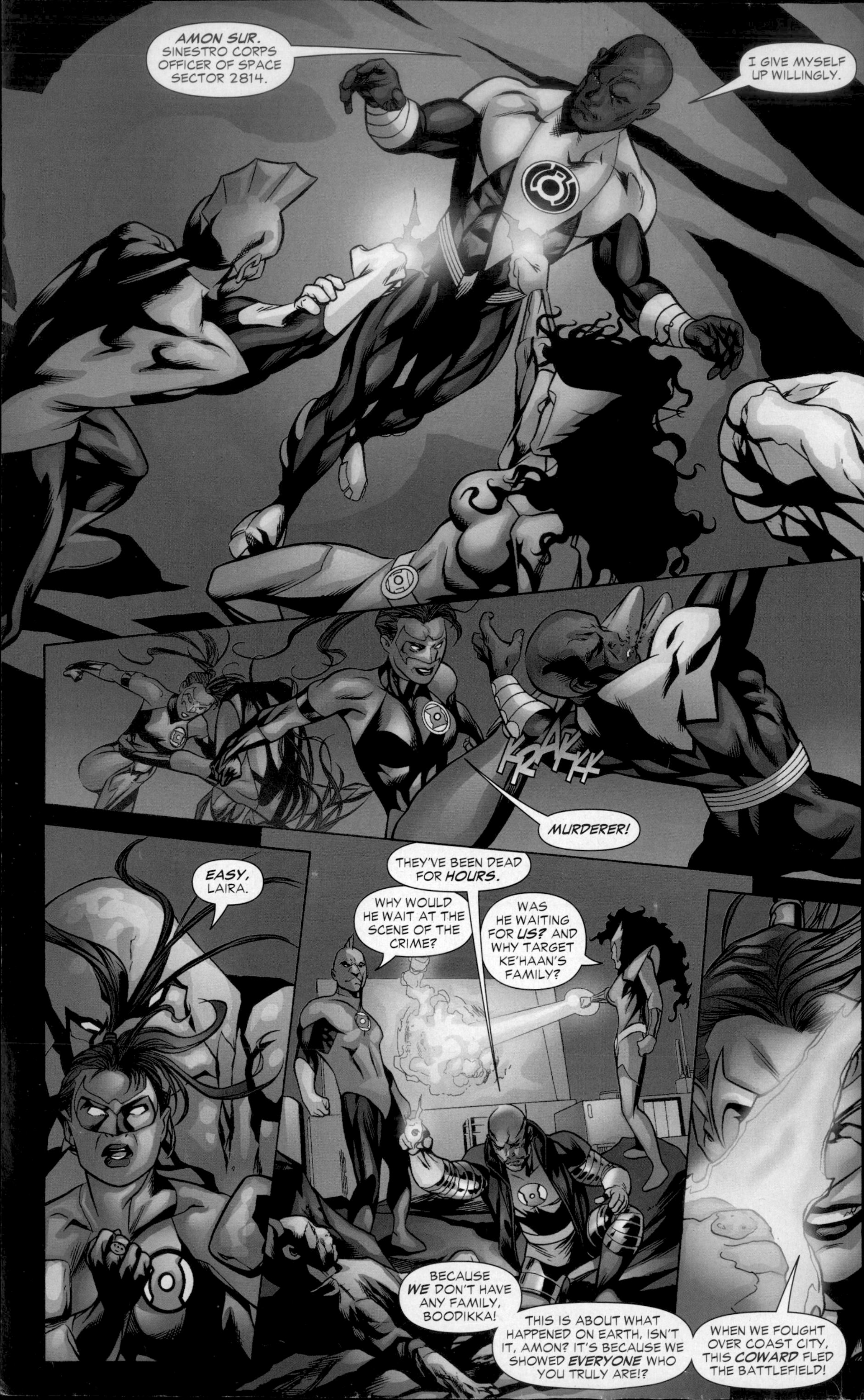
AMON SUR. SINESTRO CORPS OFFICER OF SPACE SECTOR 2814.
I GIVE MYSELF UP WILLINGLY.
KRAKKK
MURDERER!
EASY, LAIRA.
THEY'VE BEEN DEAD FOR HOURS.
WHY WOULD HE WAIT AT THE SCENE OF THE CRIME?
WAS HE WAITING FOR US? AND WHY TARGET KE'HAAN'S FAMILY?
BECAUSE WE DON'T HAVE ANY FAMILY, BOODIKKA!
THIS IS ABOUT WHAT HAPPENED ON EARTH, ISN'T IT, AMON? IT'S BECAUSE WE SHOWED EVERYONE WHO YOU TRULY ARE!?
WHEN WE FOUGHT OVER COAST CITY, THIS COWARD FLED THE BATTLEFIELD!

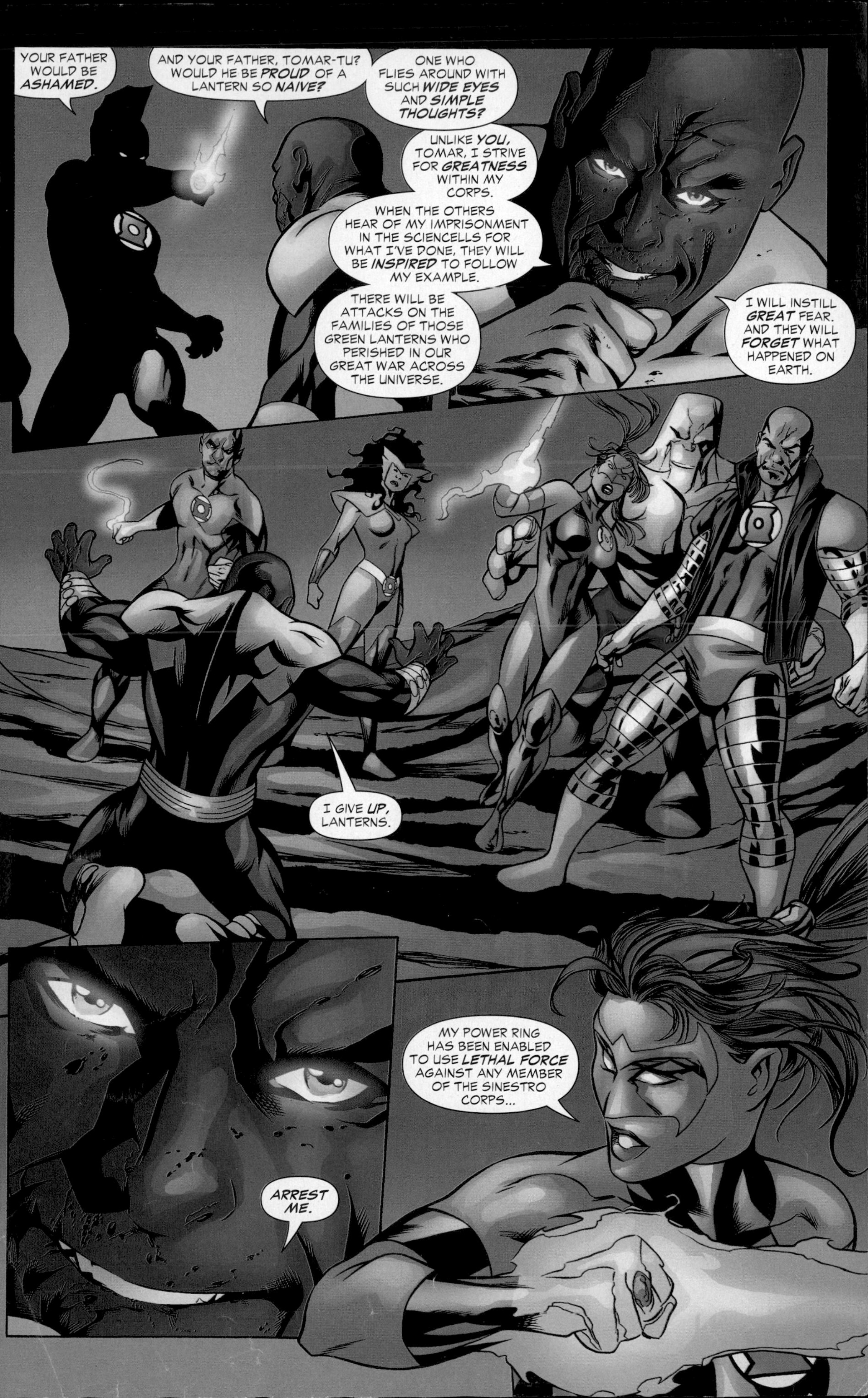
YOUR FATHER WOULD BE ASHAMED.
AND YOUR FATHER, TOMAR-TU? WOULD HE BE PROUD OF A LANTERN SO NAIVE?
ONE WHO FLIES AROUND WITH SUCH WIDE EYES AND SIMPLE THOUGHTS?
UNLIKE YOU, TOMAR, I STRIVE FOR GREATNESS WITHIN MY CORPS.
WHEN THE OTHERS HEAR OF MY IMPRISONMENT IN THE SCIENCELLS FOR WHAT I'VE DONE, THEY WILL BE INSPIRED TO FOLLOW MY EXAMPLE.
THERE WILL BE ATTACKS ON THE FAMILIES OF THOSE GREEN LANTERNS WHO PERISHED IN OUR GREAT WAR ACROSS THE UNIVERSE.
I WILL INSTILL GREAT FEAR. AND THEY WILL FORGET WHAT HAPPENED ON EARTH.
I GIVE UP, LANTERNS.
MY POWER RING HAS BEEN ENABLED TO USE LETHAL FORCE AGAINST ANY MEMBER OF THE SINESTRO CORPS...
ARREST ME.

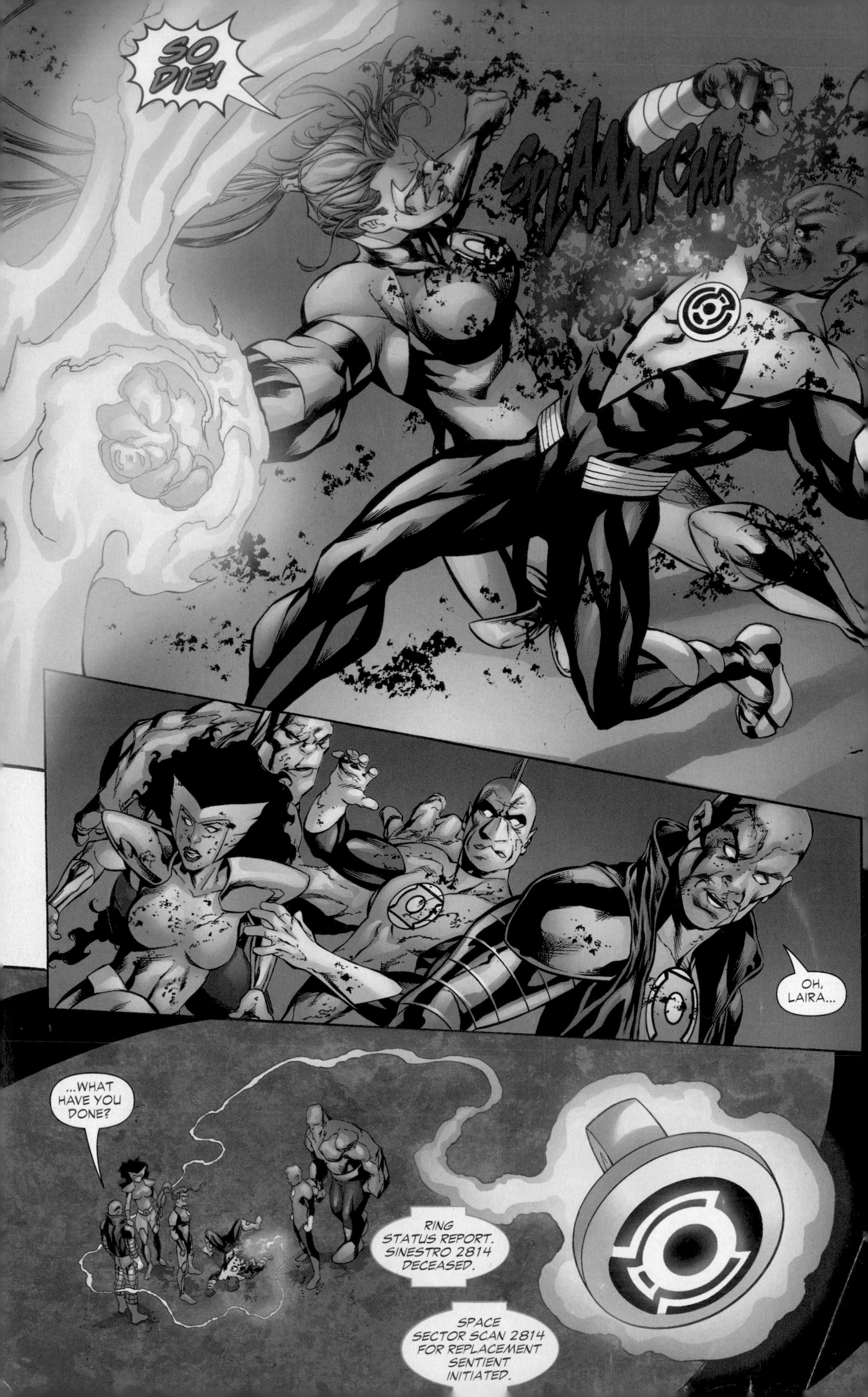
SO DIE!
SPLAAAATCHH
OH, LAIRA...
...WHAT HAVE YOU DONE?
RING STATUS REPORT. SINESTRO 2814 DECEASED.
SPACE SECTOR SCAN 2814 FOR REPLACEMENT SENTIENT INITIATED.

GREEN LANTERN 27 Cover by Mike McKone, Andy Lanning and Moose Baumann

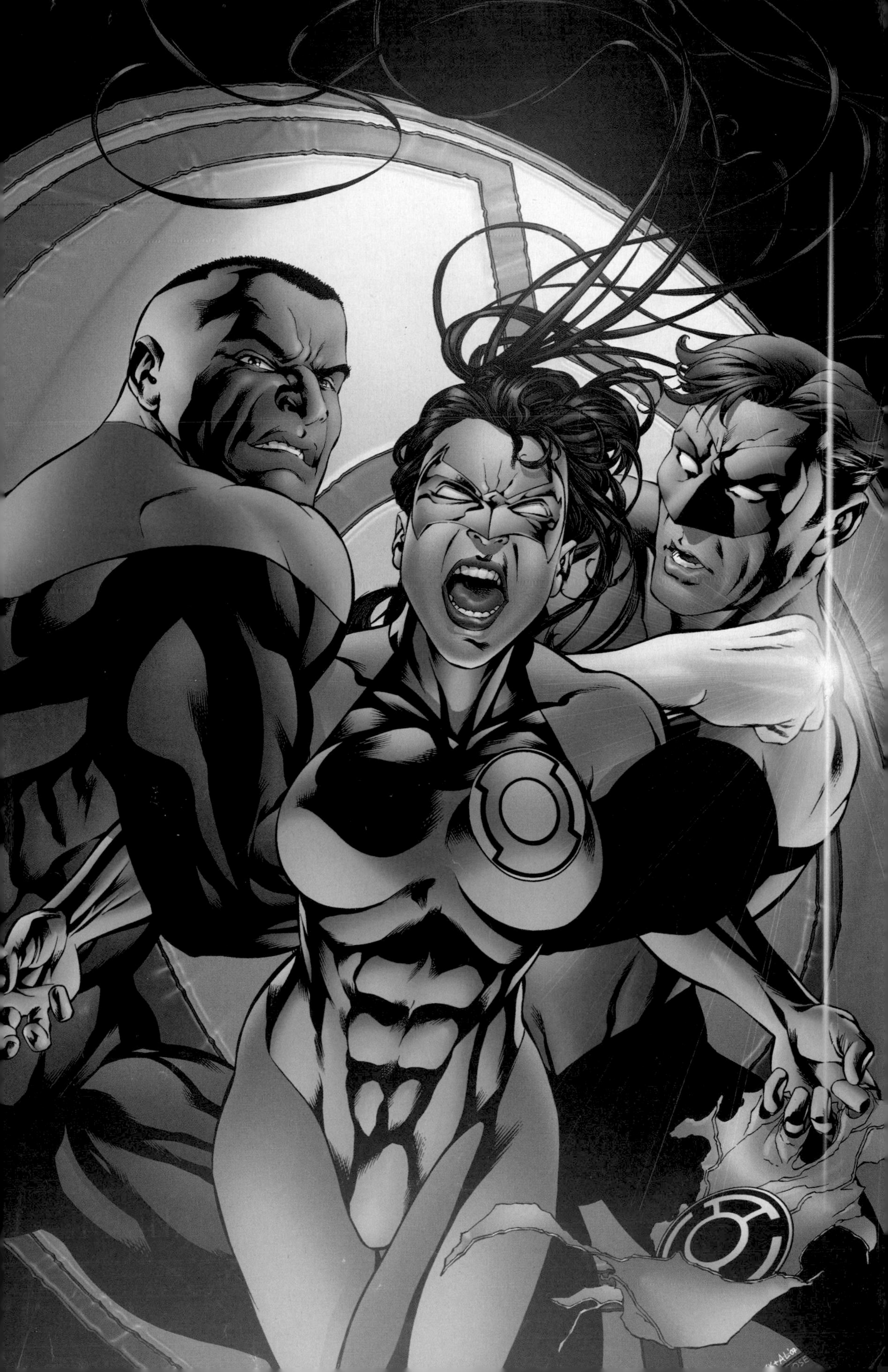

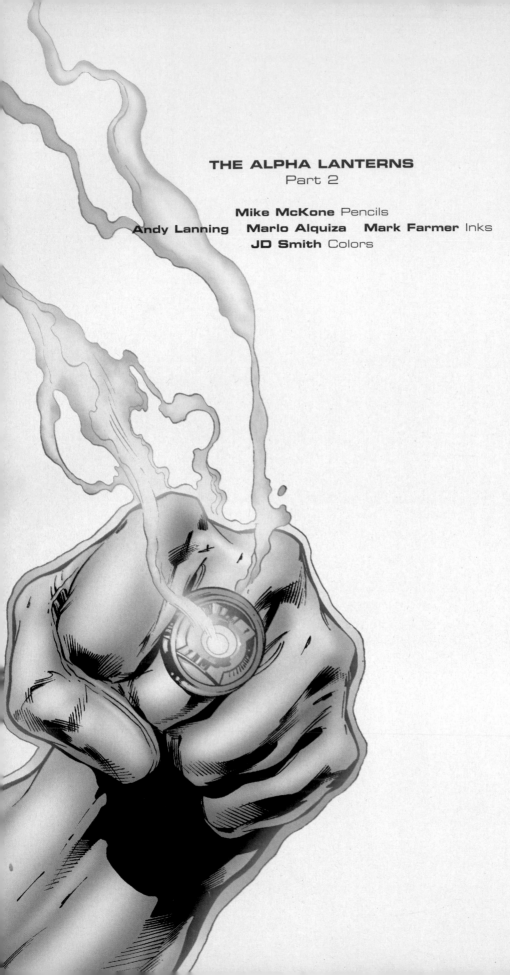

THE ALPHA LANTERNS
Part 2

Mike McKone Pencils

Andy Lanning   **Marlo Alquiza**   **Mark Farmer** Inks

JD Smith Colors

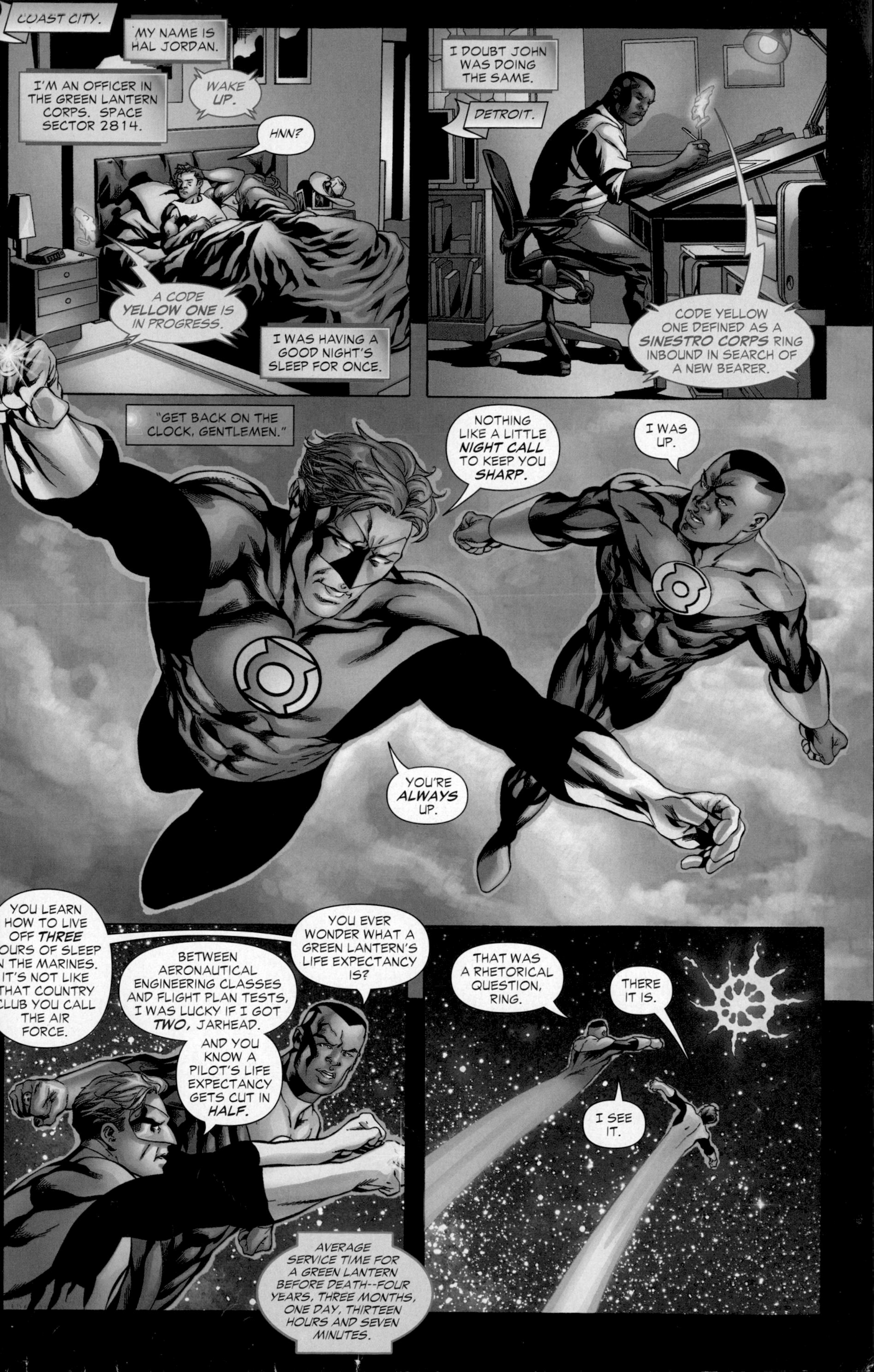
COAST CITY.
MY NAME IS HAL JORDAN.
I'M AN OFFICER IN THE GREEN LANTERN CORPS. SPACE SECTOR 2814.
WAKE UP.
HNN?
A CODE YELLOW ONE IS IN PROGRESS.
I WAS HAVING A GOOD NIGHT'S SLEEP FOR ONCE.
I DOUBT JOHN WAS DOING THE SAME.
DETROIT.
CODE YELLOW ONE DEFINED AS A SINESTRO CORPS RING INBOUND IN SEARCH OF A NEW BEARER.
"GET BACK ON THE CLOCK, GENTLEMEN."
NOTHING LIKE A LITTLE NIGHT CALL TO KEEP YOU SHARP.
I WAS UP.
YOU'RE ALWAYS UP.
YOU LEARN HOW TO LIVE OFF THREE OURS OF SLEEP N THE MARINES. IT'S NOT LIKE THAT COUNTRY CLUB YOU CALL THE AIR FORCE.
BETWEEN AERONAUTICAL ENGINEERING CLASSES AND FLIGHT PLAN TESTS, I WAS LUCKY IF I GOT TWO, JARHEAD.
AND YOU KNOW A PILOT'S LIFE EXPECTANCY GETS CUT IN HALF.
YOU EVER WONDER WHAT A GREEN LANTERN'S LIFE EXPECTANCY IS?
AVERAGE SERVICE TIME FOR A GREEN LANTERN BEFORE DEATH--FOUR YEARS, THREE MONTHS, ONE DAY, THIRTEEN HOURS AND SEVEN MINUTES.
THAT WAS A RHETORICAL QUESTION, RING.
THERE IT IS.
I SEE IT.

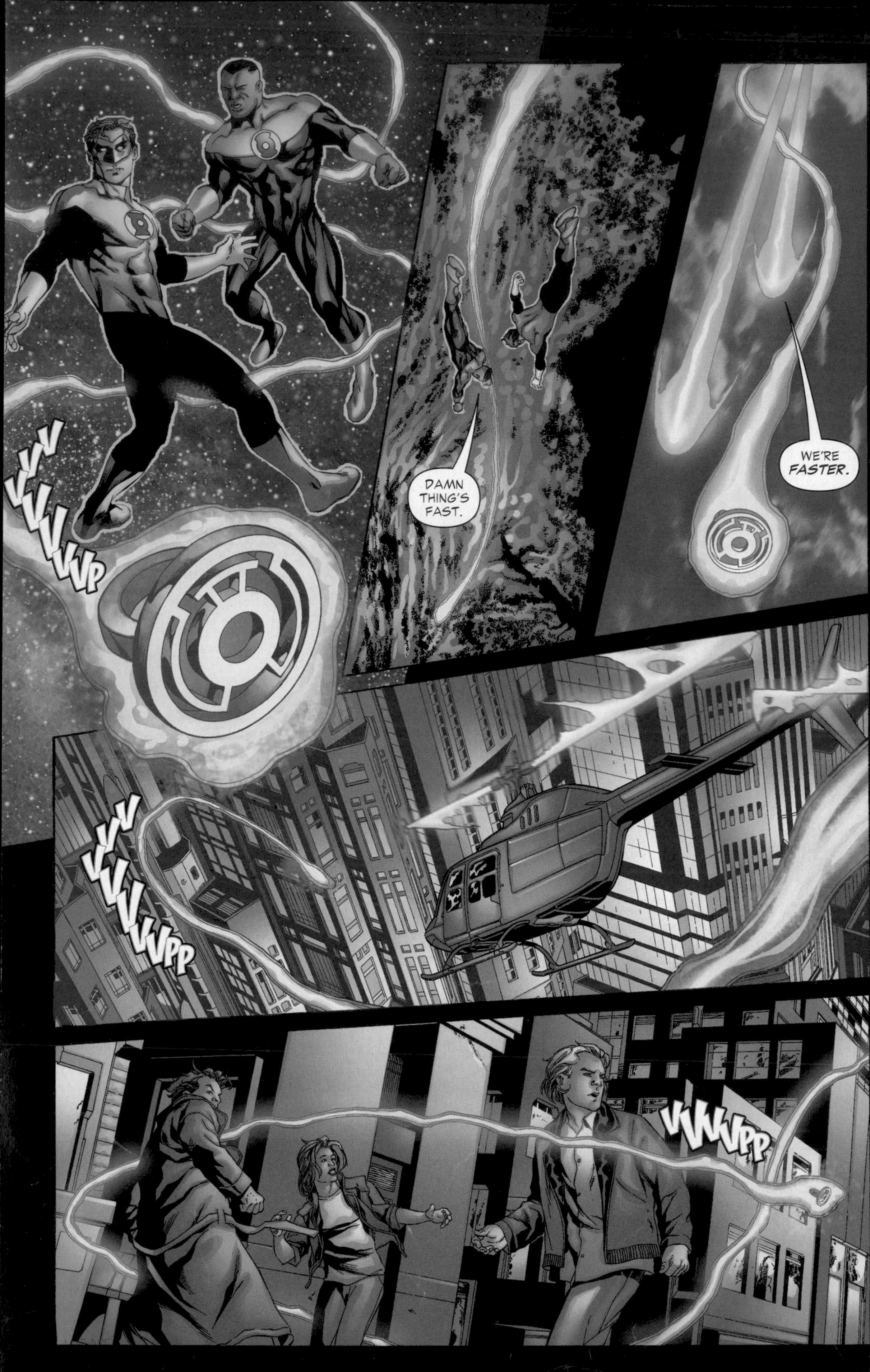
VVVVVVVVP
DAMN THING'S FAST.
WE'RE FASTER.
VVVVVVVVPP
VVVVVPP

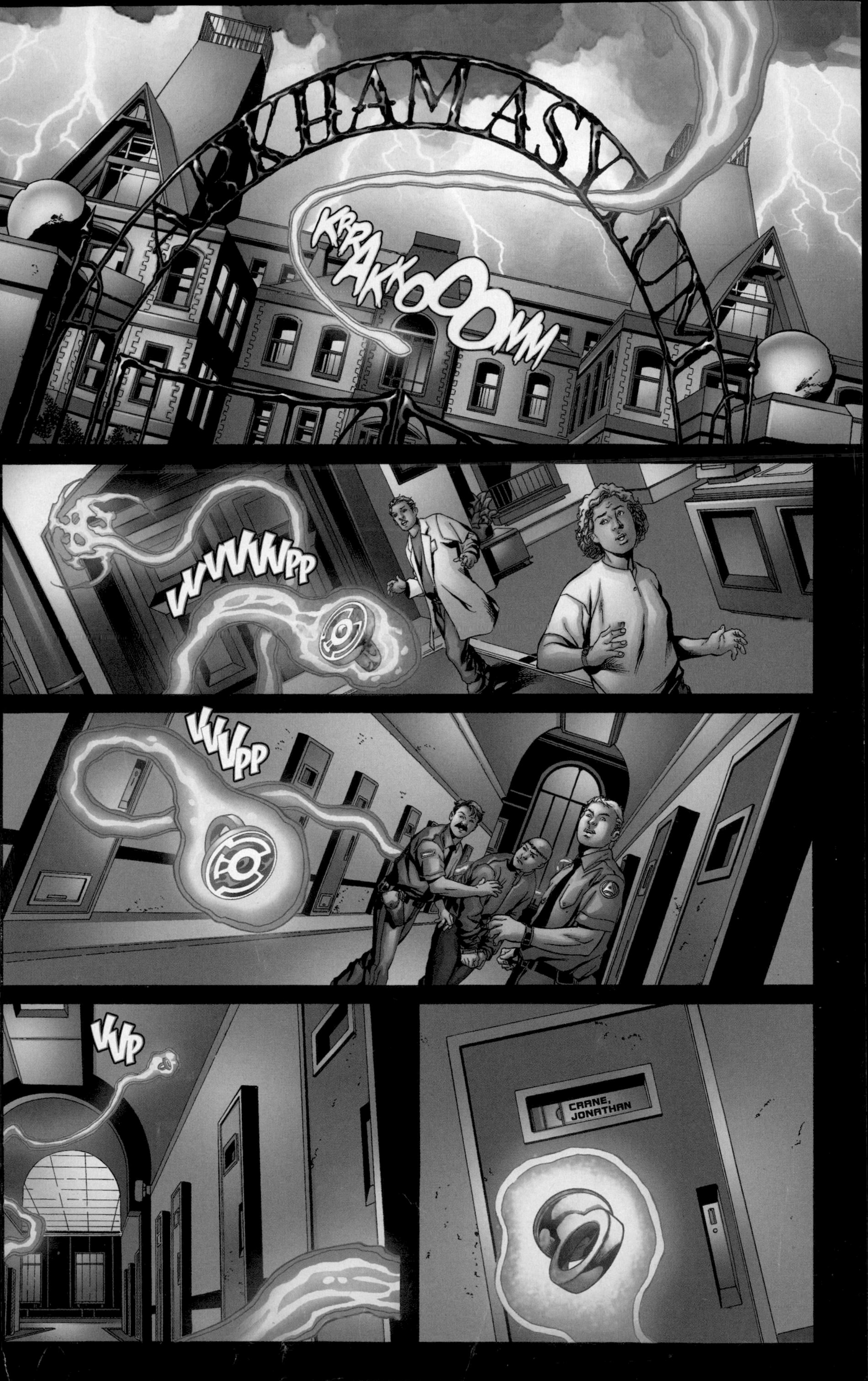
KRRAKKOOOMM
VVVVVVPP
VVVPP
VVP
CRANE, JONATHAN

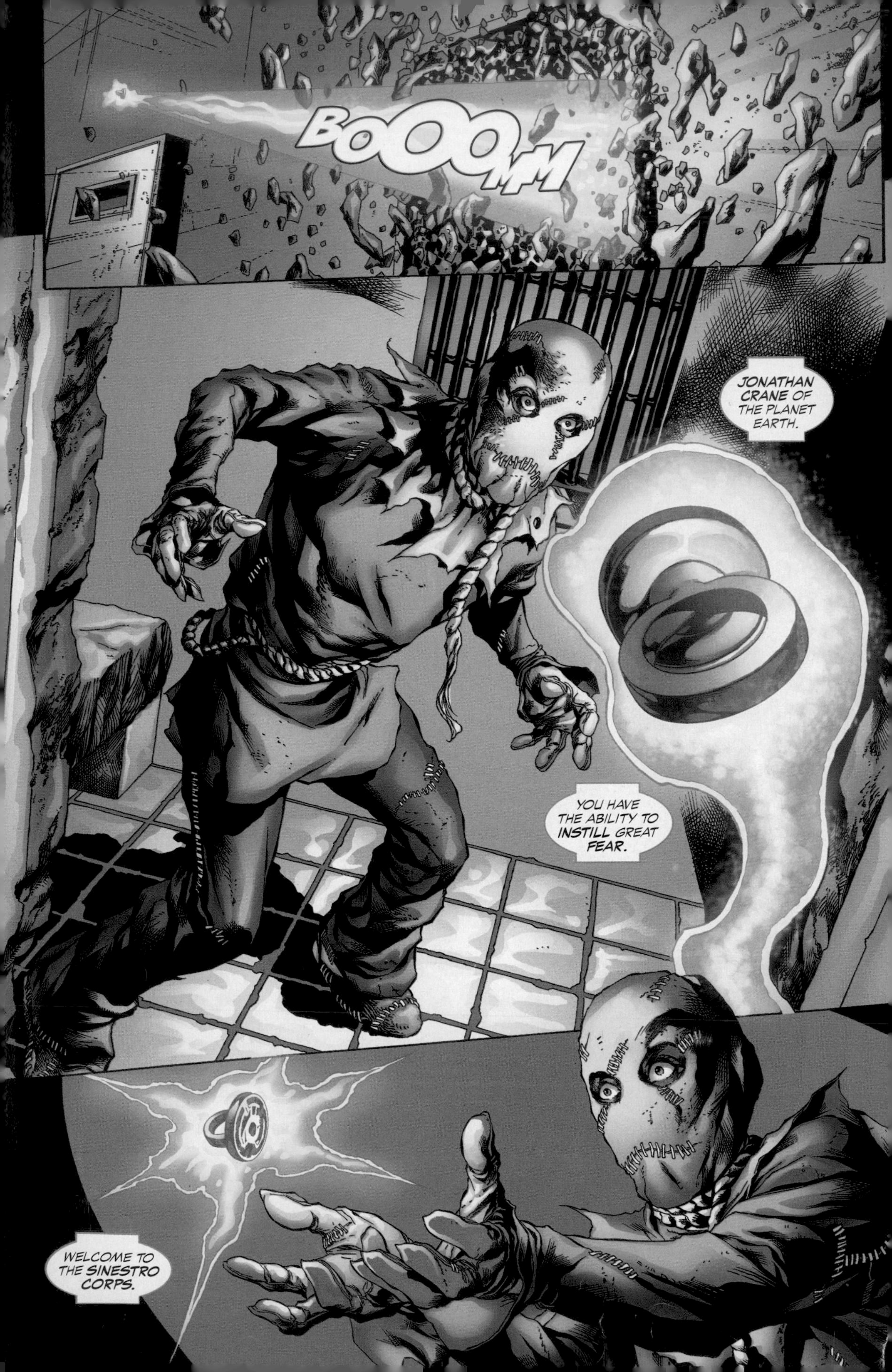
BOOOMM
JONATHAN CRANE OF THE PLANET EARTH.
YOU HAVE THE ABILITY TO INSTILL GREAT FEAR.
WELCOME TO THE SINESTRO CORPS.

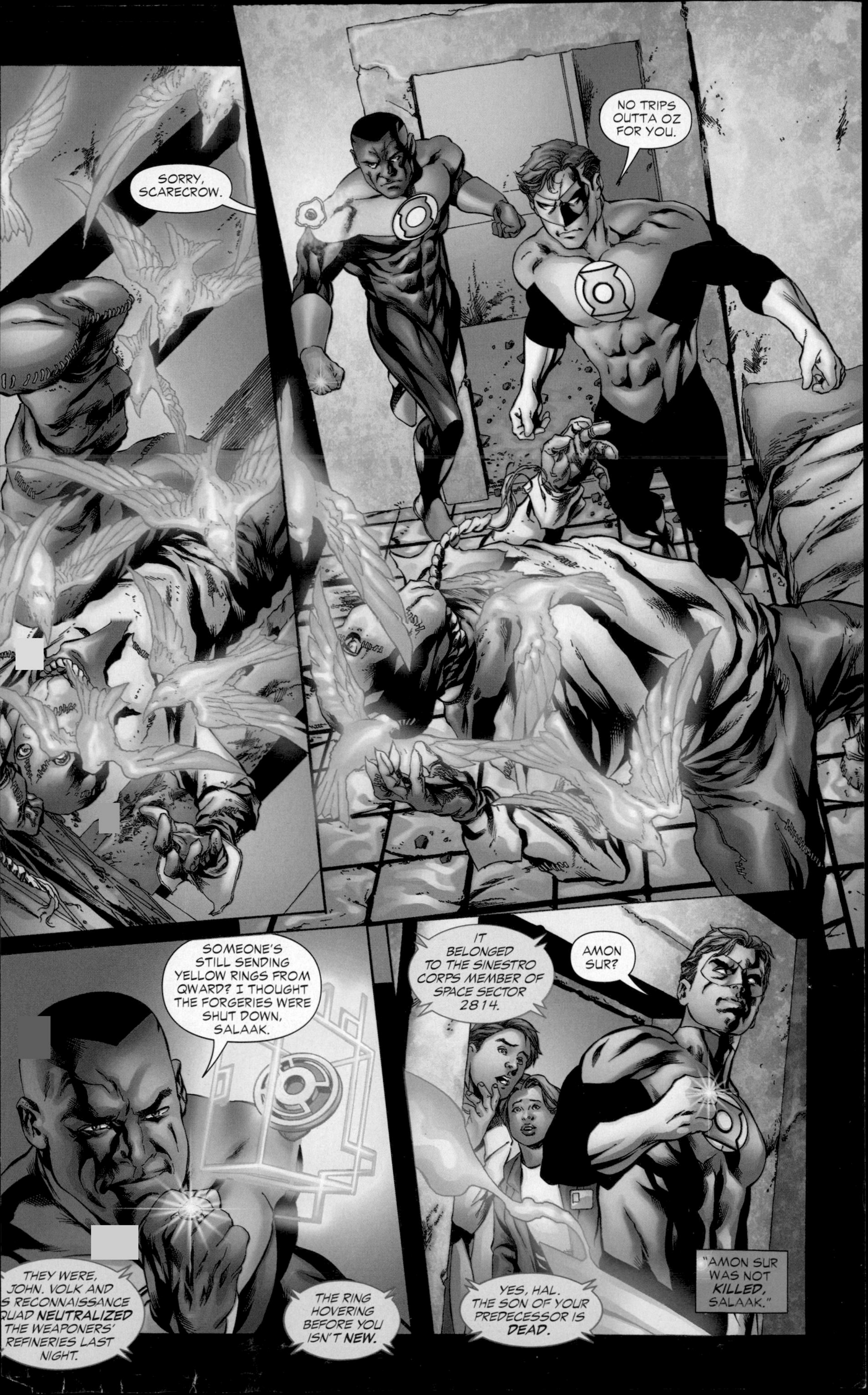
SORRY, SCARECROW.
NO TRIPS OUTTA OZ FOR YOU.
SOMEONE'S STILL SENDING YELLOW RINGS FROM QWARD? I THOUGHT THE FORGERIES WERE SHUT DOWN, SALAAK.
THEY WERE, JOHN. VOLK AND S RECONNAISSANCE QUAD **NEUTRALIZED** THE WEAPONERS' REFINERIES LAST NIGHT.
THE RING HOVERING BEFORE YOU ISN'T **NEW**.
IT BELONGED TO THE SINESTRO CORPS MEMBER OF SPACE SECTOR 2814.
AMON SUR?
YES, HAL. THE SON OF YOUR PREDECESSOR IS **DEAD**.
"AMON SUR WAS NOT **KILLED**, SALAAK."

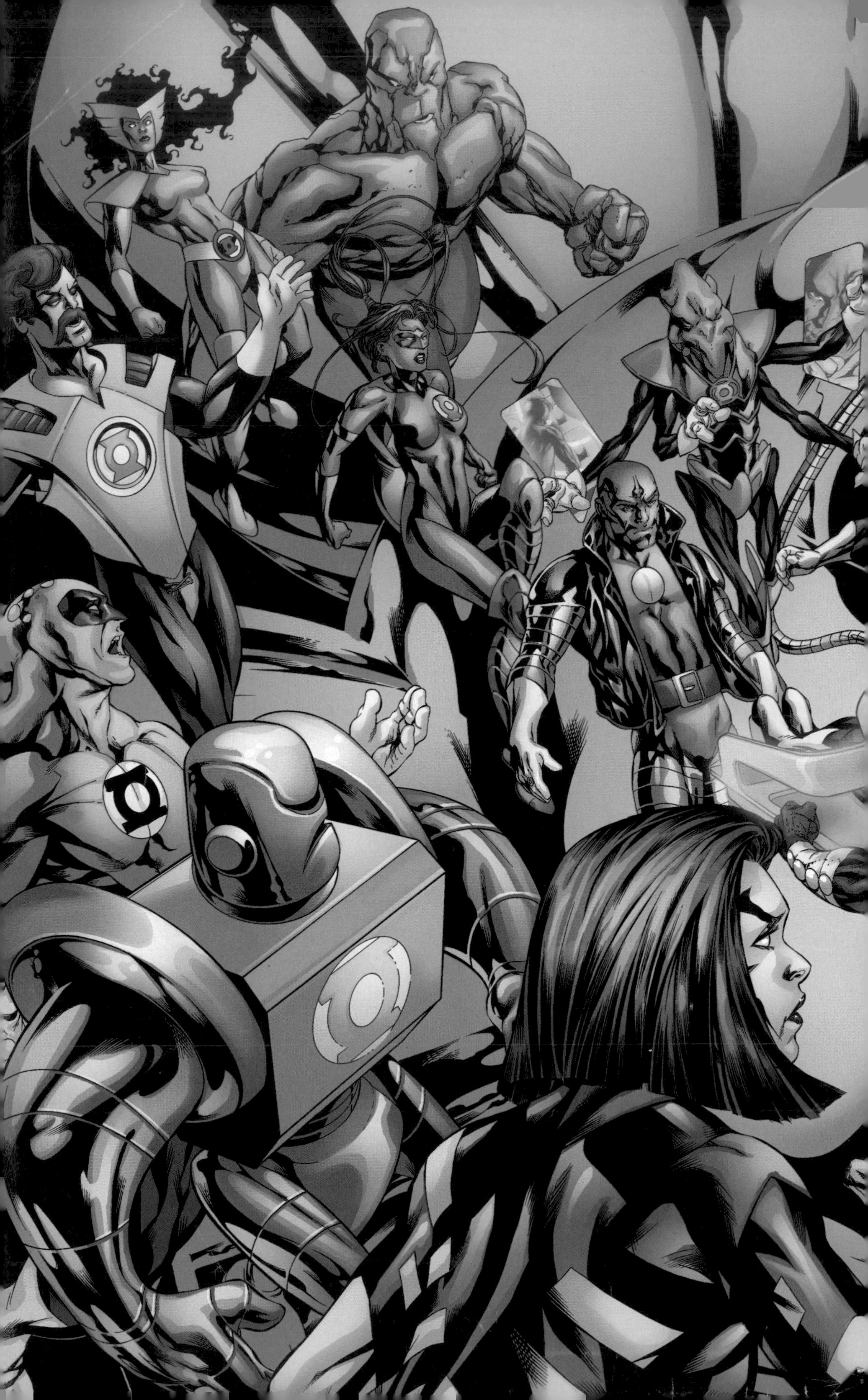

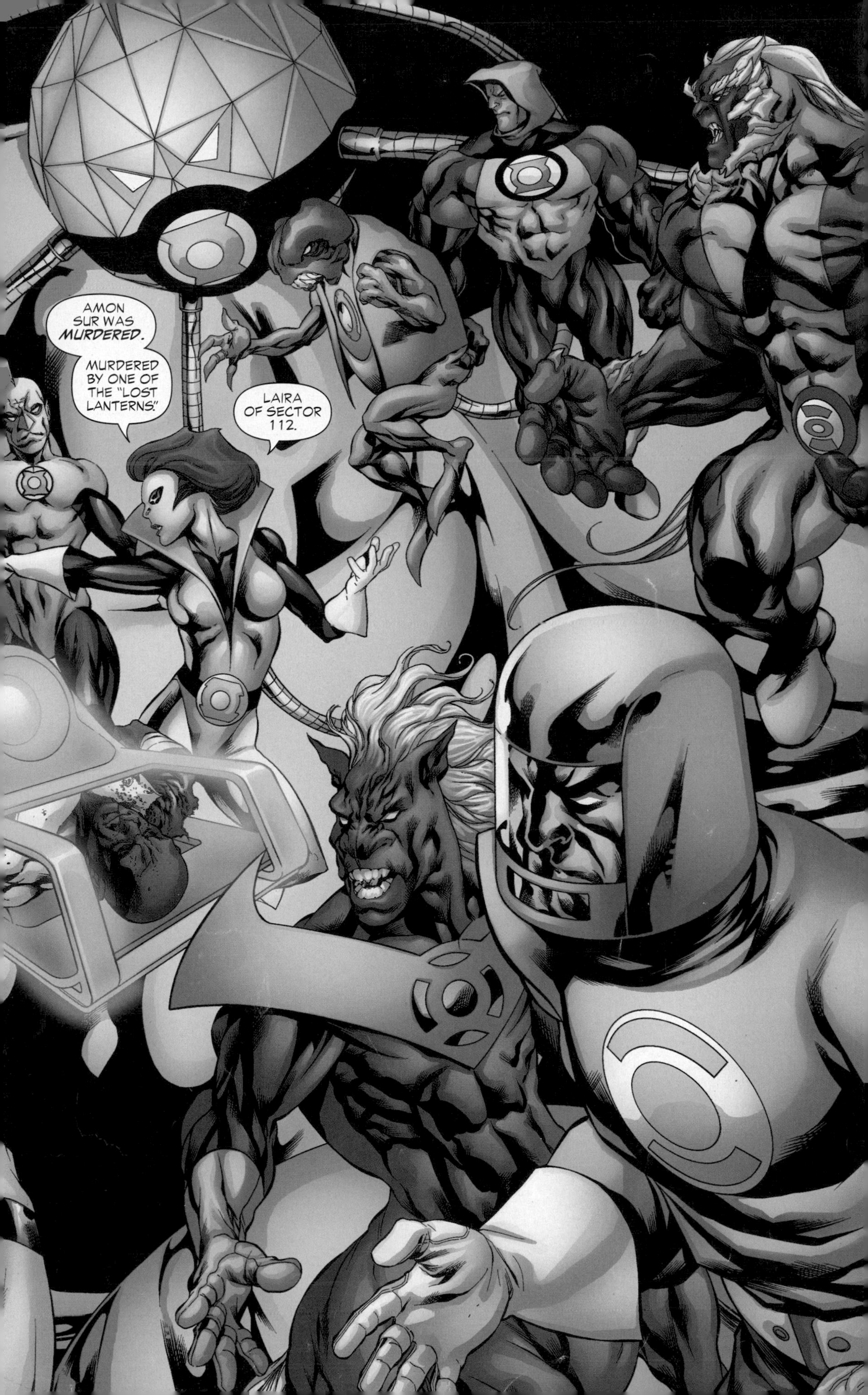
AMON SUR WAS *MURDERED*.
MURDERED BY ONE OF THE "LOST LANTERNS."
LAIRA OF SECTOR 112.

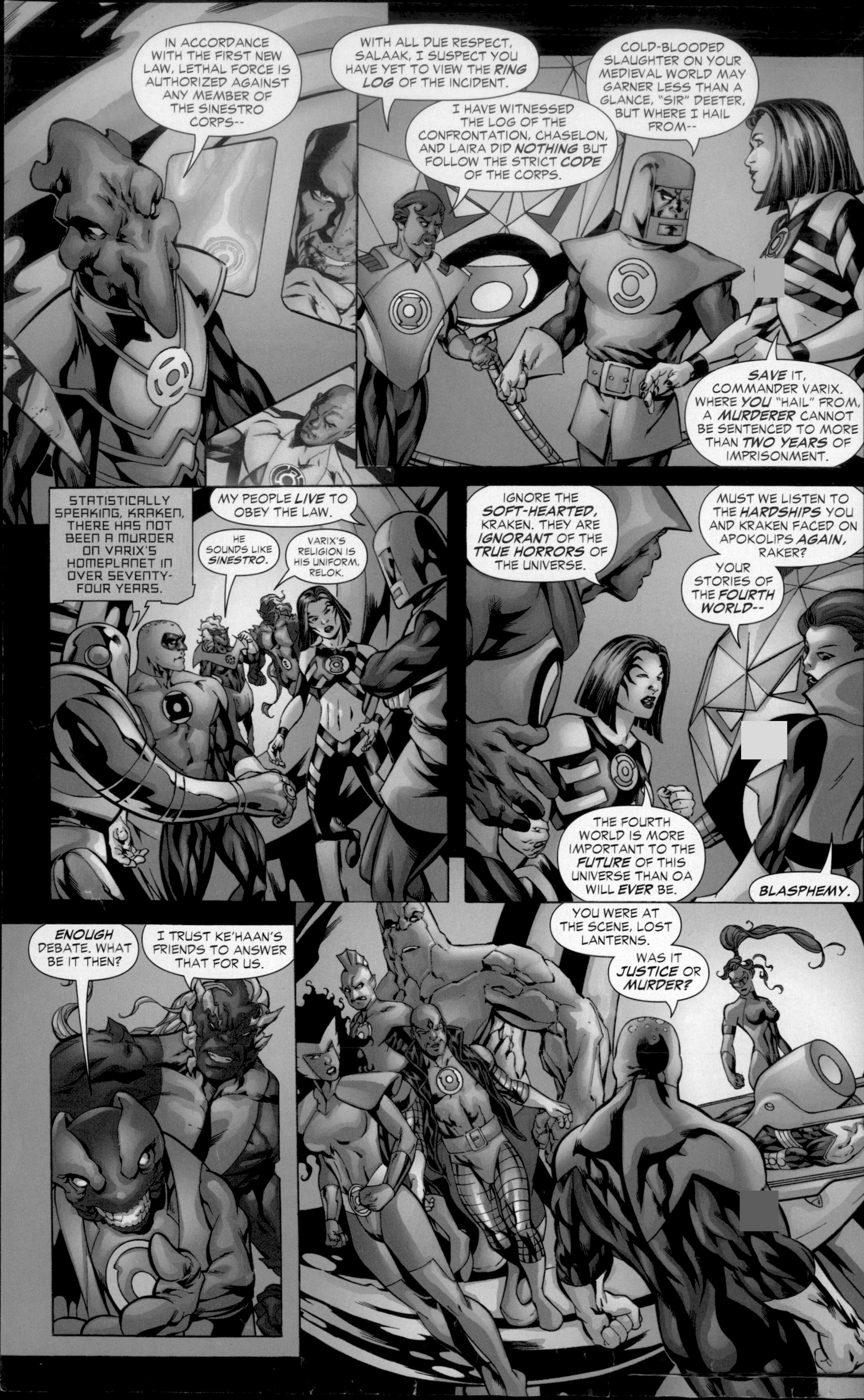
IN ACCORDANCE WITH THE FIRST NEW LAW, LETHAL FORCE IS AUTHORIZED AGAINST ANY MEMBER OF THE SINESTRO CORPS--
WITH ALL DUE RESPECT, SALAAK, I SUSPECT YOU HAVE YET TO VIEW THE RING LOG OF THE INCIDENT.
I HAVE WITNESSED THE LOG OF THE CONFRONTATION, CHASELON, AND LAIRA DID NOTHING BUT FOLLOW THE STRICT CODE OF THE CORPS.
COLD-BLOODED SLAUGHTER ON YOUR MEDIEVAL WORLD MAY GARNER LESS THAN A GLANCE, "SIR" DEETER, BUT WHERE I HAIL FROM--
SAVE IT, COMMANDER VARIX. WHERE YOU "HAIL" FROM, A MURDERER CANNOT BE SENTENCED TO MORE THAN TWO YEARS OF IMPRISONMENT.
STATISTICALLY SPEAKING, KRAKEN, THERE HAS NOT BEEN A MURDER ON VARIX'S HOMEPLANET IN OVER SEVENTY-FOUR YEARS.
MY PEOPLE LIVE TO OBEY THE LAW.
HE SOUNDS LIKE SINESTRO.
VARIX'S RELIGION IS HIS UNIFORM, RELOK.
IGNORE THE SOFT-HEARTED, KRAKEN. THEY ARE IGNORANT OF THE TRUE HORRORS OF THE UNIVERSE.
MUST WE LISTEN TO THE HARDSHIPS YOU AND KRAKEN FACED ON APOKOLIPS AGAIN, RAKER?
YOUR STORIES OF THE FOURTH WORLD--
THE FOURTH WORLD IS MORE IMPORTANT TO THE FUTURE OF THIS UNIVERSE THAN OA WILL EVER BE.
BLASPHEMY.
ENOUGH DEBATE. WHAT BE IT THEN?
I TRUST KE'HAAN'S FRIENDS TO ANSWER THAT FOR US.
YOU WERE AT THE SCENE, LOST LANTERNS.
WAS IT JUSTICE OR MURDER?

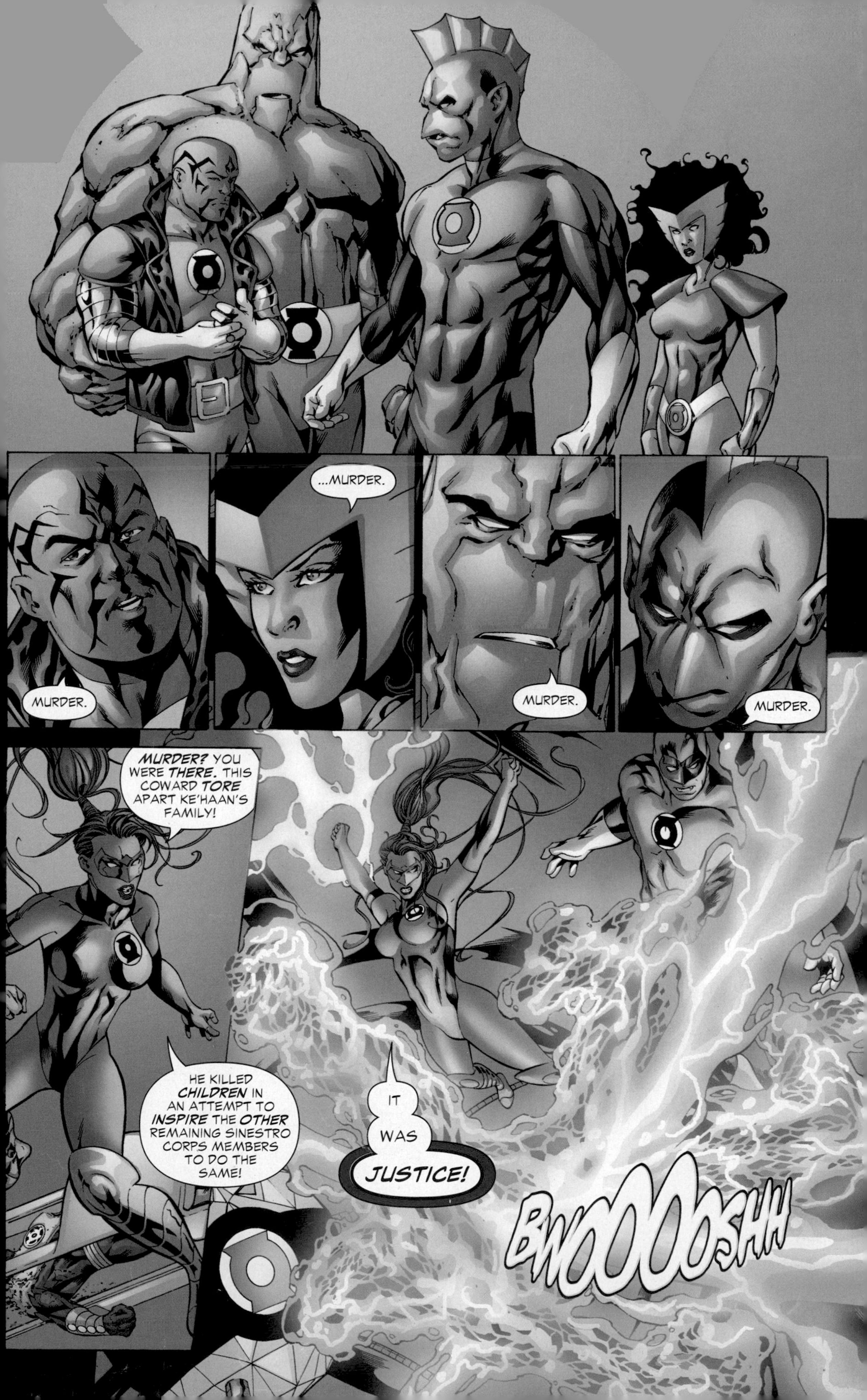
MURDER.
...MURDER.
MURDER.
MURDER.
MURDER? YOU WERE THERE. THIS COWARD TORE APART KE'HAAN'S FAMILY!
HE KILLED CHILDREN IN AN ATTEMPT TO INSPIRE THE OTHER REMAINING SINESTRO CORPS MEMBERS TO DO THE SAME!
IT WAS JUSTICE!
BWOOOOSHH

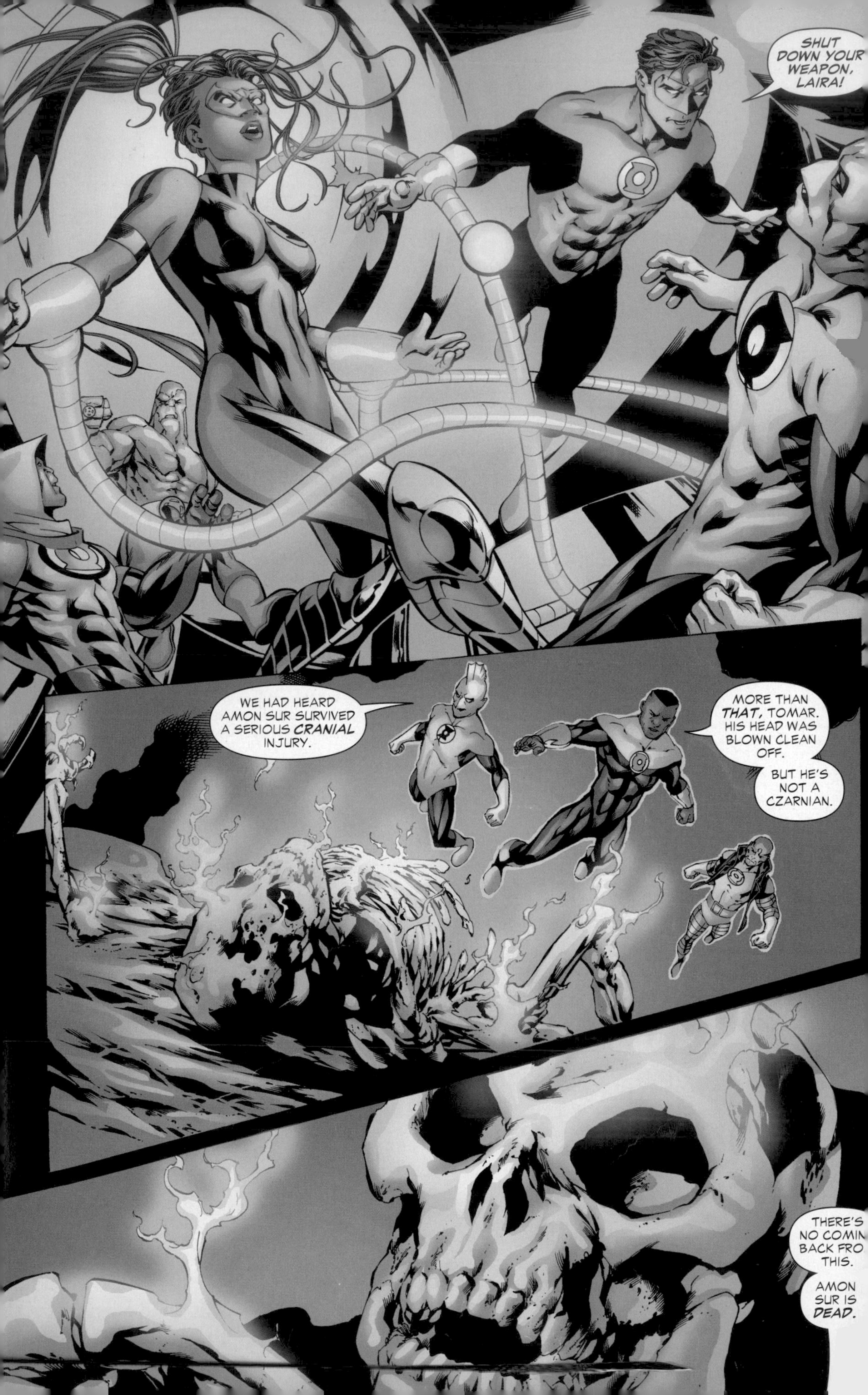
SHUT DOWN YOUR WEAPON, LAIRA!
WE HAD HEARD AMON SUR SURVIVED A SERIOUS CRANIAL INJURY.
MORE THAN THAT, TOMAR. HIS HEAD WAS BLOWN CLEAN OFF.
BUT HE'S NOT A CZARNIAN.
THERE'S NO COMIN BACK FRO THIS.
AMON SUR IS DEAD.

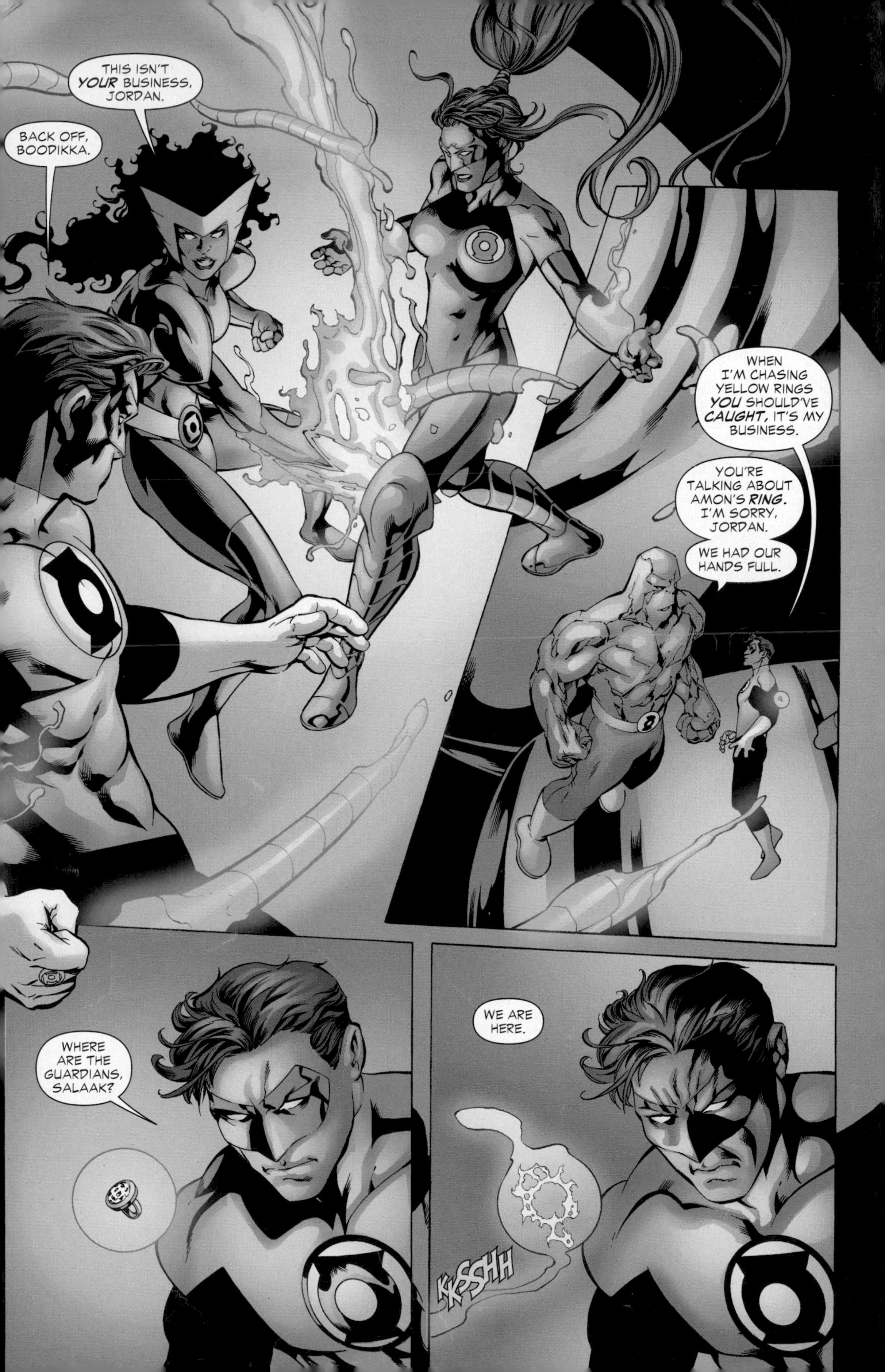
THIS ISN'T *YOUR* BUSINESS, JORDAN.
BACK OFF, BOODIKKA.
WHEN I'M CHASING YELLOW RINGS *YOU* SHOULD'VE *CAUGHT*, IT'S MY BUSINESS.
YOU'RE TALKING ABOUT AMON'S *RING*. I'M SORRY, JORDAN.
WE HAD OUR HANDS FULL.
WHERE ARE THE GUARDIANS, SALAAK?
WE ARE HERE.
KKSSHH

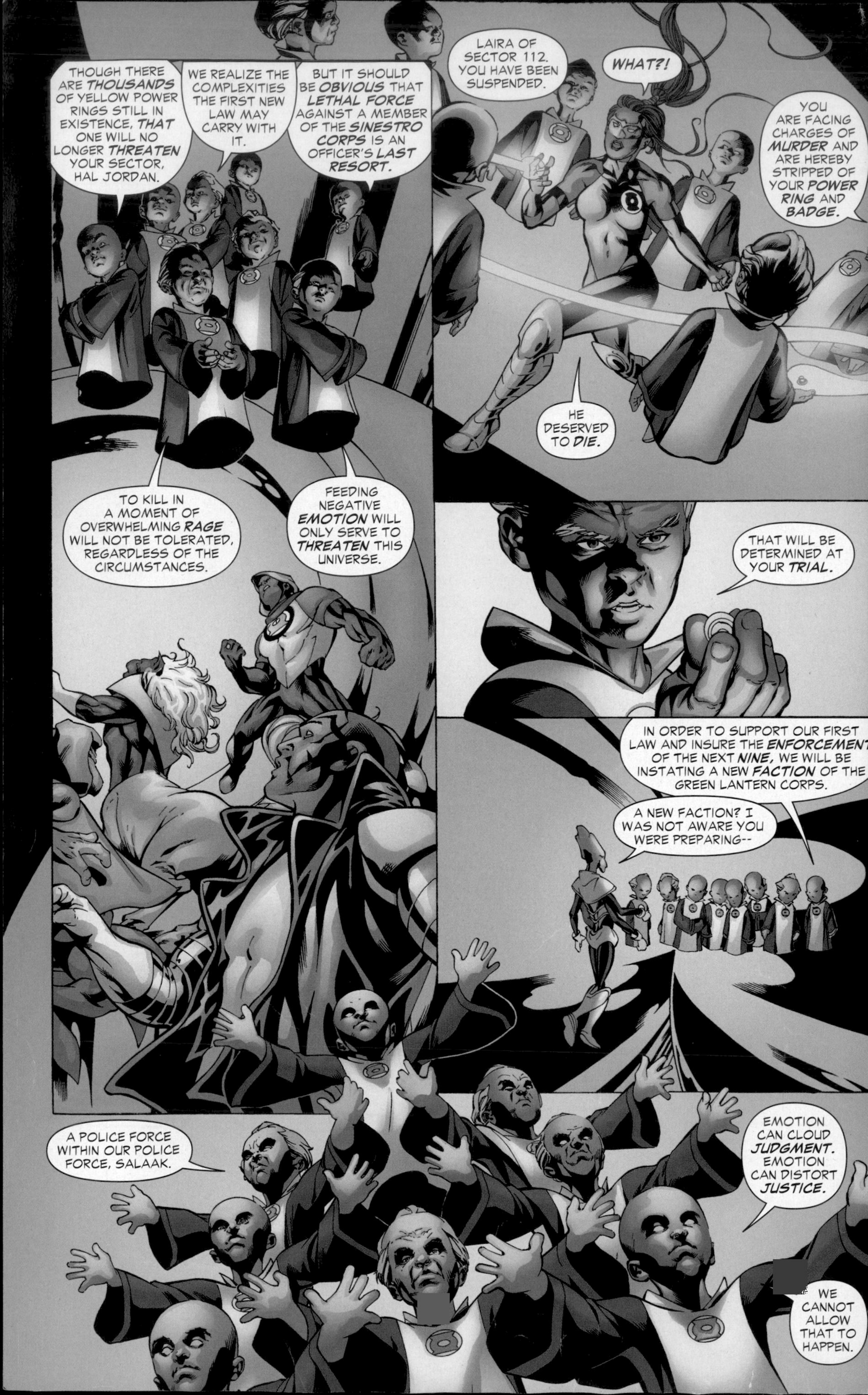
THOUGH THERE ARE THOUSANDS OF YELLOW POWER RINGS STILL IN EXISTENCE, THAT ONE WILL NO LONGER THREATEN YOUR SECTOR, HAL JORDAN.
WE REALIZE THE COMPLEXITIES THE FIRST NEW LAW MAY CARRY WITH IT.
BUT IT SHOULD BE OBVIOUS THAT LETHAL FORCE AGAINST A MEMBER OF THE SINESTRO CORPS IS AN OFFICER'S LAST RESORT.
LAIRA OF SECTOR 112. YOU HAVE BEEN SUSPENDED.
WHAT?!
YOU ARE FACING CHARGES OF MURDER AND ARE HEREBY STRIPPED OF YOUR POWER RING AND BADGE.
HE DESERVED TO DIE.
TO KILL IN A MOMENT OF OVERWHELMING RAGE WILL NOT BE TOLERATED, REGARDLESS OF THE CIRCUMSTANCES.
FEEDING NEGATIVE EMOTION WILL ONLY SERVE TO THREATEN THIS UNIVERSE.
THAT WILL BE DETERMINED AT YOUR TRIAL.
IN ORDER TO SUPPORT OUR FIRST LAW AND INSURE THE ENFORCEMENT OF THE NEXT NINE, WE WILL BE INSTATING A NEW FACTION OF THE GREEN LANTERN CORPS.
A NEW FACTION? I WAS NOT AWARE YOU WERE PREPARING--
A POLICE FORCE WITHIN OUR POLICE FORCE, SALAAK.
EMOTION CAN CLOUD JUDGMENT. EMOTION CAN DISTORT JUSTICE.
WE CANNOT ALLOW THAT TO HAPPEN.

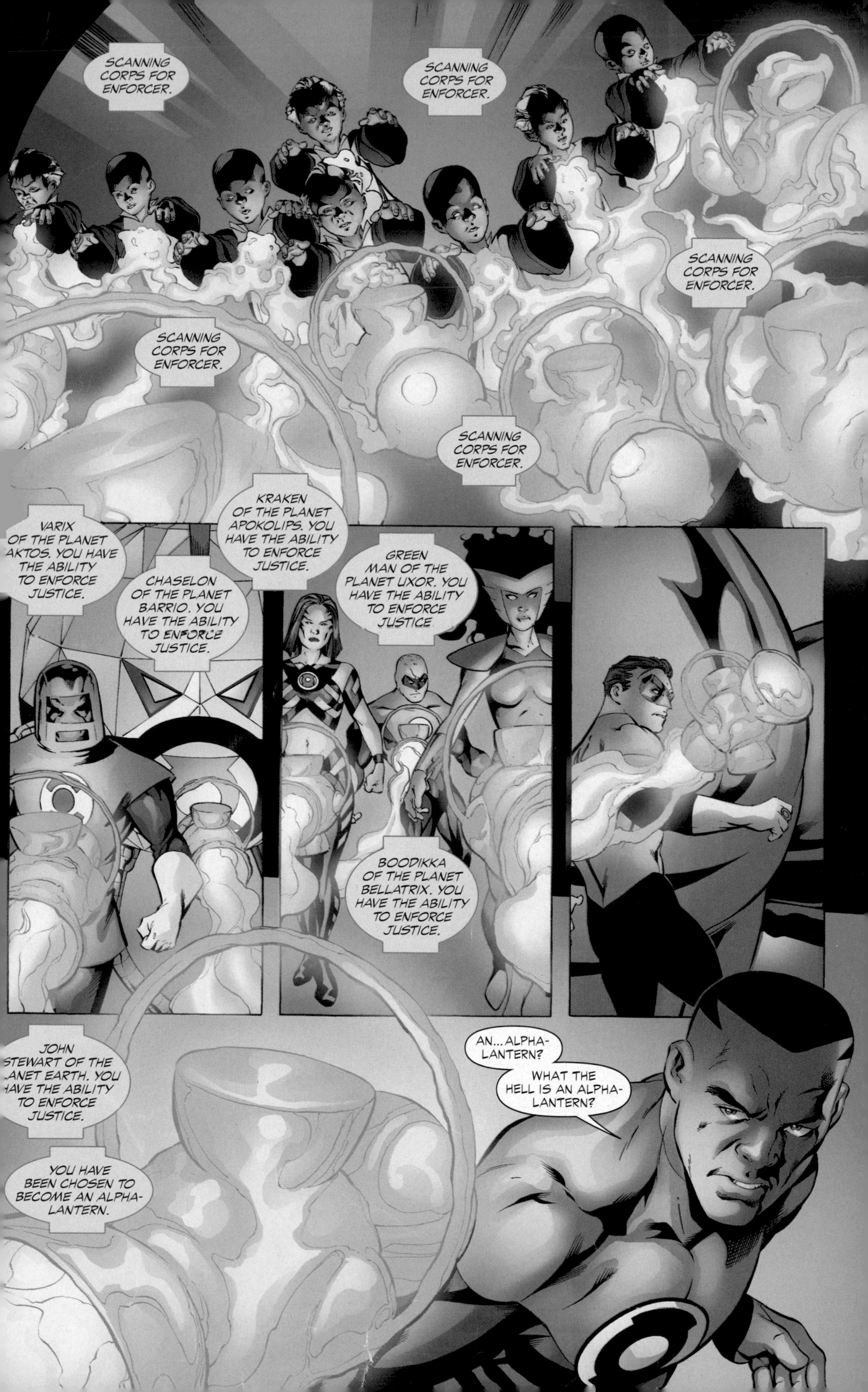
SCANNING CORPS FOR ENFORCER.
SCANNING CORPS FOR ENFORCER.
SCANNING CORPS FOR ENFORCER.
SCANNING CORPS FOR ENFORCER.
SCANNING CORPS FOR ENFORCER.
VARIX OF THE PLANET AKTOS. YOU HAVE THE ABILITY TO ENFORCE JUSTICE.
KRAKEN OF THE PLANET APOKOLIPS. YOU HAVE THE ABILITY TO ENFORCE JUSTICE.
CHASELON OF THE PLANET BARRIO. YOU HAVE THE ABILITY TO ENFORCE JUSTICE.
GREEN MAN OF THE PLANET UXOR. YOU HAVE THE ABILITY TO ENFORCE JUSTICE.
BOODIKKA OF THE PLANET BELLATRIX. YOU HAVE THE ABILITY TO ENFORCE JUSTICE.
JOHN STEWART OF THE LANET EARTH. YOU AVE THE ABILITY TO ENFORCE JUSTICE.
YOU HAVE BEEN CHOSEN TO BECOME AN ALPHA-LANTERN.
AN...ALPHA-LANTERN?
WHAT THE HELL IS AN ALPHA-LANTERN?

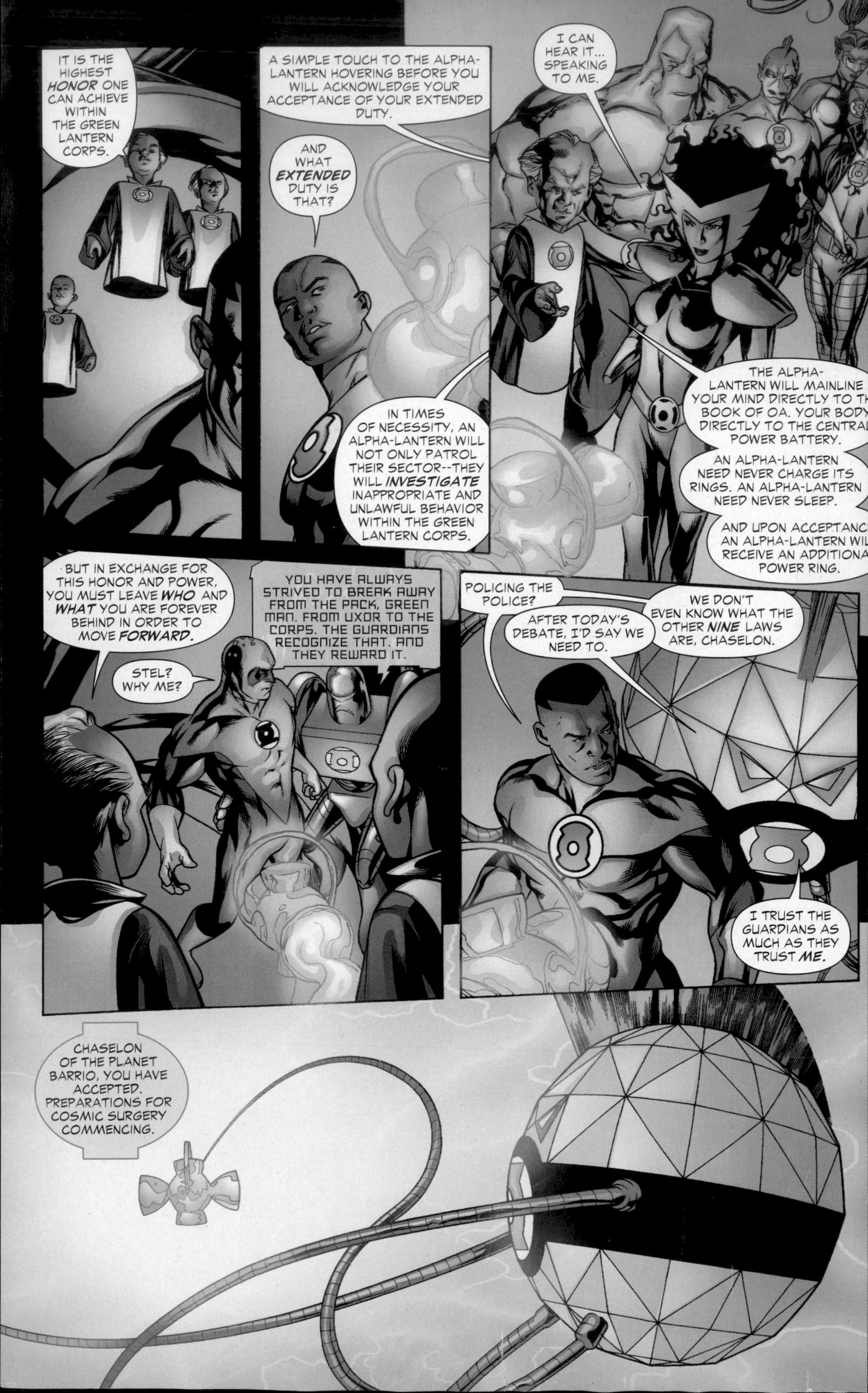
IT IS THE HIGHEST HONOR ONE CAN ACHIEVE WITHIN THE GREEN LANTERN CORPS.
A SIMPLE TOUCH TO THE ALPHA-LANTERN HOVERING BEFORE YOU WILL ACKNOWLEDGE YOUR ACCEPTANCE OF YOUR EXTENDED DUTY.
AND WHAT EXTENDED DUTY IS THAT?
IN TIMES OF NECESSITY, AN ALPHA-LANTERN WILL NOT ONLY PATROL THEIR SECTOR--THEY WILL INVESTIGATE INAPPROPRIATE AND UNLAWFUL BEHAVIOR WITHIN THE GREEN LANTERN CORPS.
I CAN HEAR IT... SPEAKING TO ME.
THE ALPHA-LANTERN WILL MAINLINE YOUR MIND DIRECTLY TO TH BOOK OF OA. YOUR BODY DIRECTLY TO THE CENTRAL POWER BATTERY.
AN ALPHA-LANTERN NEED NEVER CHARGE ITS RINGS. AN ALPHA-LANTERN NEED NEVER SLEEP.
AND UPON ACCEPTANC AN ALPHA-LANTERN WIL RECEIVE AN ADDITIONA POWER RING.
BUT IN EXCHANGE FOR THIS HONOR AND POWER, YOU MUST LEAVE WHO AND WHAT YOU ARE FOREVER BEHIND IN ORDER TO MOVE FORWARD.
STEL? WHY ME?
YOU HAVE ALWAYS STRIVED TO BREAK AWAY FROM THE PACK, GREEN MAN. FROM UXOR TO THE CORPS. THE GUARDIANS RECOGNIZE THAT. AND THEY REWARD IT.
POLICING THE POLICE?
AFTER TODAY'S DEBATE, I'D SAY WE NEED TO.
WE DON'T EVEN KNOW WHAT THE OTHER NINE LAWS ARE, CHASELON.
I TRUST THE GUARDIANS AS MUCH AS THEY TRUST ME.
CHASELON OF THE PLANET BARRIO, YOU HAVE ACCEPTED. PREPARATIONS FOR COSMIC SURGERY COMMENCING.

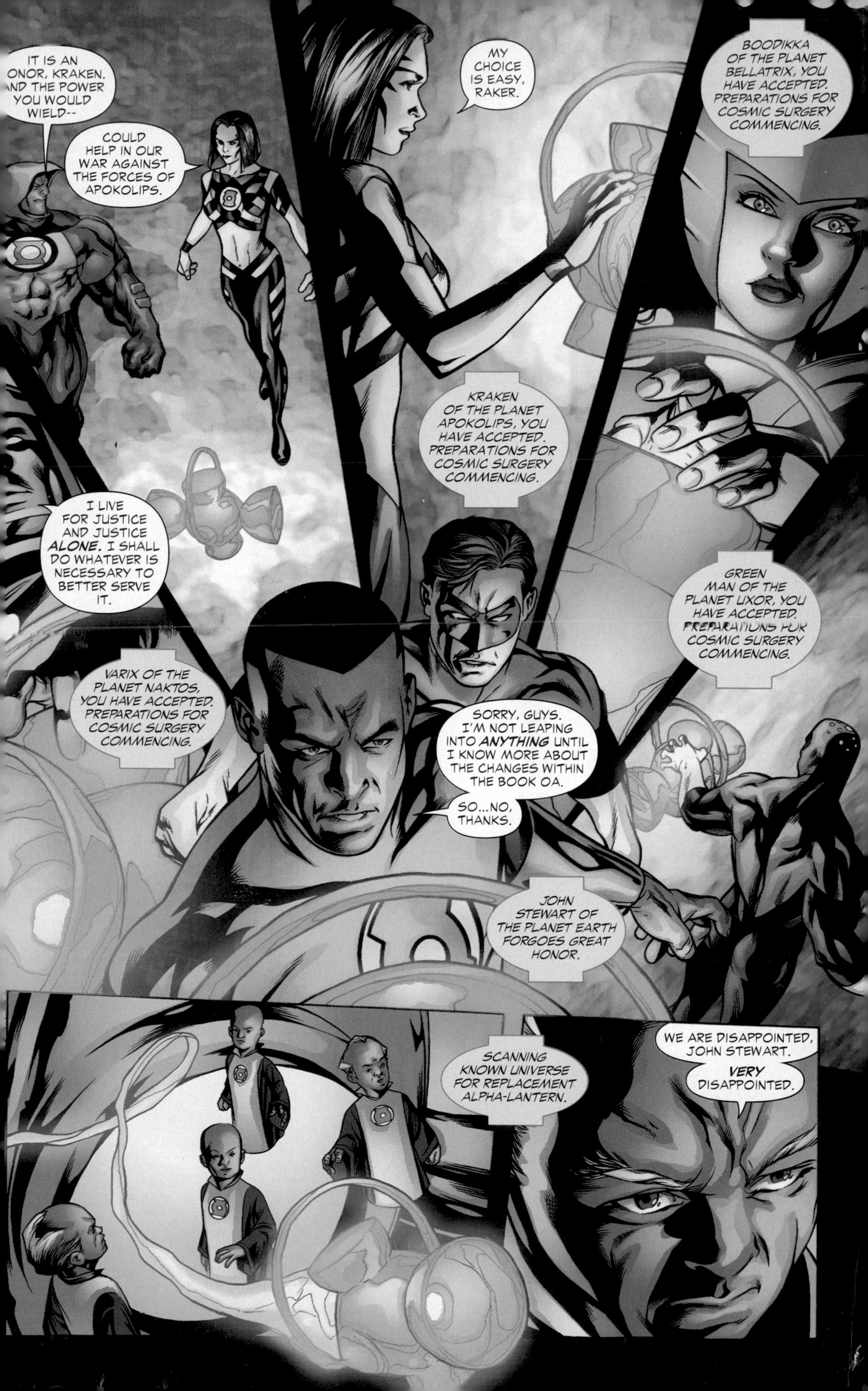

IT IS AN ONOR, KRAKEN. AND THE POWER YOU WOULD WIELD--
COULD HELP IN OUR WAR AGAINST THE FORCES OF APOKOLIPS.
MY CHOICE IS EASY, RAKER.
BOODIKKA OF THE PLANET BELLATRIX, YOU HAVE ACCEPTED. PREPARATIONS FOR COSMIC SURGERY COMMENCING.
KRAKEN OF THE PLANET APOKOLIPS, YOU HAVE ACCEPTED. PREPARATIONS FOR COSMIC SURGERY COMMENCING.
I LIVE FOR JUSTICE AND JUSTICE ALONE. I SHALL DO WHATEVER IS NECESSARY TO BETTER SERVE IT.
GREEN MAN OF THE PLANET UXOR, YOU HAVE ACCEPTED. PREPARATIONS FOR COSMIC SURGERY COMMENCING.
VARIX OF THE PLANET NAKTOS, YOU HAVE ACCEPTED. PREPARATIONS FOR COSMIC SURGERY COMMENCING.
SORRY, GUYS. I'M NOT LEAPING INTO ANYTHING UNTIL I KNOW MORE ABOUT THE CHANGES WITHIN THE BOOK OA.
SO...NO, THANKS.
JOHN STEWART OF THE PLANET EARTH FORGOES GREAT HONOR.
SCANNING KNOWN UNIVERSE FOR REPLACEMENT ALPHA-LANTERN.
WE ARE DISAPPOINTED, JOHN STEWART.
VERY DISAPPOINTED.

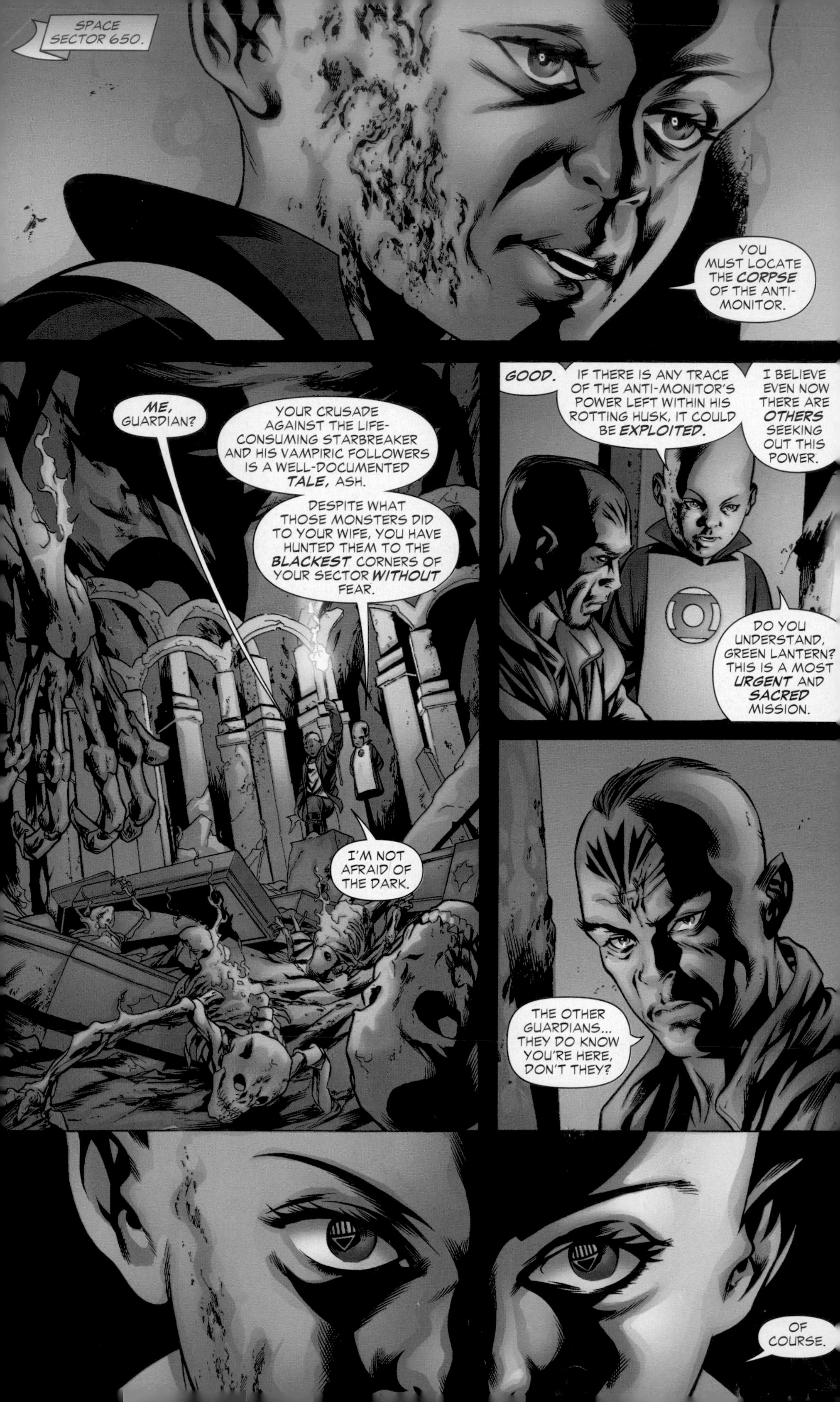
SPACE SECTOR 650.
YOU MUST LOCATE THE *CORPSE* OF THE ANTI-MONITOR.
ME, GUARDIAN?
YOUR CRUSADE AGAINST THE LIFE-CONSUMING STARBREAKER AND HIS VAMPIRIC FOLLOWERS IS A WELL-DOCUMENTED *TALE,* ASH.
DESPITE WHAT THOSE MONSTERS DID TO YOUR WIFE, YOU HAVE HUNTED THEM TO THE *BLACKEST* CORNERS OF YOUR SECTOR *WITHOUT* FEAR.
I'M NOT AFRAID OF THE DARK.
GOOD.
IF THERE IS ANY TRACE OF THE ANTI-MONITOR'S POWER LEFT WITHIN HIS ROTTING HUSK, IT COULD BE *EXPLOITED.*
I BELIEVE EVEN NOW THERE ARE *OTHERS* SEEKING OUT THIS POWER.
DO YOU UNDERSTAND, GREEN LANTERN? THIS IS A MOST *URGENT* AND *SACRED* MISSION.
THE OTHER GUARDIANS... THEY DO KNOW YOU'RE HERE, DON'T THEY?
OF COURSE.

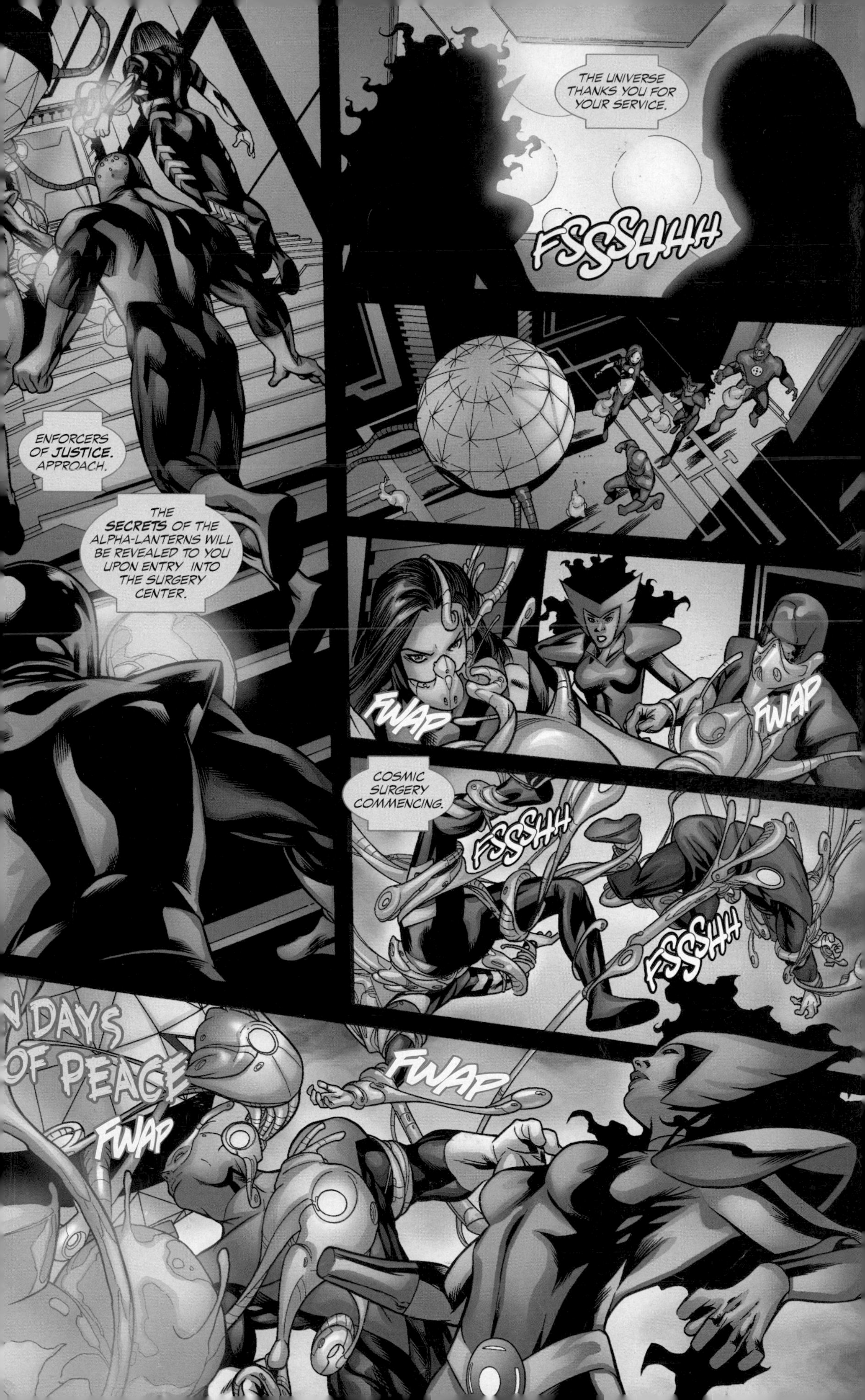
ENFORCERS OF JUSTICE. APPROACH.
THE SECRETS OF THE ALPHA-LANTERNS WILL BE REVEALED TO YOU UPON ENTRY INTO THE SURGERY CENTER.
THE UNIVERSE THANKS YOU FOR YOUR SERVICE.
FSSSHHH
FWAP
FWAP
COSMIC SURGERY COMMENCING.
FSSSHH
FSSSHH
FWAP
FWAP
DAYS OF PEACE

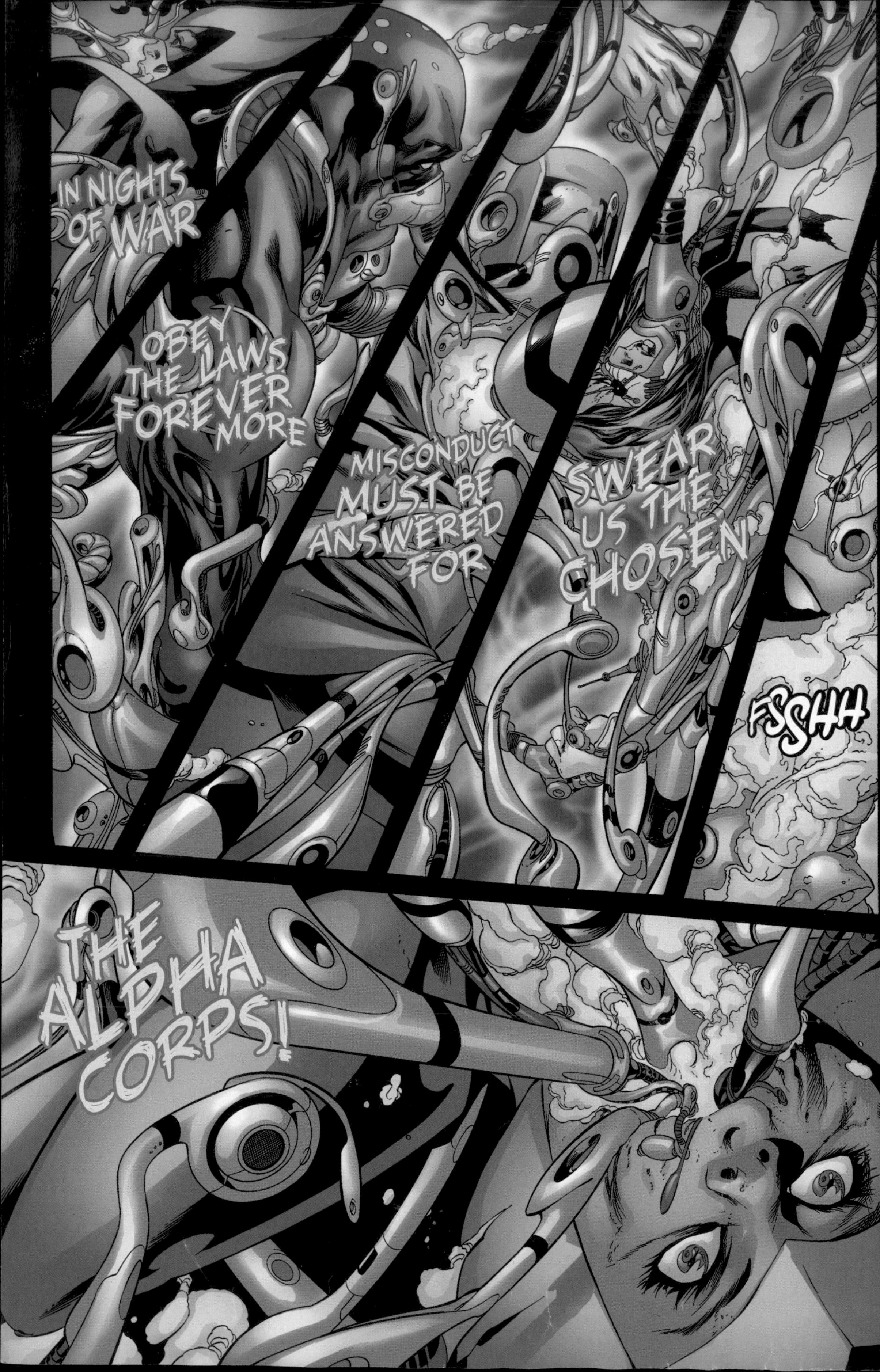
IN NIGHTS OF WAR
OBEY THE LAWS FOREVER MORE
MISCONDUCT MUST BE ANSWERED FOR
SWEAR US THE CHOSEN
FSSHH
THE ALPHA CORPS!

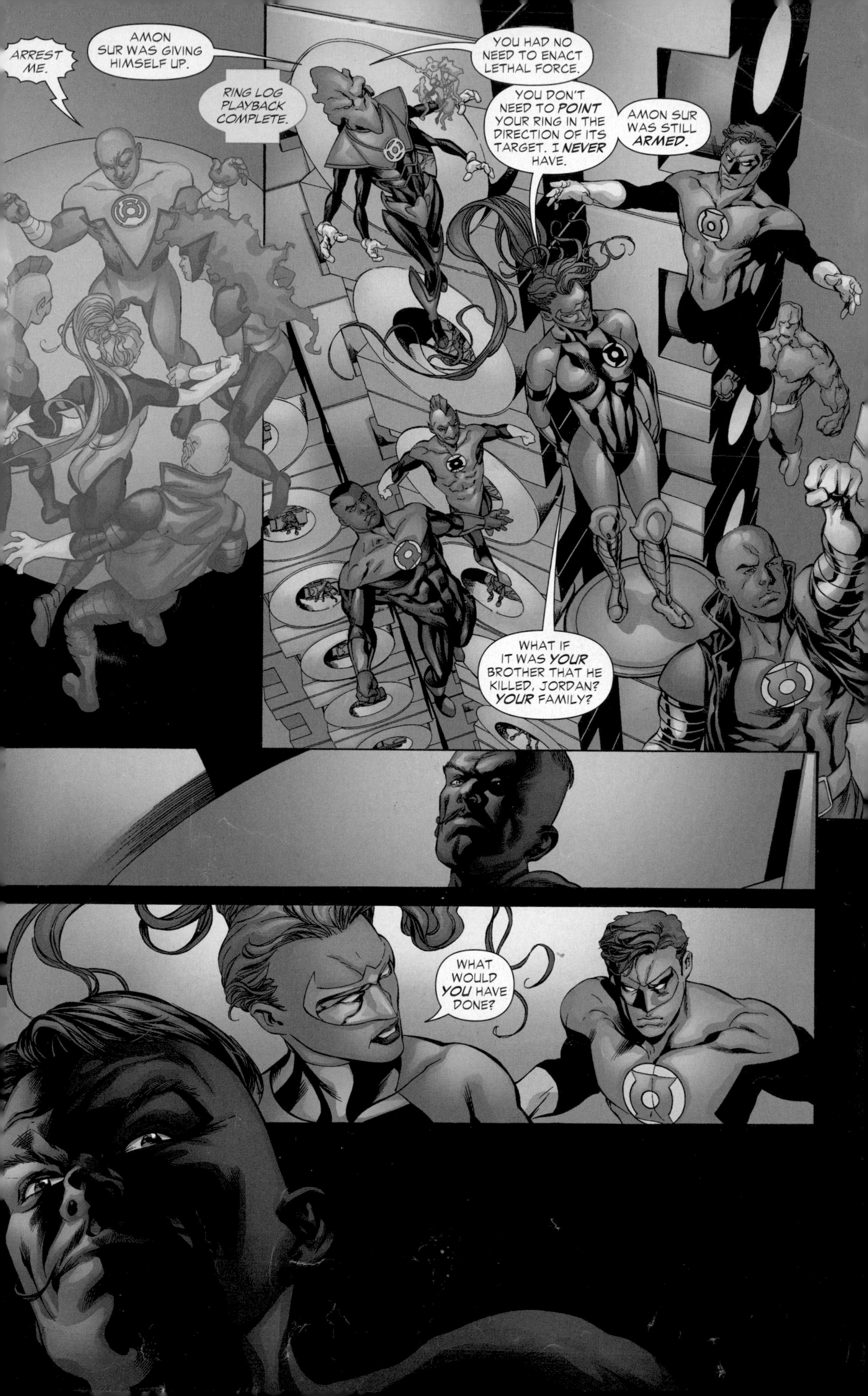

ARREST ME.
AMON SUR WAS GIVING HIMSELF UP.
RING LOG PLAYBACK COMPLETE.
YOU HAD NO NEED TO ENACT LETHAL FORCE.
YOU DON'T NEED TO POINT YOUR RING IN THE DIRECTION OF ITS TARGET. I NEVER HAVE.
AMON SUR WAS STILL ARMED.
WHAT IF IT WAS YOUR BROTHER THAT HE KILLED, JORDAN? YOUR FAMILY?
WHAT WOULD YOU HAVE DONE?

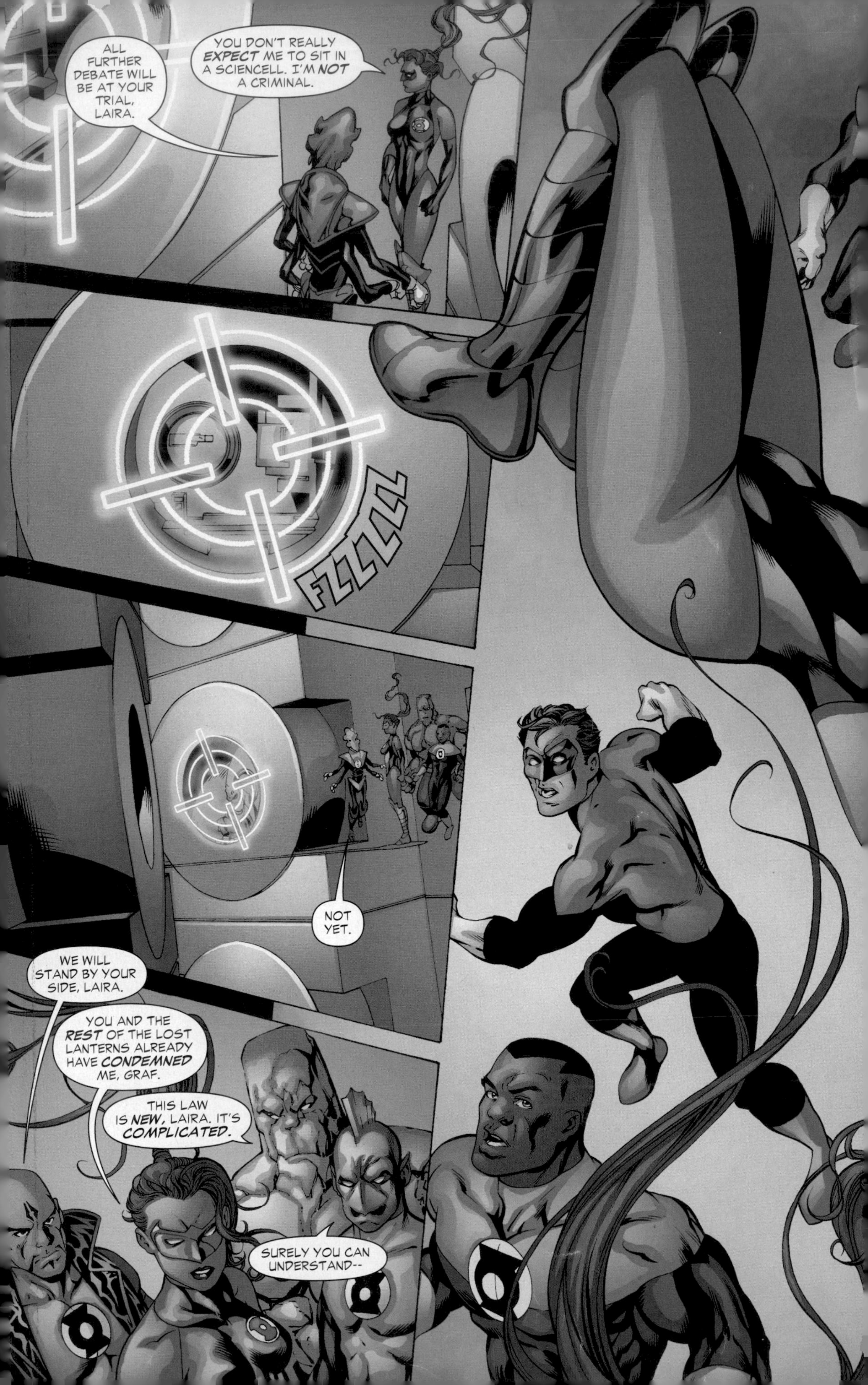
ALL FURTHER DEBATE WILL BE AT YOUR TRIAL, LAIRA.
YOU DON'T REALLY *EXPECT* ME TO SIT IN A SCIENCELL. I'M *NOT* A CRIMINAL.
FZZZZZL
NOT YET.
WE WILL STAND BY YOUR SIDE, LAIRA.
YOU AND THE *REST* OF THE LOST LANTERNS ALREADY HAVE *CONDEMNED* ME, GRAF.
THIS LAW IS *NEW*, LAIRA. IT'S *COMPLICATED*.
SURELY YOU CAN UNDERSTAND--

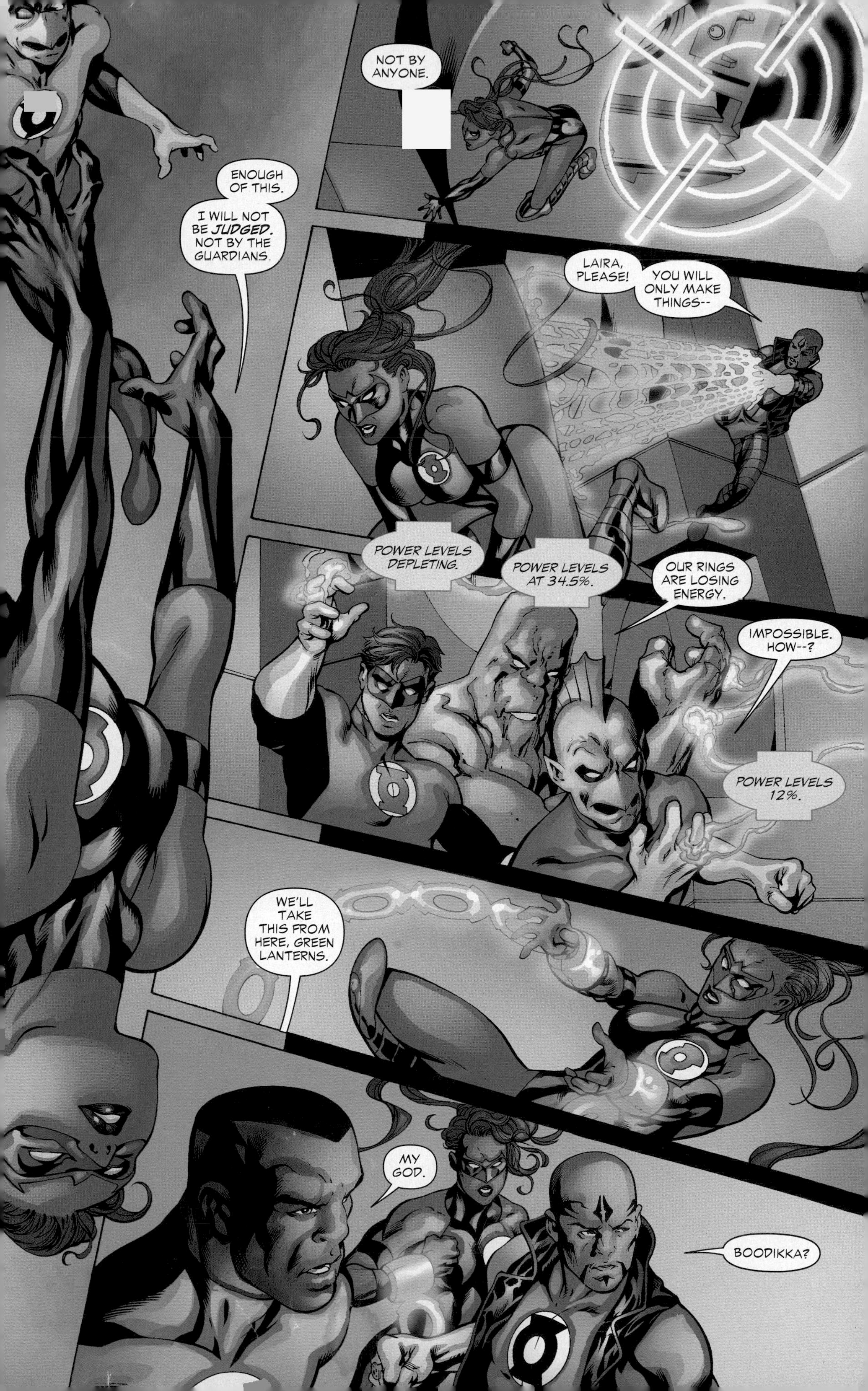
ENOUGH OF THIS.
I WILL NOT BE JUDGED. NOT BY THE GUARDIANS.
NOT BY ANYONE.
LAIRA, PLEASE!
YOU WILL ONLY MAKE THINGS--
POWER LEVELS DEPLETING.
POWER LEVELS AT 34.5%.
OUR RINGS ARE LOSING ENERGY.
IMPOSSIBLE. HOW--?
POWER LEVELS 12%.
WE'LL TAKE THIS FROM HERE, GREEN LANTERNS.
MY GOD.
BOODIKKA?

GREEN LANTERN 28 Cover by Mike McKone, Andy Lanning and Moose Baumann

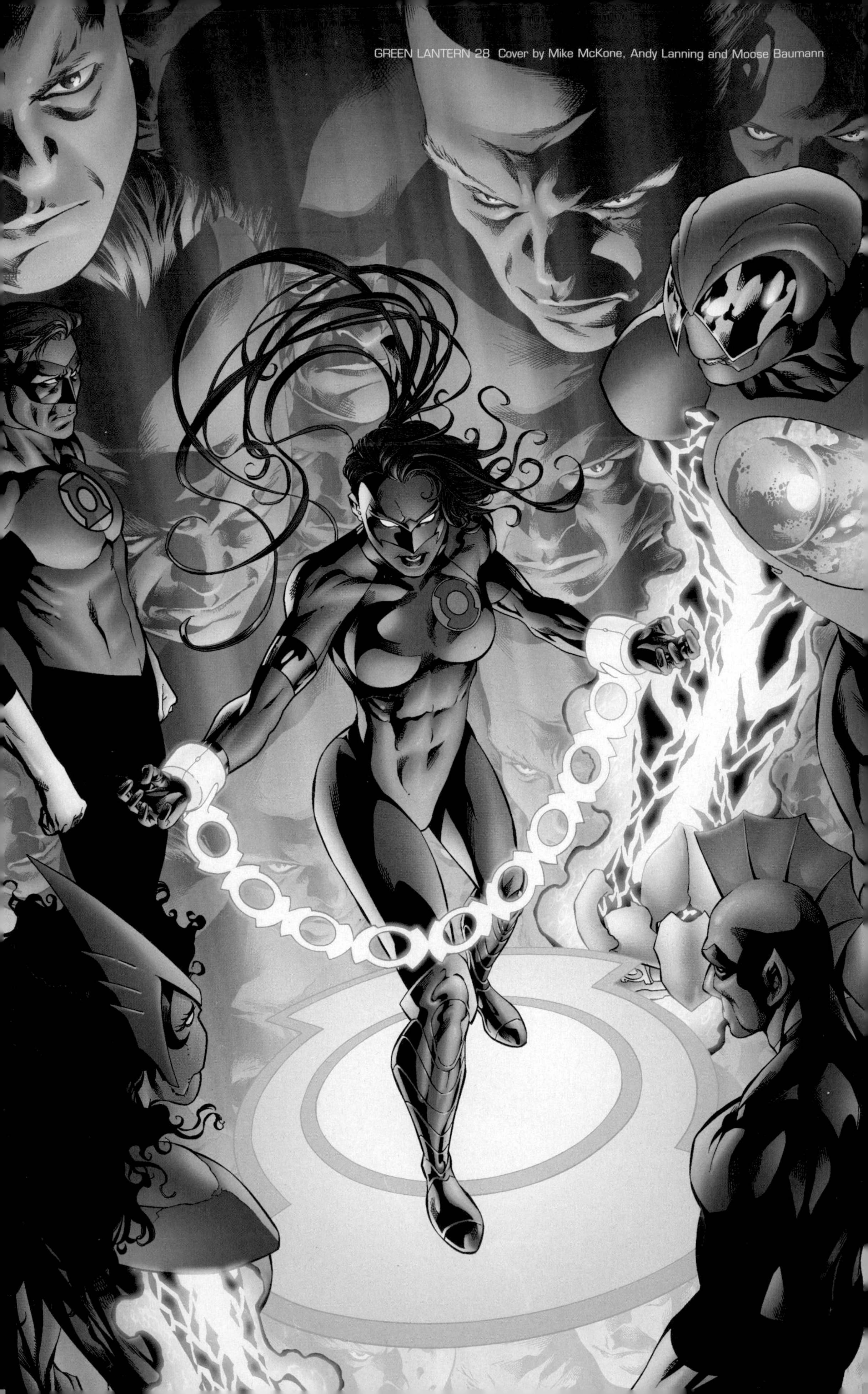

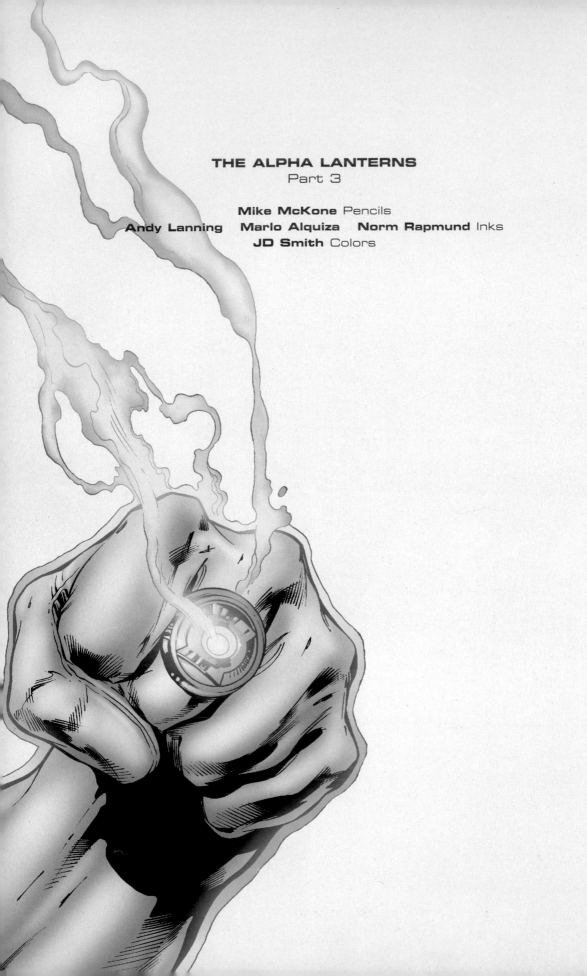

THE ALPHA LANTERNS
Part 3

Mike McKone Pencils
Andy Lanning   **Marlo Alquiza**   **Norm Rapmund** Inks
JD Smith Colors

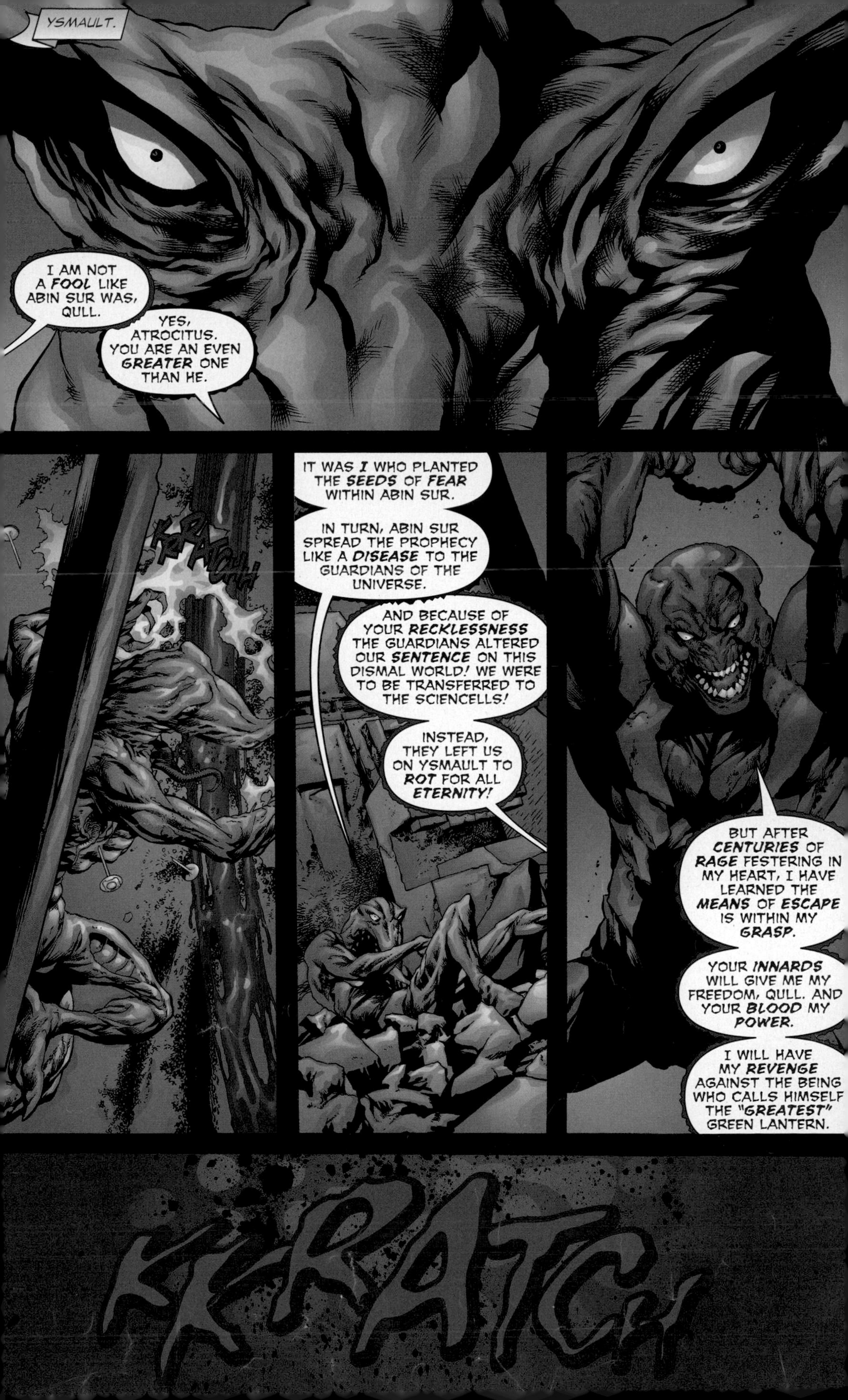
YSMAULT.
I AM NOT A **FOOL** LIKE ABIN SUR WAS, QULL.
YES, ATROCITUS. YOU ARE AN EVEN **GREATER** ONE THAN HE.
KRATCH!
IT WAS **I** WHO PLANTED THE **SEEDS** OF **FEAR** WITHIN ABIN SUR.
IN TURN, ABIN SUR SPREAD THE PROPHECY LIKE A **DISEASE** TO THE GUARDIANS OF THE UNIVERSE.
AND BECAUSE OF YOUR **RECKLESSNESS** THE GUARDIANS ALTERED OUR **SENTENCE** ON THIS DISMAL WORLD! WE WERE TO BE TRANSFERRED TO THE SCIENCELLS!
INSTEAD, THEY LEFT US ON YSMAULT TO **ROT** FOR ALL **ETERNITY**!
BUT AFTER **CENTURIES** OF **RAGE** FESTERING IN MY HEART, I HAVE LEARNED THE **MEANS** OF **ESCAPE** IS WITHIN MY **GRASP**.
YOUR **INNARDS** WILL GIVE ME MY FREEDOM, QULL. AND YOUR **BLOOD** MY **POWER**.
I WILL HAVE MY **REVENGE** AGAINST THE BEING WHO CALLS HIMSELF THE "**GREATEST**" GREEN LANTERN.
KKRATCH

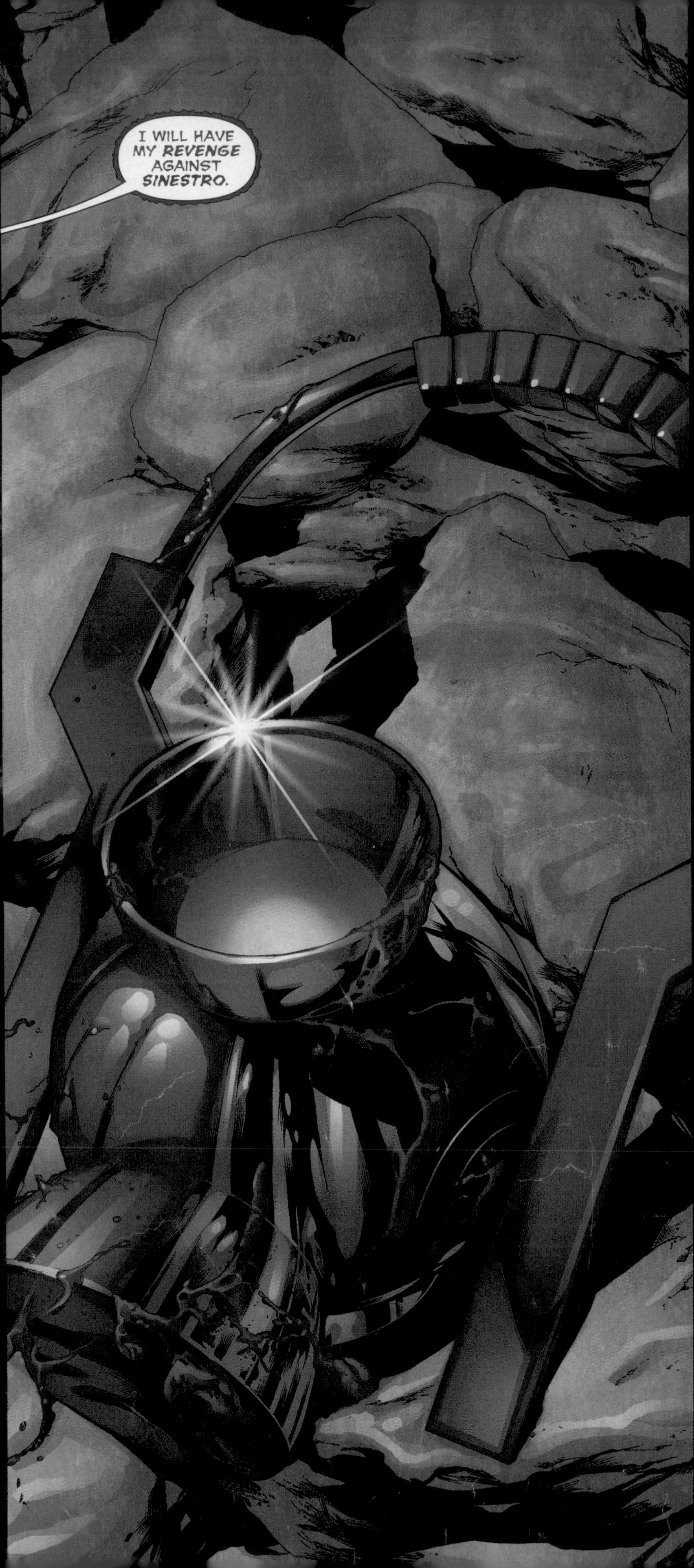
I WILL HAVE MY REVENGE AGAINST SINESTRO.

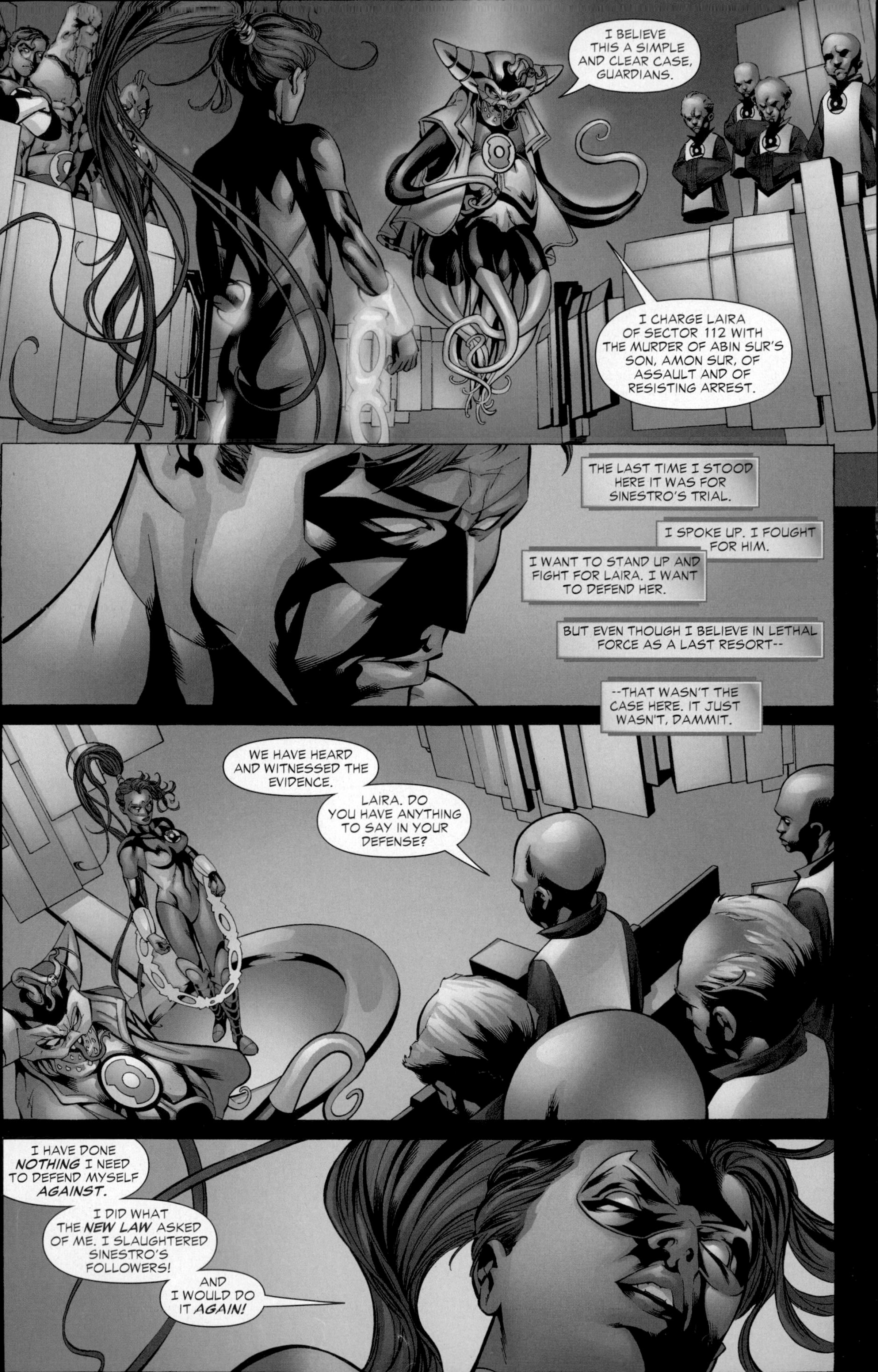
I BELIEVE THIS A SIMPLE AND CLEAR CASE, GUARDIANS.
I CHARGE LAIRA OF SECTOR 112 WITH THE MURDER OF ABIN SUR'S SON, AMON SUR, OF ASSAULT AND OF RESISTING ARREST.
THE LAST TIME I STOOD HERE IT WAS FOR SINESTRO'S TRIAL.
I SPOKE UP. I FOUGHT FOR HIM.
I WANT TO STAND UP AND FIGHT FOR LAIRA. I WANT TO DEFEND HER.
BUT EVEN THOUGH I BELIEVE IN LETHAL FORCE AS A LAST RESORT--
--THAT WASN'T THE CASE HERE. IT JUST WASN'T, DAMMIT.
WE HAVE HEARD AND WITNESSED THE EVIDENCE.
LAIRA. DO YOU HAVE ANYTHING TO SAY IN YOUR DEFENSE?
I HAVE DONE *NOTHING* I NEED TO DEFEND MYSELF *AGAINST*.
I DID WHAT THE *NEW LAW* ASKED OF ME. I SLAUGHTERED SINESTRO'S FOLLOWERS!
AND I WOULD DO IT *AGAIN!*

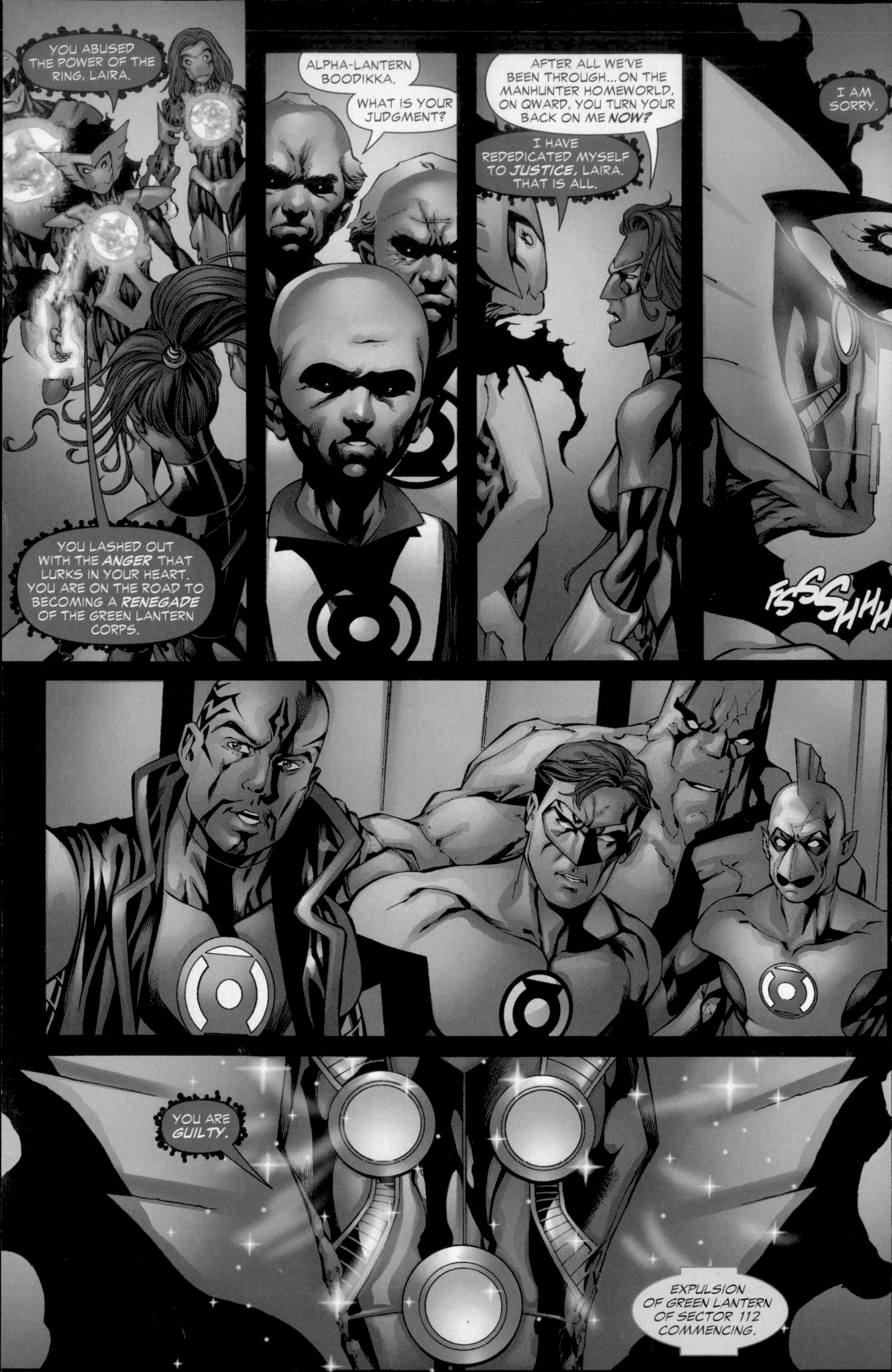
YOU ABUSED THE POWER OF THE RING, LAIRA.
YOU LASHED OUT WITH THE ANGER THAT LURKS IN YOUR HEART. YOU ARE ON THE ROAD TO BECOMING A RENEGADE OF THE GREEN LANTERN CORPS.
ALPHA-LANTERN BOODIKKA.
WHAT IS YOUR JUDGMENT?
AFTER ALL WE'VE BEEN THROUGH...ON THE MANHUNTER HOMEWORLD, ON QWARD, YOU TURN YOUR BACK ON ME NOW?
I HAVE REDEDICATED MYSELF TO JUSTICE, LAIRA. THAT IS ALL.
I AM SORRY.
FSSSHHH
YOU ARE GUILTY.
EXPULSION OF GREEN LANTERN OF SECTOR 112 COMMENCING.

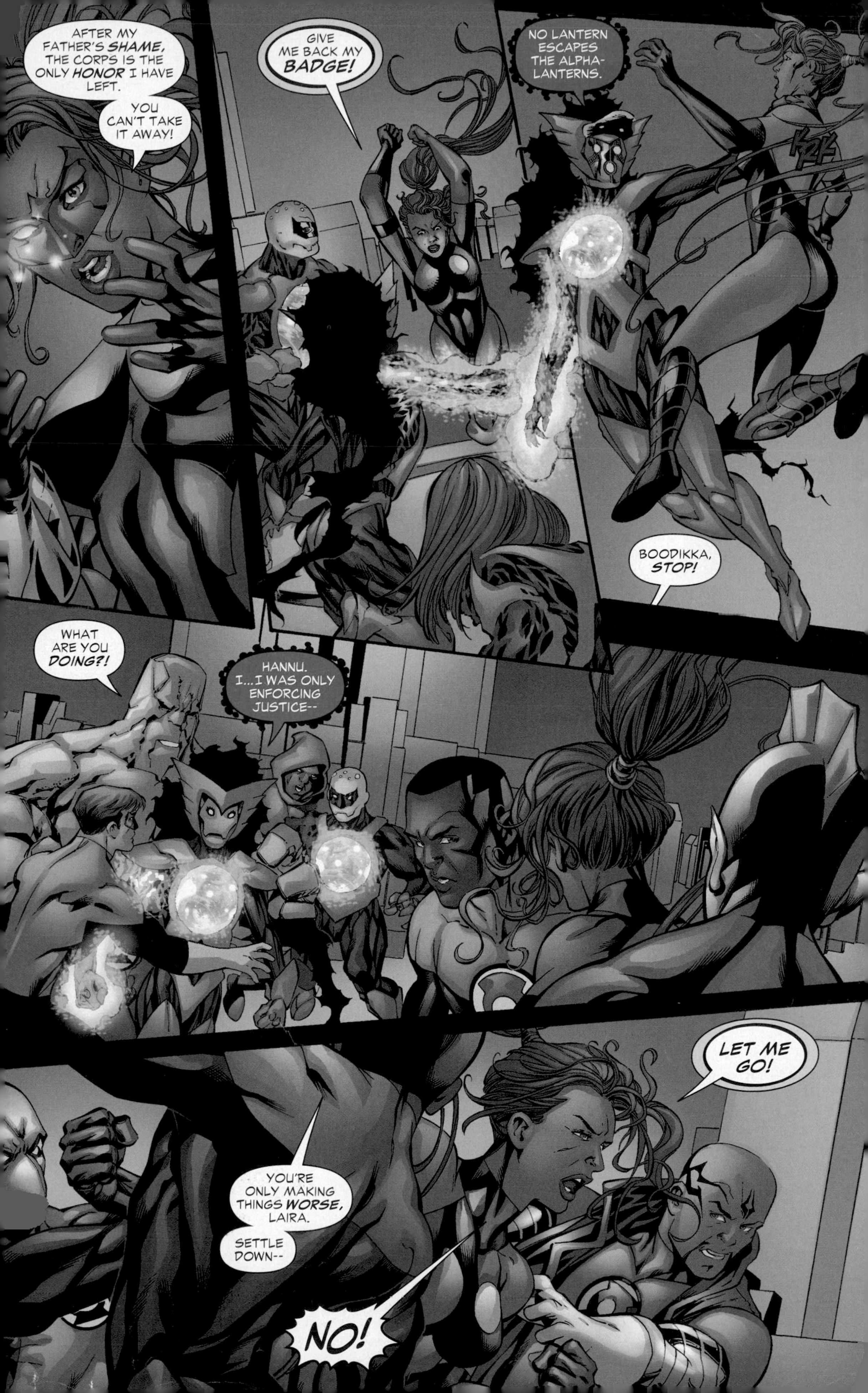
AFTER MY FATHER'S SHAME, THE CORPS IS THE ONLY HONOR I HAVE LEFT.
YOU CAN'T TAKE IT AWAY!
GIVE ME BACK MY BADGE!
NO LANTERN ESCAPES THE ALPHA-LANTERNS.
BOODIKKA, STOP!
WHAT ARE YOU DOING?!
HANNU. I...I WAS ONLY ENFORCING JUSTICE--
LET ME GO!
YOU'RE ONLY MAKING THINGS WORSE, LAIRA.
SETTLE DOWN--
NO!

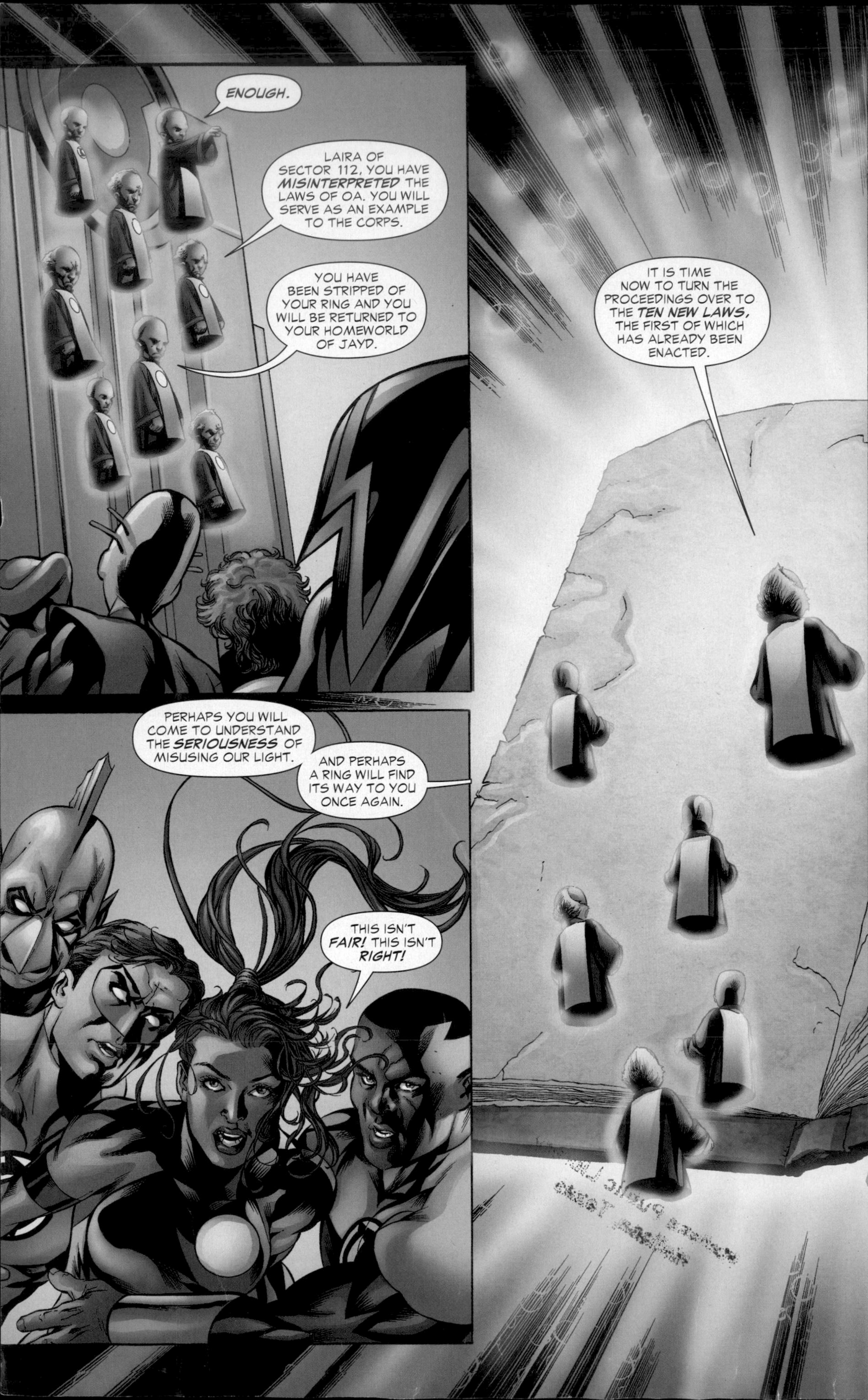

ENOUGH.
LAIRA OF SECTOR 112, YOU HAVE *MISINTERPRETED* THE LAWS OF OA. YOU WILL SERVE AS AN EXAMPLE TO THE CORPS.
YOU HAVE BEEN STRIPPED OF YOUR RING AND YOU WILL BE RETURNED TO YOUR HOMEWORLD OF JAYD.
PERHAPS YOU WILL COME TO UNDERSTAND THE *SERIOUSNESS* OF MISUSING OUR LIGHT.
AND PERHAPS A RING WILL FIND ITS WAY TO YOU ONCE AGAIN.
THIS ISN'T *FAIR!* THIS ISN'T *RIGHT!*
IT IS TIME NOW TO TURN THE PROCEEDINGS OVER TO THE *TEN NEW LAWS,* THE FIRST OF WHICH HAS ALREADY BEEN ENACTED.

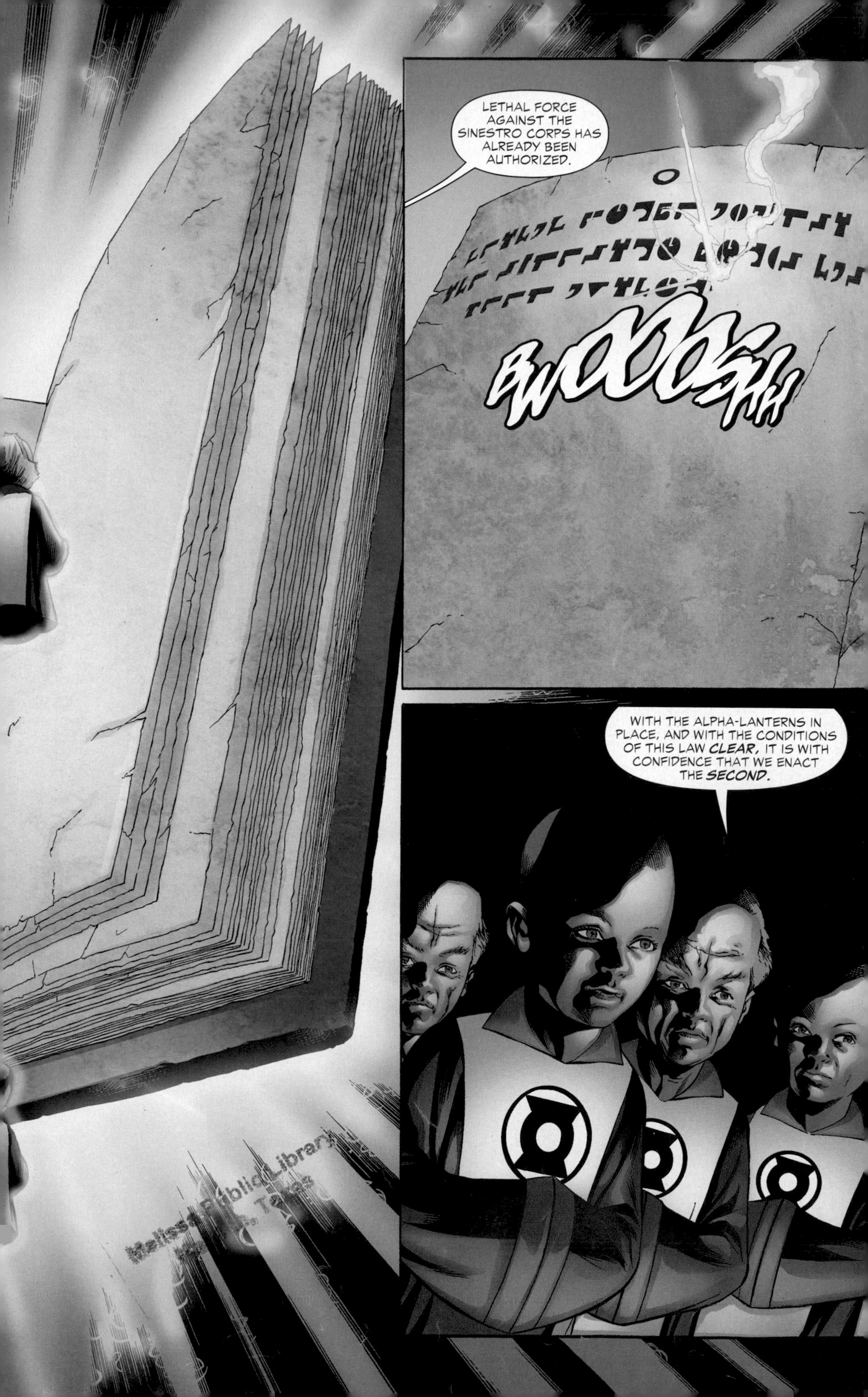
LETHAL FORCE AGAINST THE SINESTRO CORPS HAS ALREADY BEEN AUTHORIZED.
BWOOOSHH
WITH THE ALPHA-LANTERNS IN PLACE, AND WITH THE CONDITIONS OF THIS LAW CLEAR, IT IS WITH CONFIDENCE THAT WE ENACT THE SECOND.

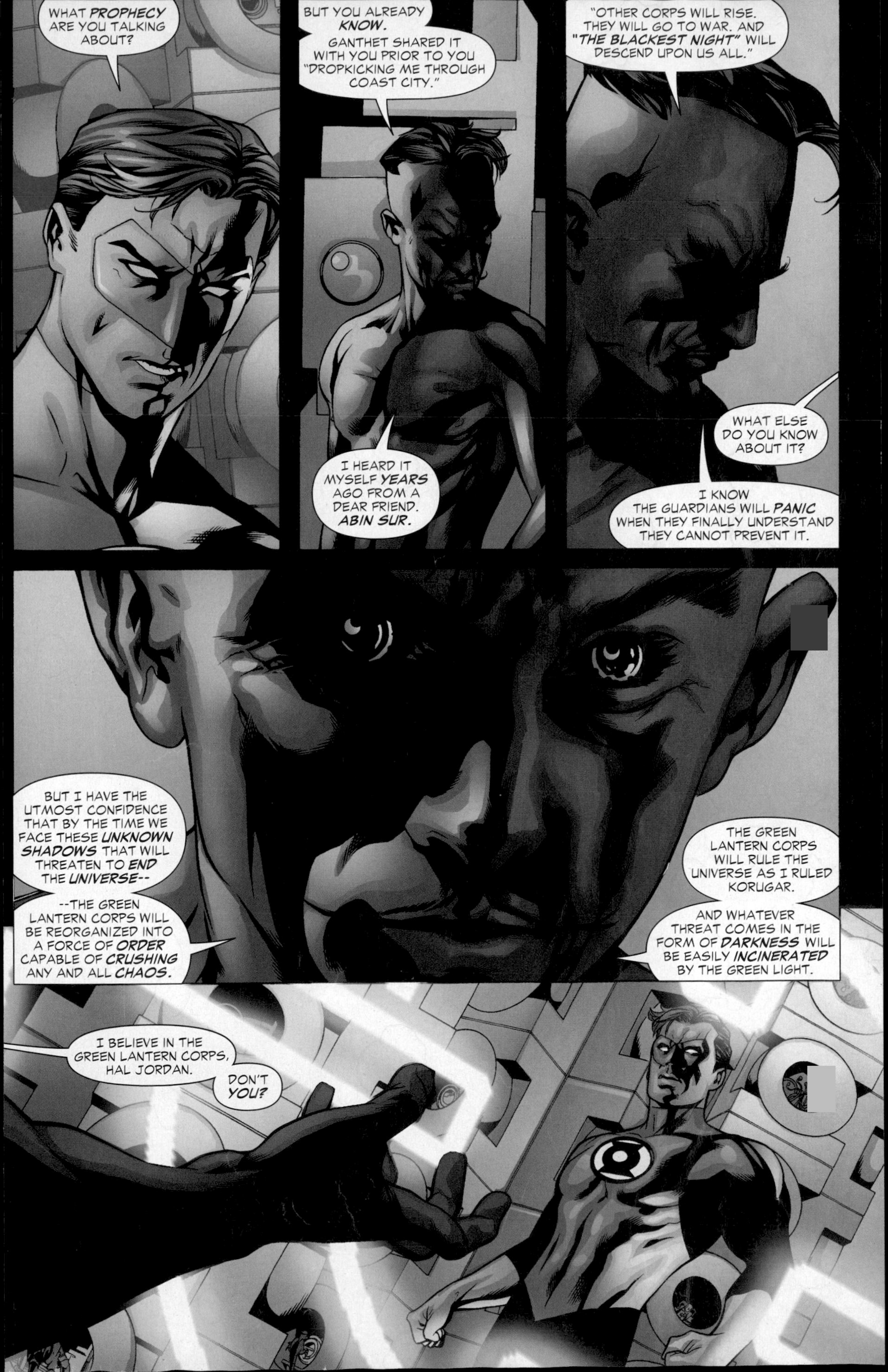
WHAT PROPHECY ARE YOU TALKING ABOUT?
BUT YOU ALREADY KNOW.
GANTHET SHARED IT WITH YOU PRIOR TO YOU "DROPKICKING ME THROUGH COAST CITY."
I HEARD IT MYSELF YEARS AGO FROM A DEAR FRIEND. ABIN SUR.
"OTHER CORPS WILL RISE. THEY WILL GO TO WAR. AND "THE BLACKEST NIGHT" WILL DESCEND UPON US ALL."
WHAT ELSE DO YOU KNOW ABOUT IT?
I KNOW THE GUARDIANS WILL PANIC WHEN THEY FINALLY UNDERSTAND THEY CANNOT PREVENT IT.
BUT I HAVE THE UTMOST CONFIDENCE THAT BY THE TIME WE FACE THESE UNKNOWN SHADOWS THAT WILL THREATEN TO END THE UNIVERSE--
--THE GREEN LANTERN CORPS WILL BE REORGANIZED INTO A FORCE OF ORDER CAPABLE OF CRUSHING ANY AND ALL CHAOS.
THE GREEN LANTERN CORPS WILL RULE THE UNIVERSE AS I RULED KORUGAR.
AND WHATEVER THREAT COMES IN THE FORM OF DARKNESS WILL BE EASILY INCINERATED BY THE GREEN LIGHT.
I BELIEVE IN THE GREEN LANTERN CORPS, HAL JORDAN.
DON'T YOU?

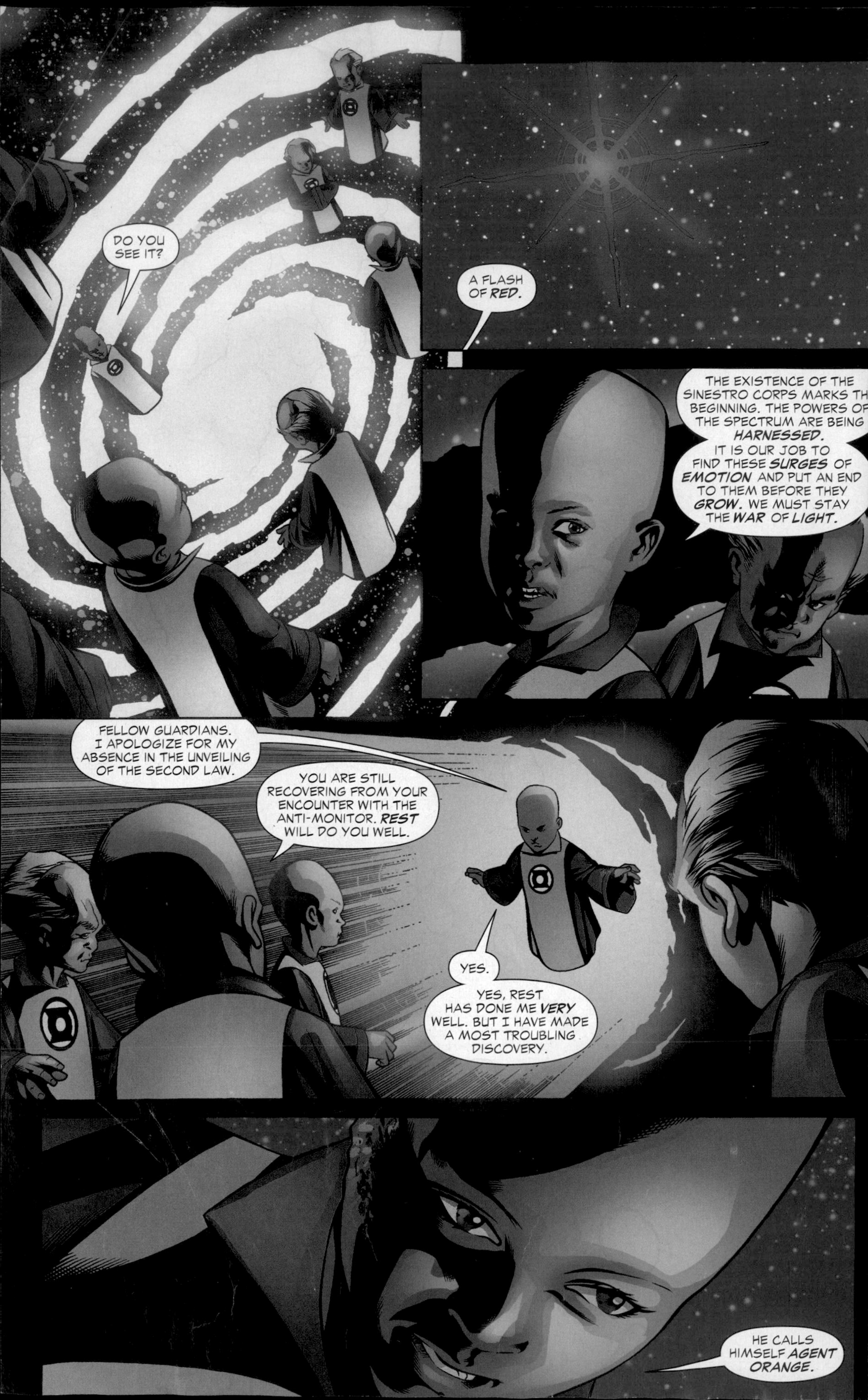
DO YOU SEE IT?
A FLASH OF RED.
THE EXISTENCE OF THE SINESTRO CORPS MARKS TH BEGINNING. THE POWERS OF THE SPECTRUM ARE BEING HARNESSED.
IT IS OUR JOB TO FIND THESE SURGES OF EMOTION AND PUT AN END TO THEM BEFORE THEY GROW. WE MUST STAY THE WAR OF LIGHT.
FELLOW GUARDIANS. I APOLOGIZE FOR MY ABSENCE IN THE UNVEILING OF THE SECOND LAW.
YOU ARE STILL RECOVERING FROM YOUR ENCOUNTER WITH THE ANTI-MONITOR. REST WILL DO YOU WELL.
YES.
YES, REST HAS DONE ME VERY WELL. BUT I HAVE MADE A MOST TROUBLING DISCOVERY.
HE CALLS HIMSELF AGENT ORANGE.

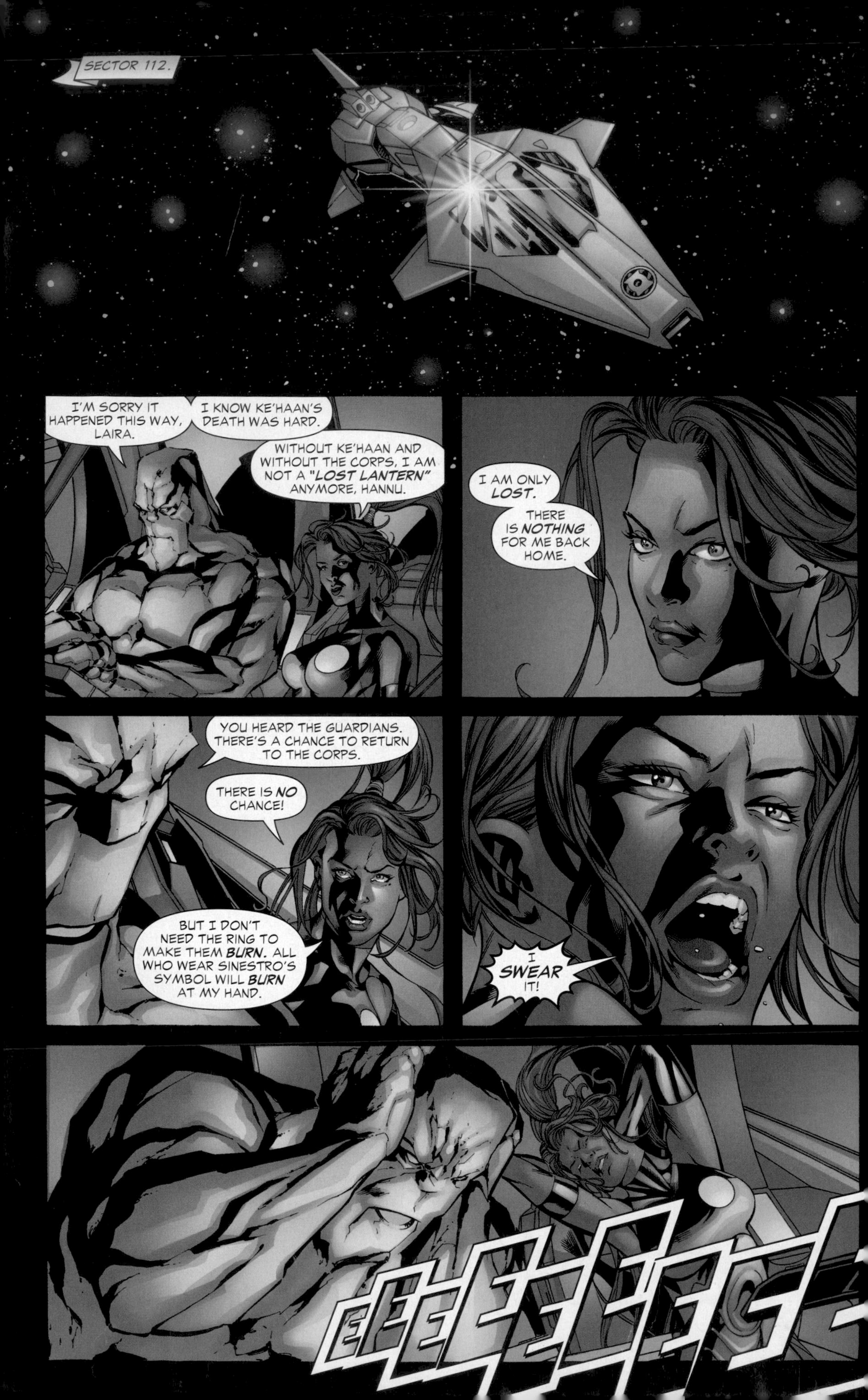
SECTOR 112.
I'M SORRY IT HAPPENED THIS WAY, LAIRA.
I KNOW KE'HAAN'S DEATH WAS HARD.
WITHOUT KE'HAAN AND WITHOUT THE CORPS, I AM NOT A "LOST LANTERN" ANYMORE, HANNU.
I AM ONLY LOST.
THERE IS NOTHING FOR ME BACK HOME.
YOU HEARD THE GUARDIANS. THERE'S A CHANCE TO RETURN TO THE CORPS.
THERE IS NO CHANCE!
BUT I DON'T NEED THE RING TO MAKE THEM BURN. ALL WHO WEAR SINESTRO'S SYMBOL WILL BURN AT MY HAND.
I SWEAR IT!

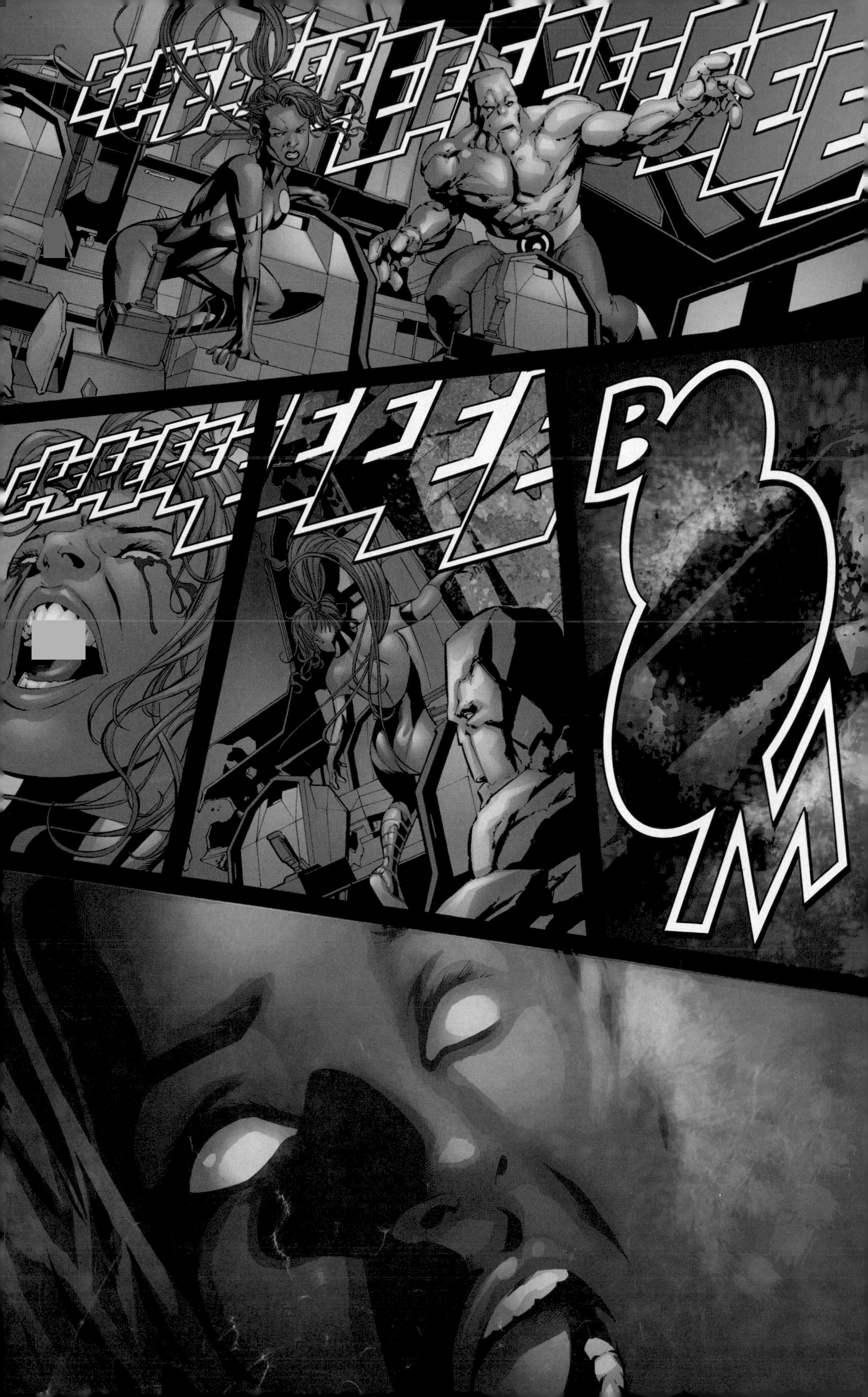

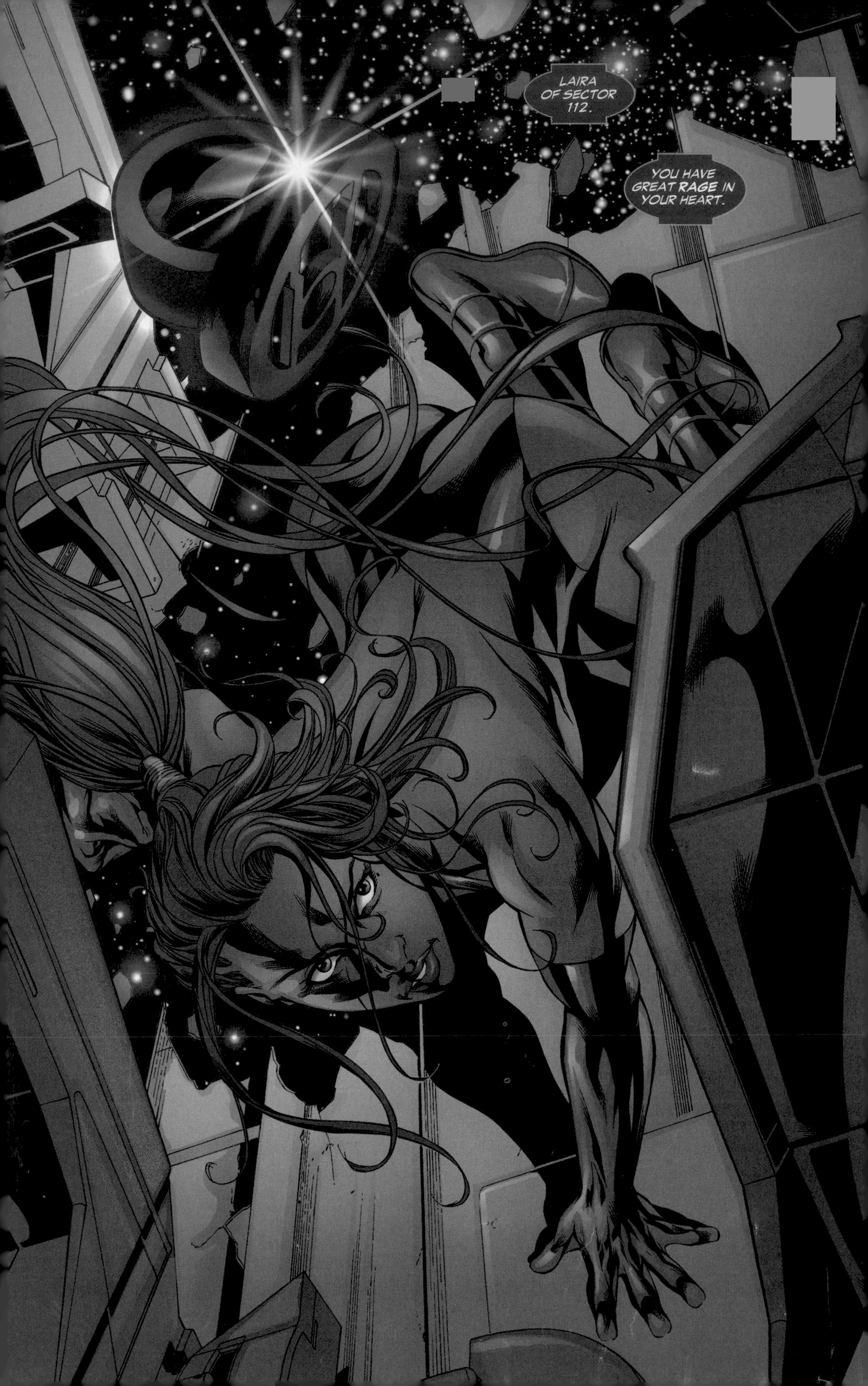
LAIRA OF SECTOR 112.
YOU HAVE GREAT RAGE IN YOUR HEART.

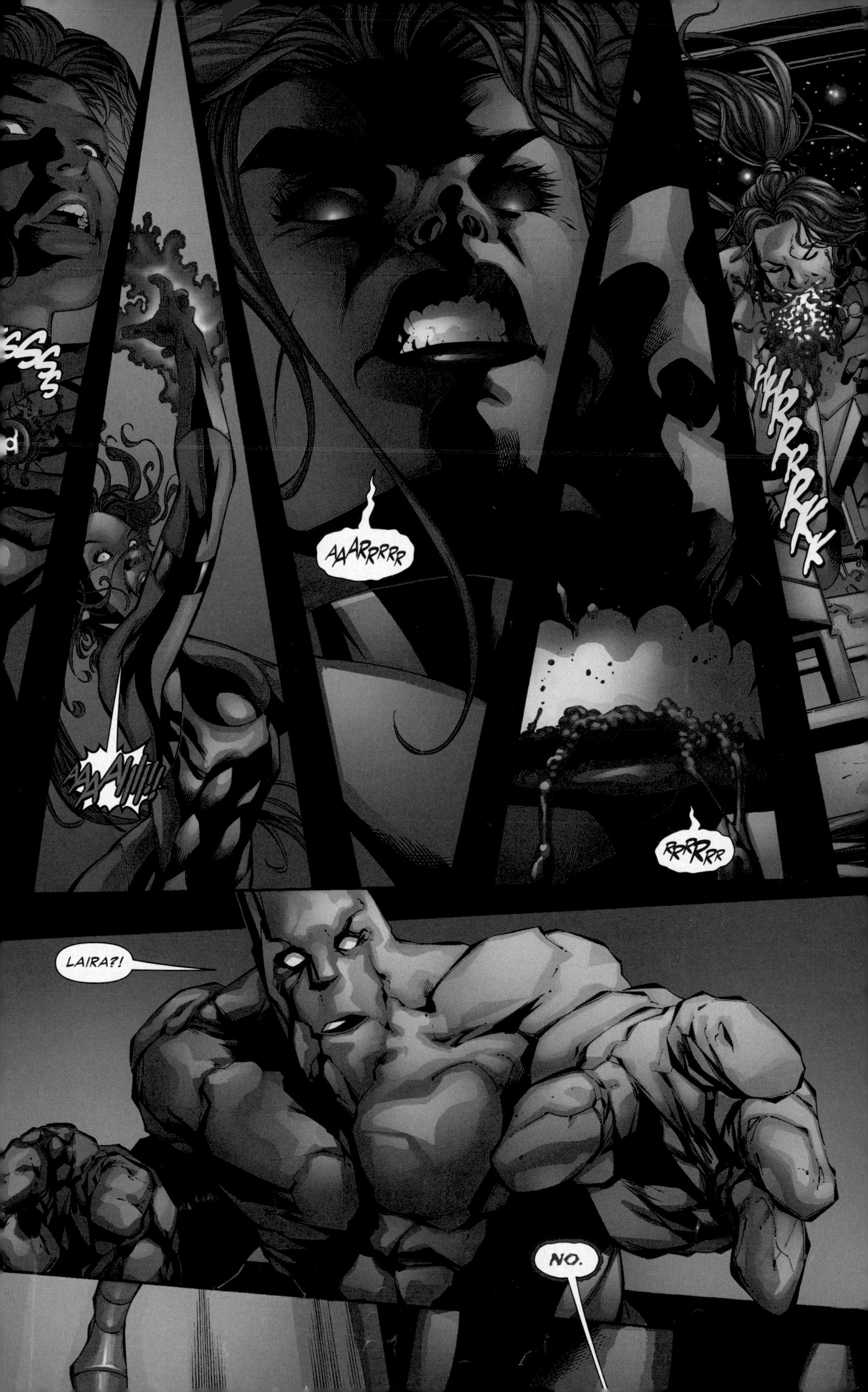

SSSS
AAAARRRR
HHRRRKKK
AAAAIIII!!
RRRRRR
LAIRA?!
NO.

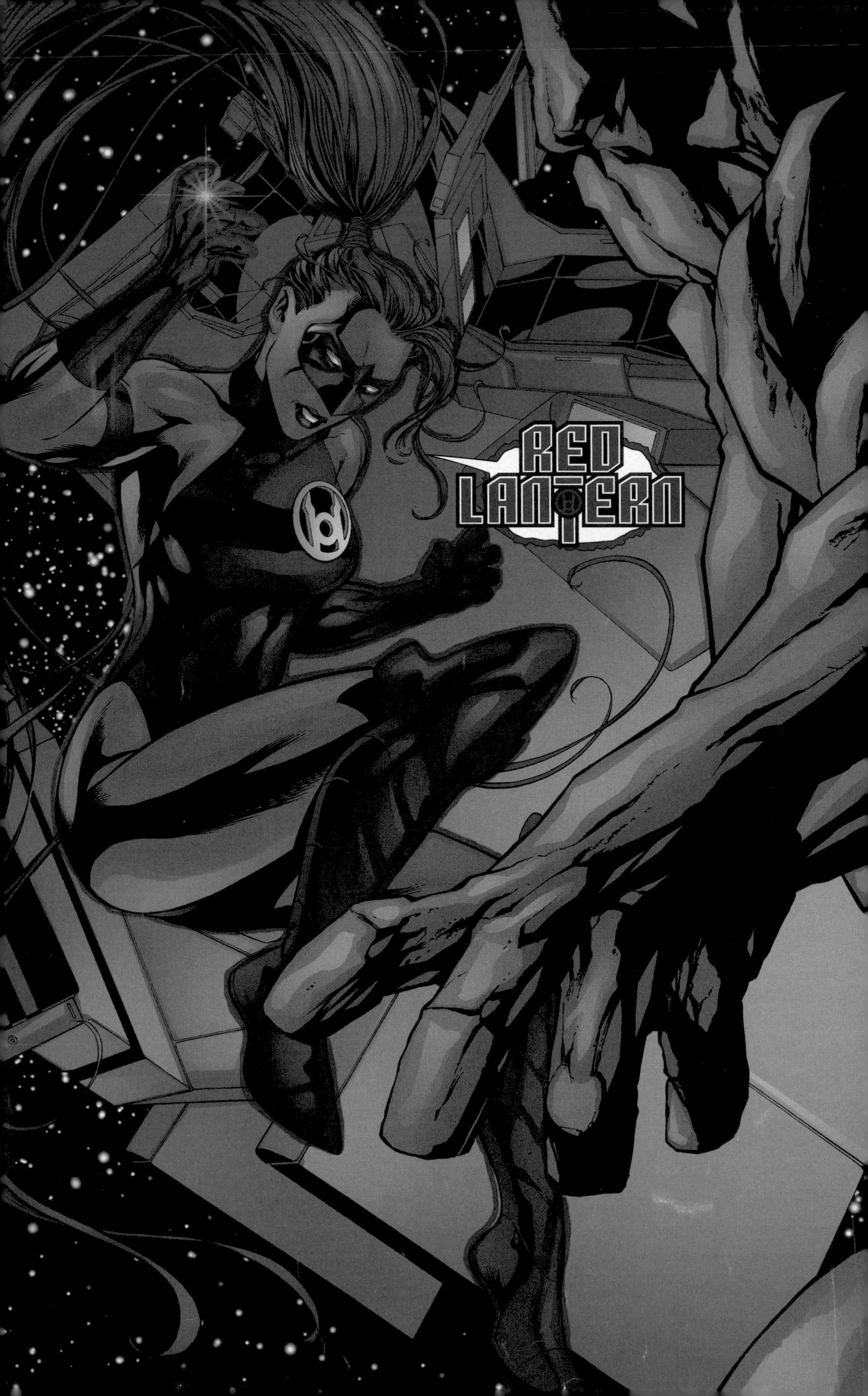
RED LANTERN

NAL CRISIS: RAGE OF THE RED LANTERNS
over by Shane Davis, Sandra Hope and Nei Ruffino

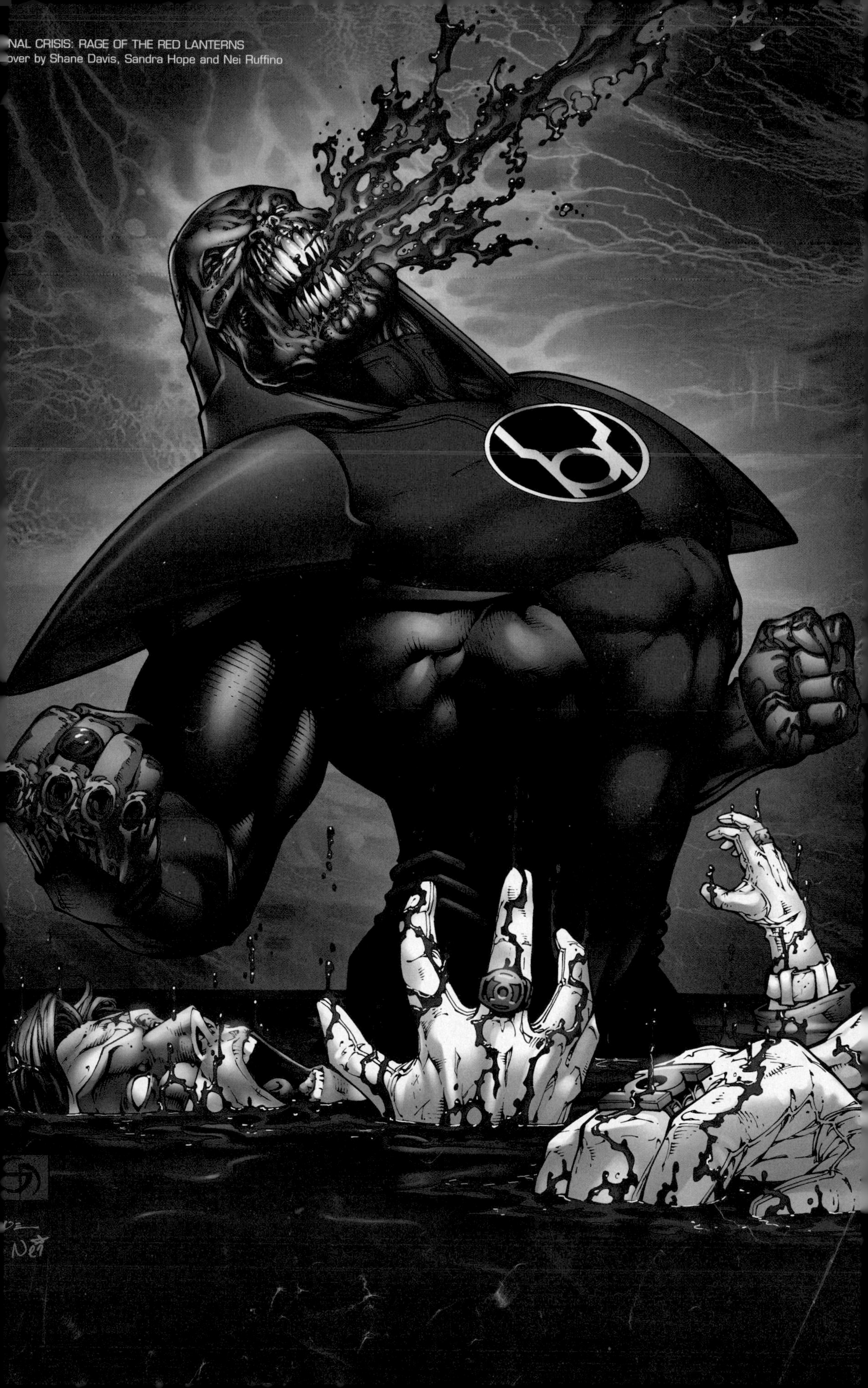

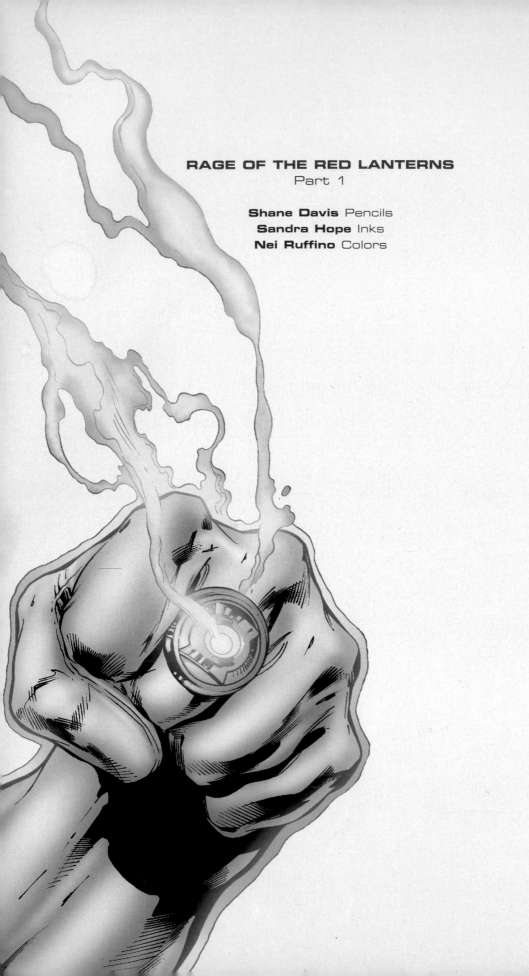

RAGE OF THE RED LANTERNS
Part 1

Shane Davis Pencils
Sandra Hope Inks
Nei Ruffino Colors

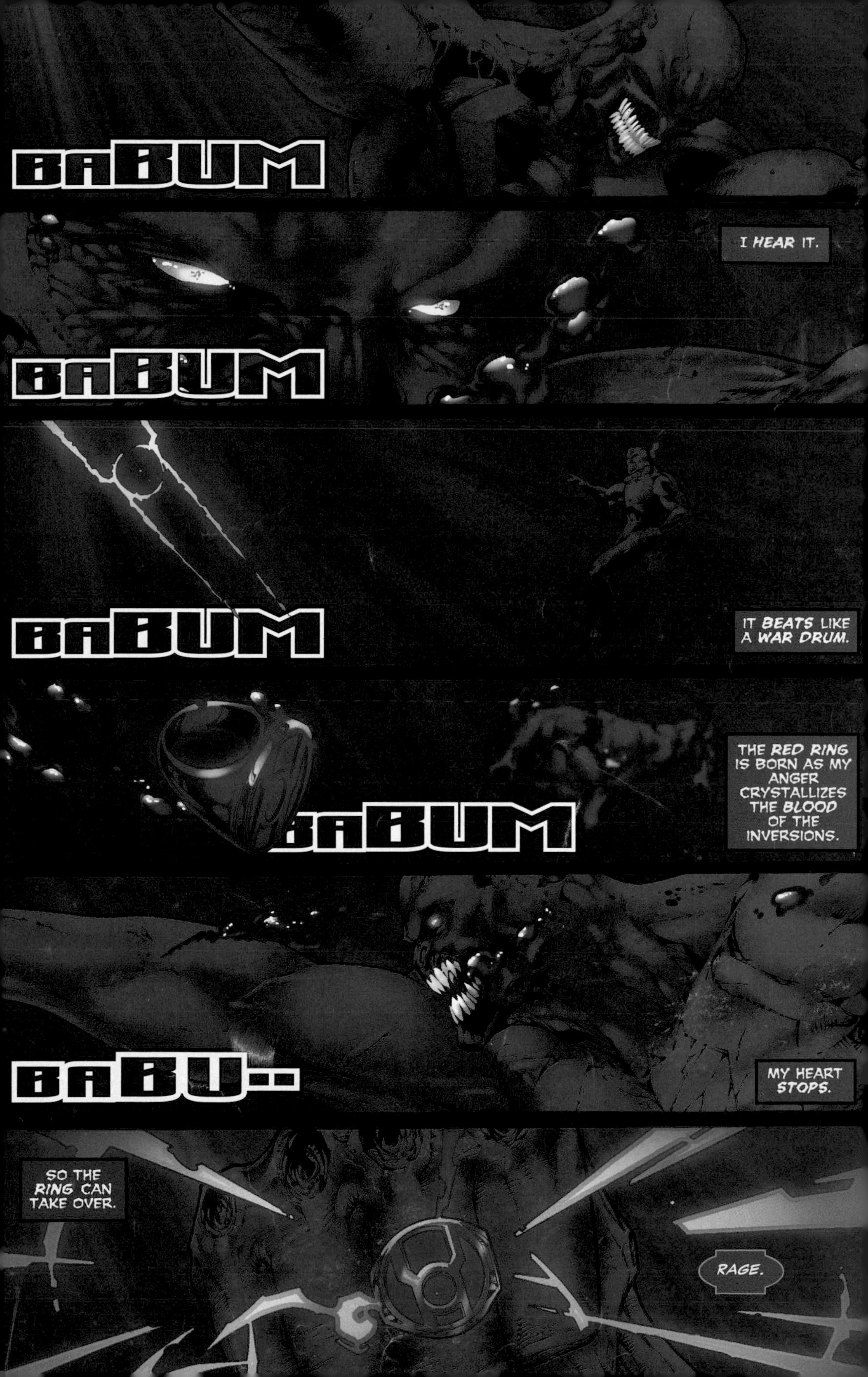
BABUM
I HEAR IT.
BABUM
BABUM
IT BEATS LIKE A WAR DRUM.
BABUM
THE RED RING IS BORN AS MY ANGER CRYSTALLIZES THE BLOOD OF THE INVERSIONS.
BABU--
MY HEART STOPS.
SO THE RING CAN TAKE OVER.
RAGE.

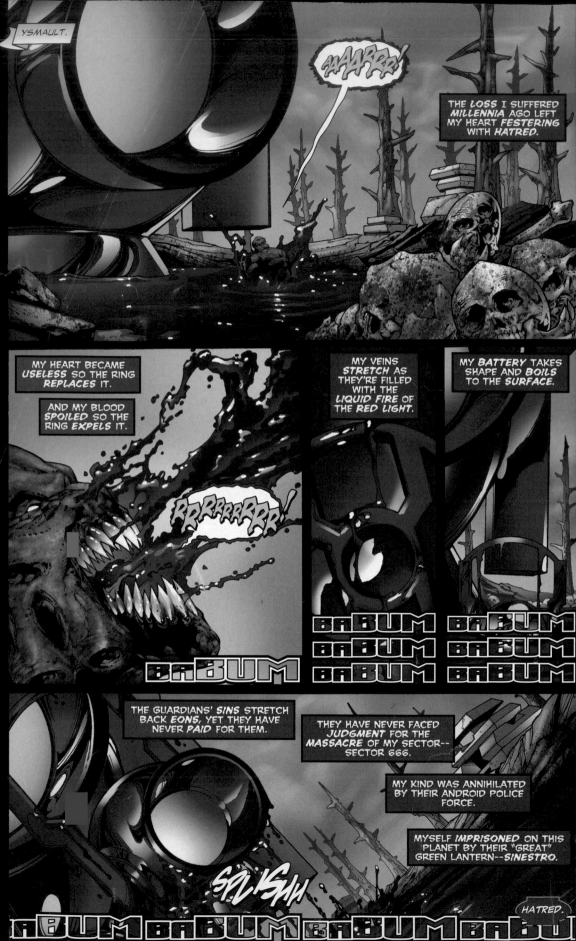

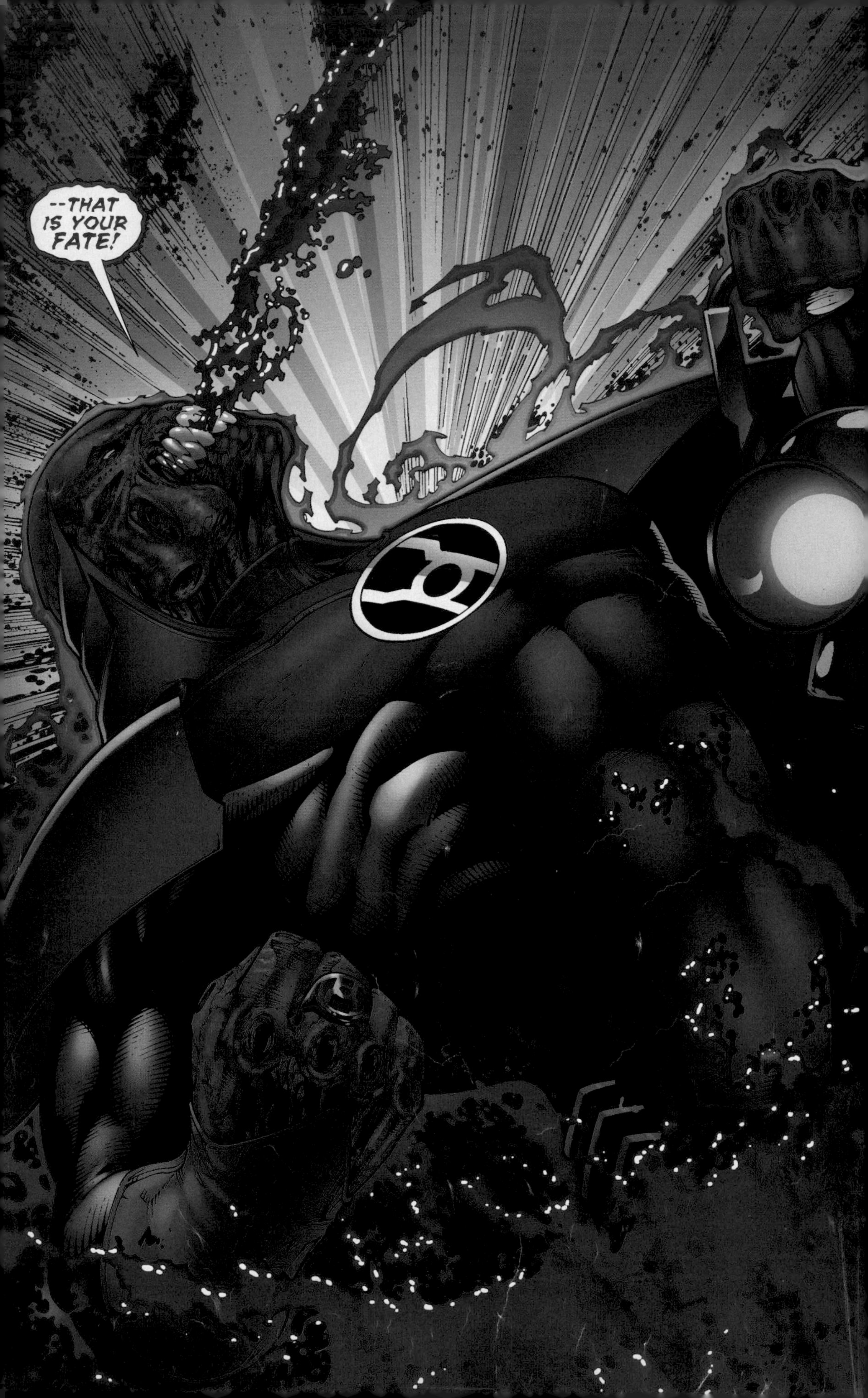
--THAT IS YOUR FATE!

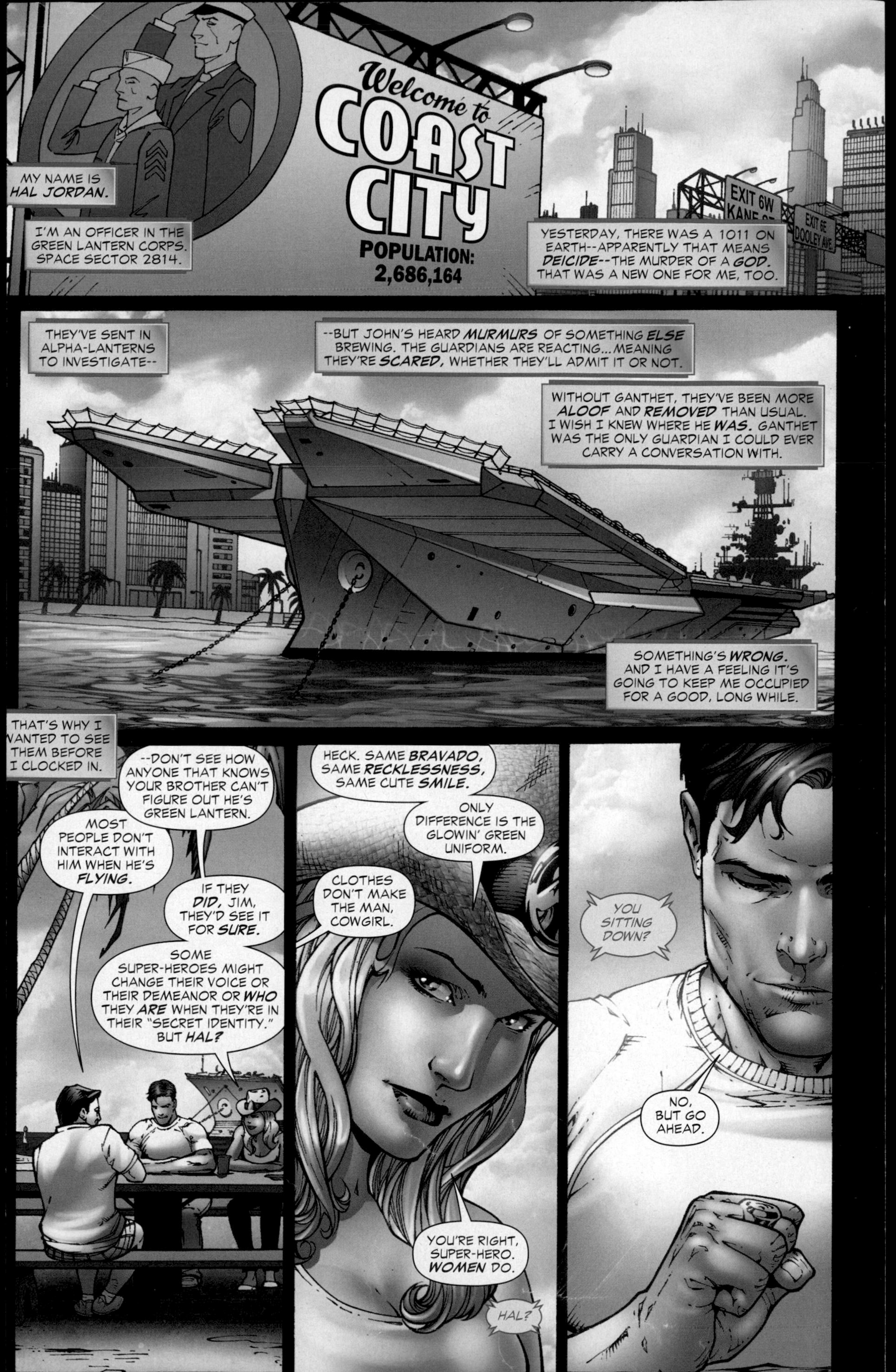

Welcome to COAST CITY
POPULATION: 2,686,164
MY NAME IS HAL JORDAN.
I'M AN OFFICER IN THE GREEN LANTERN CORPS. SPACE SECTOR 2814.
EXIT 6W
EXIT 6E DOOLEY AVE.
YESTERDAY, THERE WAS A 1011 ON EARTH--APPARENTLY THAT MEANS DEICIDE--THE MURDER OF A GOD. THAT WAS A NEW ONE FOR ME, TOO.
THEY'VE SENT IN ALPHA-LANTERNS TO INVESTIGATE--
--BUT JOHN'S HEARD MURMURS OF SOMETHING ELSE BREWING. THE GUARDIANS ARE REACTING...MEANING THEY'RE SCARED, WHETHER THEY'LL ADMIT IT OR NOT.
WITHOUT GANTHET, THEY'VE BEEN MORE ALOOF AND REMOVED THAN USUAL. I WISH I KNEW WHERE HE WAS. GANTHET WAS THE ONLY GUARDIAN I COULD EVER CARRY A CONVERSATION WITH.
SOMETHING'S WRONG. AND I HAVE A FEELING IT'S GOING TO KEEP ME OCCUPIED FOR A GOOD, LONG WHILE.
THAT'S WHY I WANTED TO SEE THEM BEFORE I CLOCKED IN.
--DON'T SEE HOW ANYONE THAT KNOWS YOUR BROTHER CAN'T FIGURE OUT HE'S GREEN LANTERN.
MOST PEOPLE DON'T INTERACT WITH HIM WHEN HE'S FLYING.
IF THEY DID, JIM, THEY'D SEE IT FOR SURE.
SOME SUPER-HEROES MIGHT CHANGE THEIR VOICE OR THEIR DEMEANOR OR WHO THEY ARE WHEN THEY'RE IN THEIR "SECRET IDENTITY." BUT HAL?
HECK. SAME BRAVADO, SAME RECKLESSNESS, SAME CUTE SMILE.
ONLY DIFFERENCE IS THE GLOWIN' GREEN UNIFORM.
CLOTHES DON'T MAKE THE MAN, COWGIRL.
YOU'RE RIGHT, SUPER-HERO. WOMEN DO.
HAL?
YOU SITTING DOWN?
NO, BUT GO AHEAD.

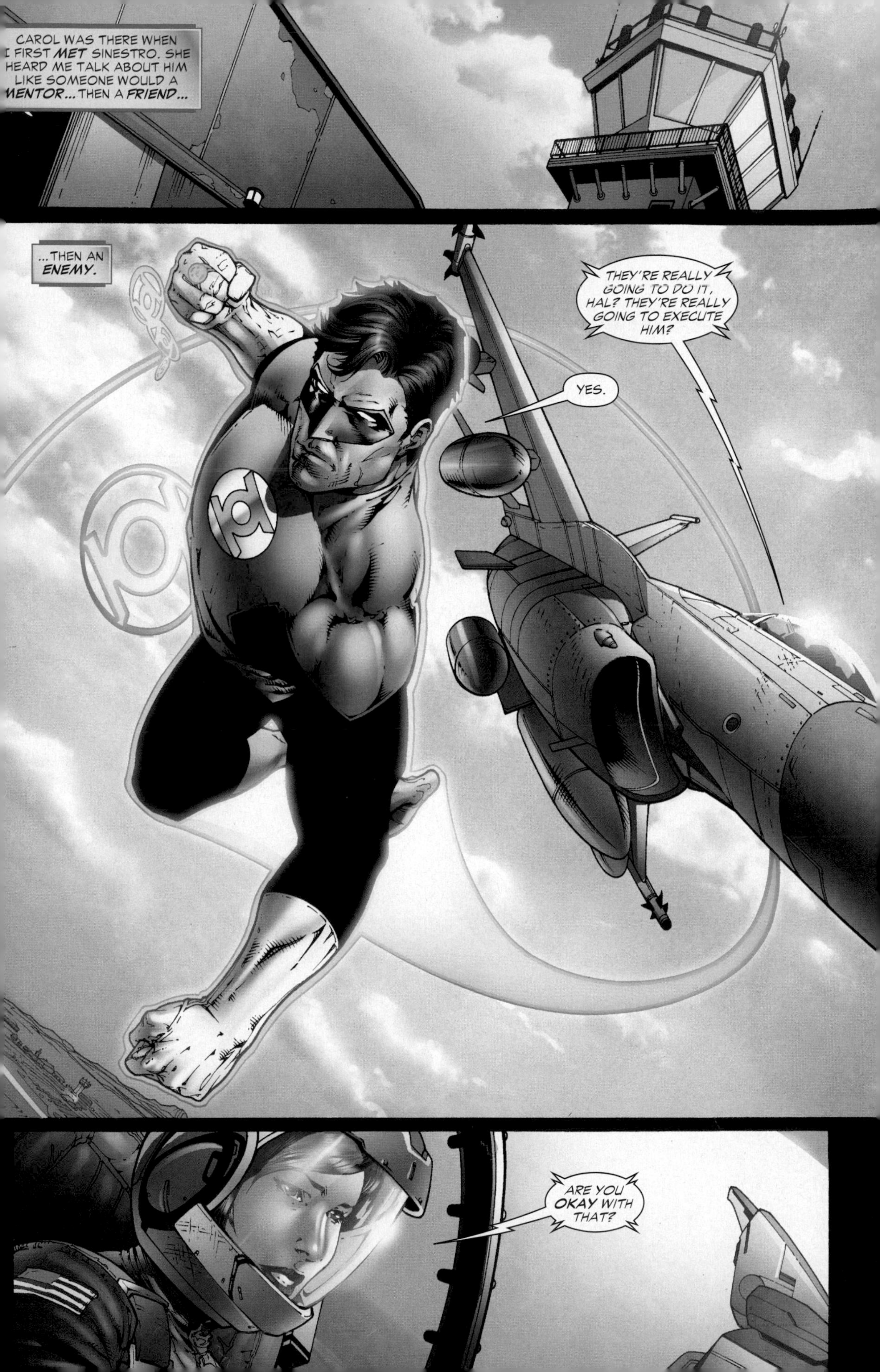
CAROL WAS THERE WHEN I FIRST MET SINESTRO. SHE HEARD ME TALK ABOUT HIM LIKE SOMEONE WOULD A MENTOR... THEN A FRIEND...
...THEN AN ENEMY.
THEY'RE REALLY GOING TO DO IT, HAL? THEY'RE REALLY GOING TO EXECUTE HIM?
YES.
ARE YOU OKAY WITH THAT?

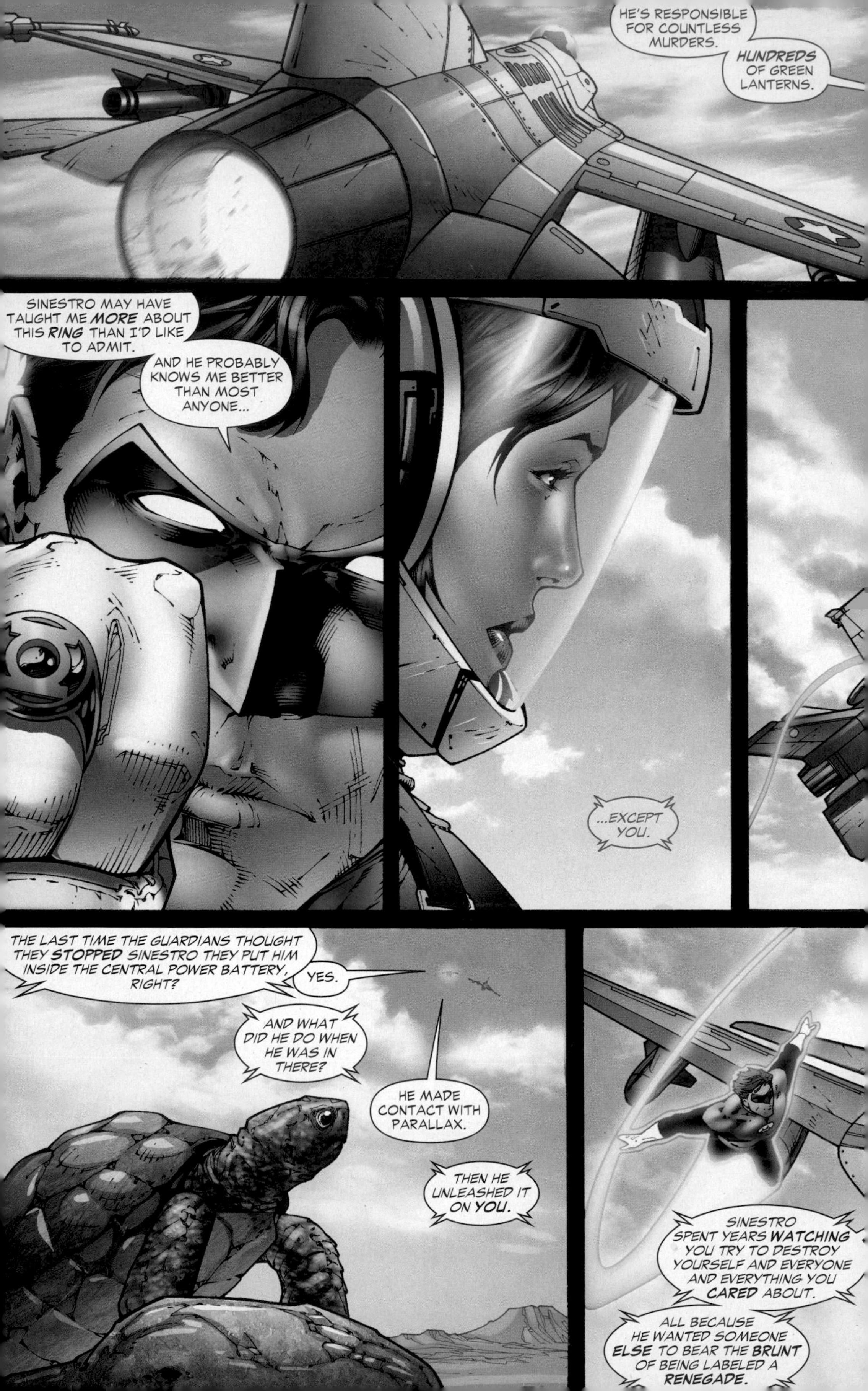
HE'S RESPONSIBLE FOR COUNTLESS MURDERS.
HUNDREDS OF GREEN LANTERNS.
SINESTRO MAY HAVE TAUGHT ME MORE ABOUT THIS RING THAN I'D LIKE TO ADMIT.
AND HE PROBABLY KNOWS ME BETTER THAN MOST ANYONE...
...EXCEPT YOU.
THE LAST TIME THE GUARDIANS THOUGHT THEY STOPPED SINESTRO THEY PUT HIM INSIDE THE CENTRAL POWER BATTERY, RIGHT?
YES.
AND WHAT DID HE DO WHEN HE WAS IN THERE?
HE MADE CONTACT WITH PARALLAX.
THEN HE UNLEASHED IT ON YOU.
SINESTRO SPENT YEARS WATCHING YOU TRY TO DESTROY YOURSELF AND EVERYONE AND EVERYTHING YOU CARED ABOUT.
ALL BECAUSE HE WANTED SOMEONE ELSE TO BEAR THE BRUNT OF BEING LABELED A RENEGADE.

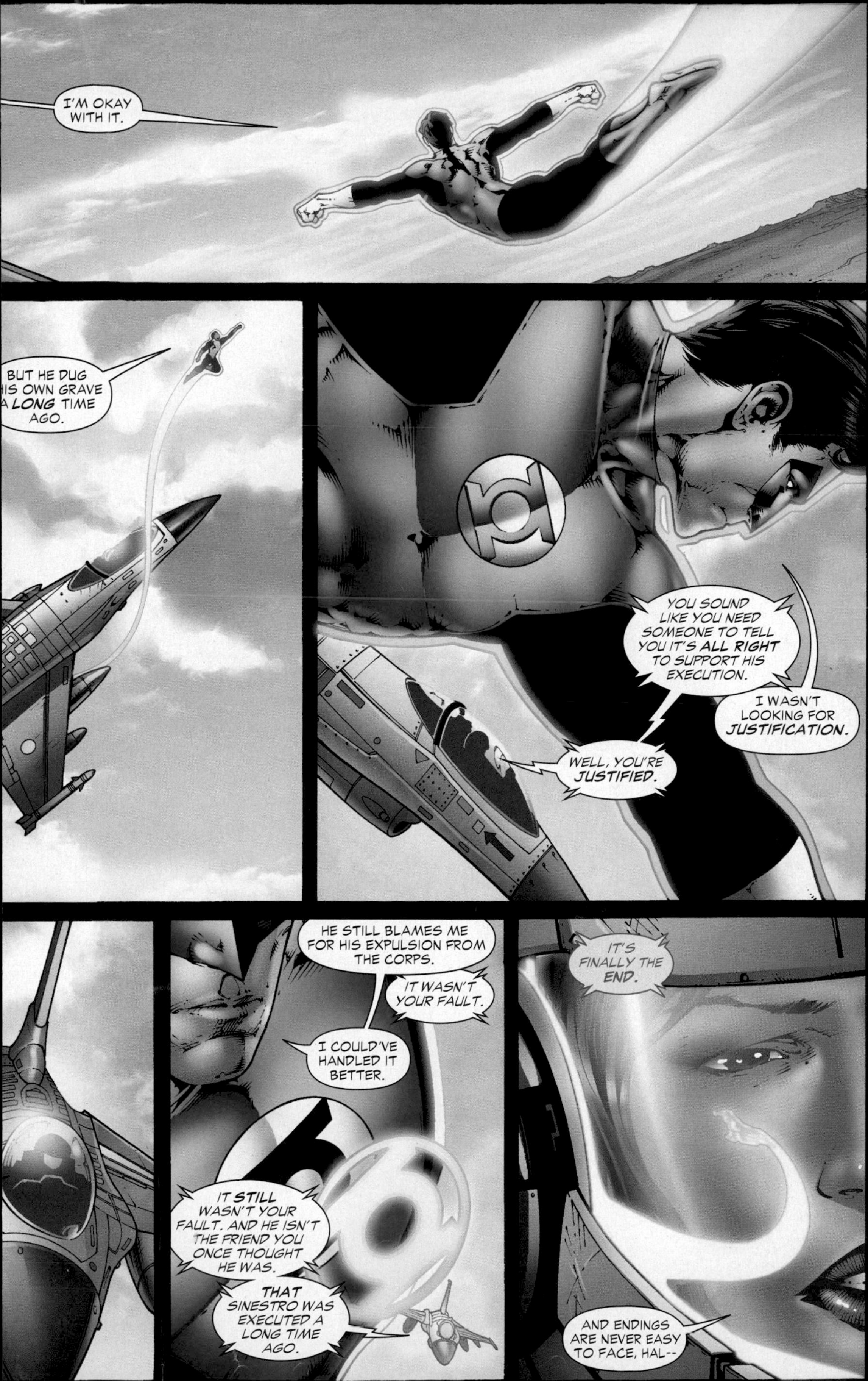

I'M OKAY WITH IT.
BUT HE DUG HIS OWN GRAVE A **LONG** TIME AGO.
YOU SOUND LIKE YOU NEED SOMEONE TO TELL YOU IT'S **ALL RIGHT** TO SUPPORT HIS EXECUTION.
I WASN'T LOOKING FOR **JUSTIFICATION**.
WELL, YOU'RE **JUSTIFIED**.
HE STILL BLAMES ME FOR HIS EXPULSION FROM THE CORPS.
IT WASN'T YOUR FAULT.
I COULD'VE HANDLED IT BETTER.
IT **STILL** WASN'T YOUR FAULT. AND HE ISN'T THE FRIEND YOU ONCE THOUGHT HE WAS.
THAT SINESTRO WAS EXECUTED A LONG TIME AGO.
IT'S FINALLY THE **END**.
AND ENDINGS ARE NEVER EASY TO FACE, HAL--

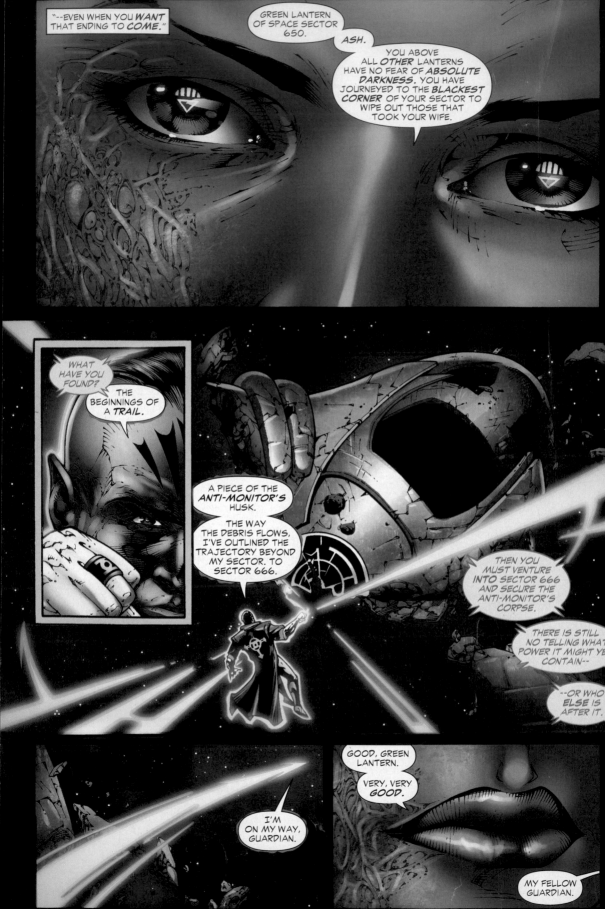

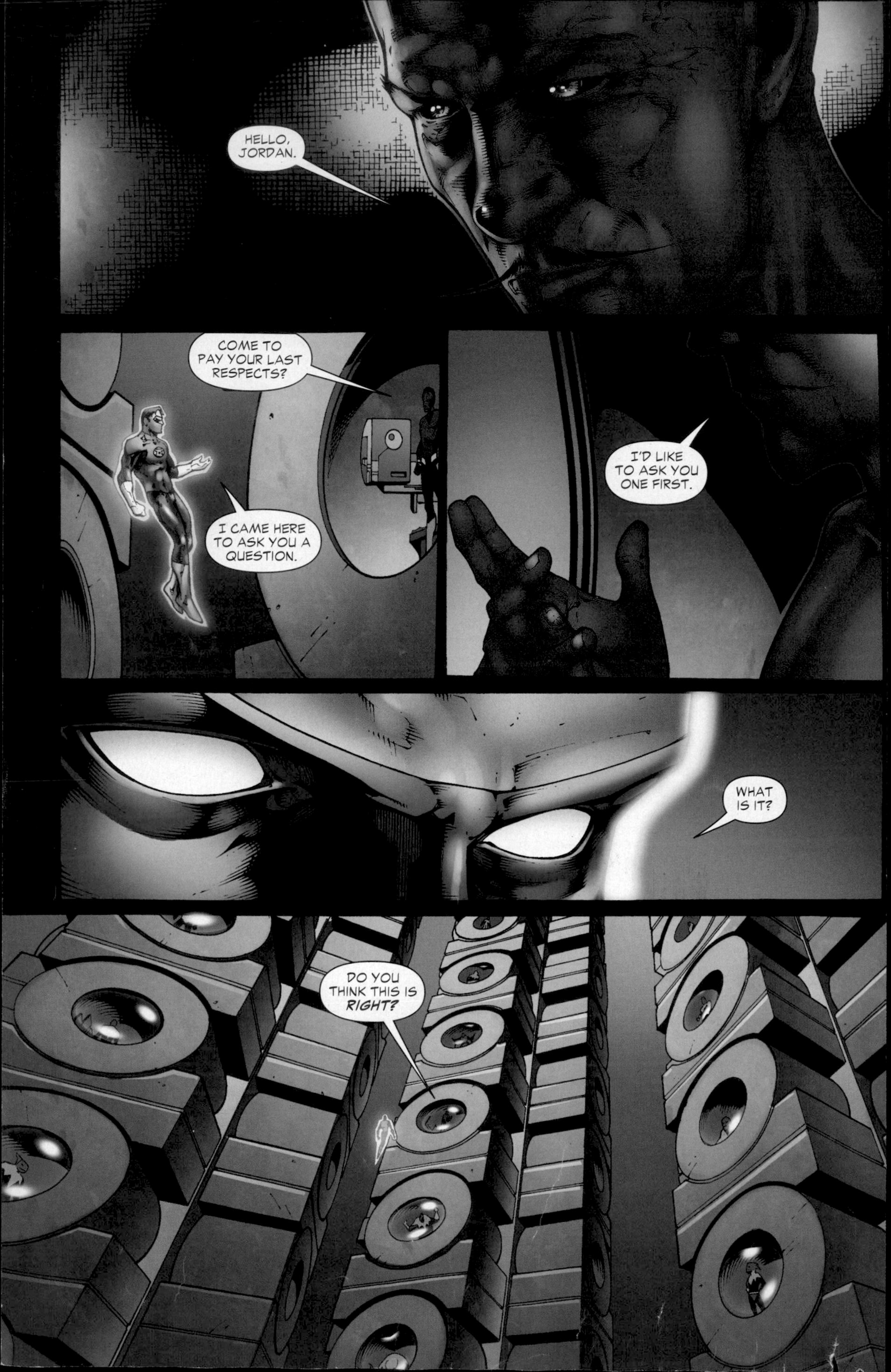
HELLO, JORDAN.
COME TO PAY YOUR LAST RESPECTS?
I CAME HERE TO ASK YOU A QUESTION.
I'D LIKE TO ASK YOU ONE FIRST.
WHAT IS IT?
DO YOU THINK THIS IS *RIGHT?*

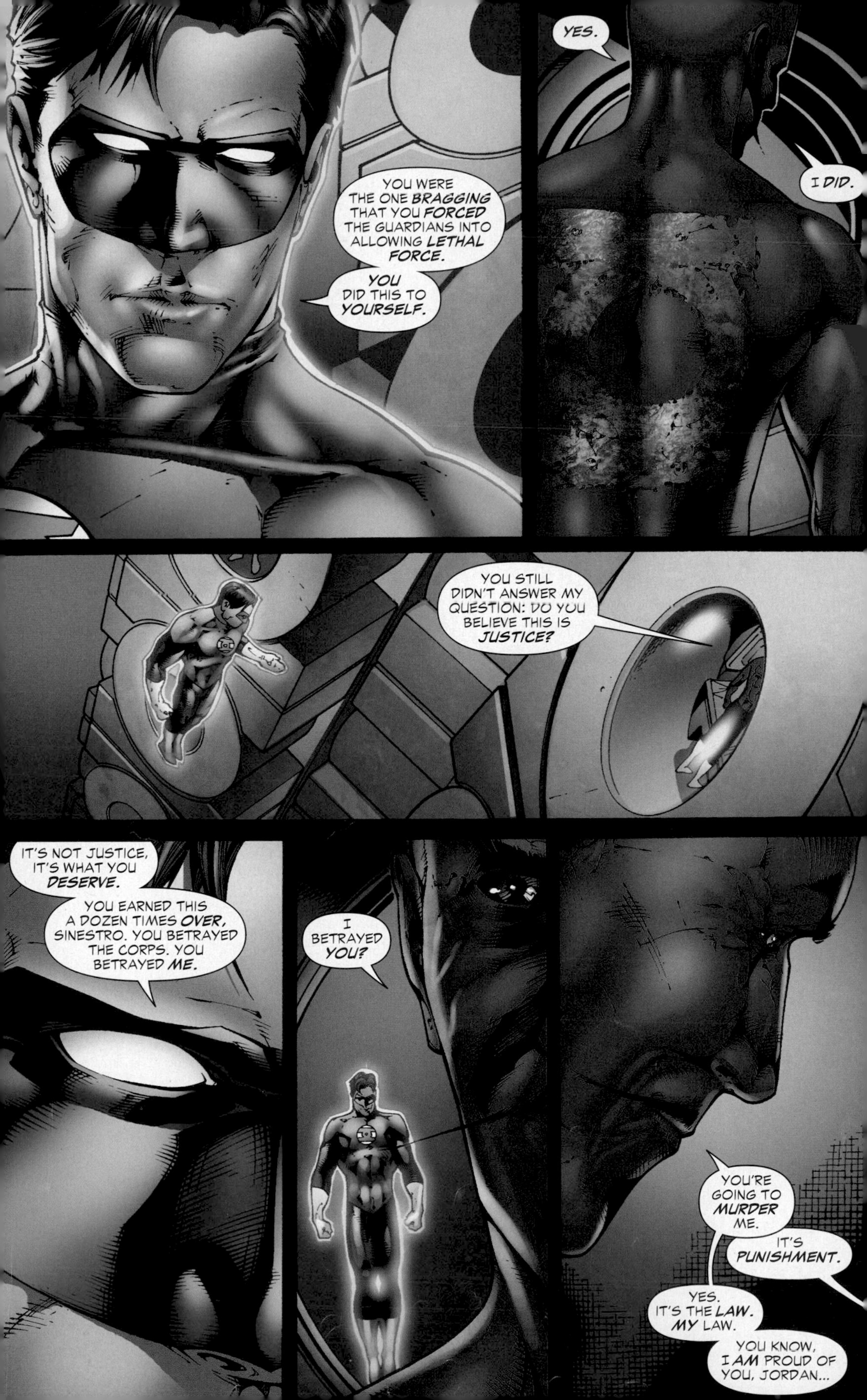
YOU WERE THE ONE BRAGGING THAT YOU FORCED THE GUARDIANS INTO ALLOWING LETHAL FORCE.
YOU DID THIS TO YOURSELF.
YES.
I DID.
YOU STILL DIDN'T ANSWER MY QUESTION: DO YOU BELIEVE THIS IS JUSTICE?
IT'S NOT JUSTICE, IT'S WHAT YOU DESERVE.
YOU EARNED THIS A DOZEN TIMES OVER, SINESTRO. YOU BETRAYED THE CORPS. YOU BETRAYED ME.
I BETRAYED YOU?
YOU'RE GOING TO MURDER ME.
IT'S PUNISHMENT.
YES. IT'S THE LAW. MY LAW.
YOU KNOW, I AM PROUD OF YOU, JORDAN...

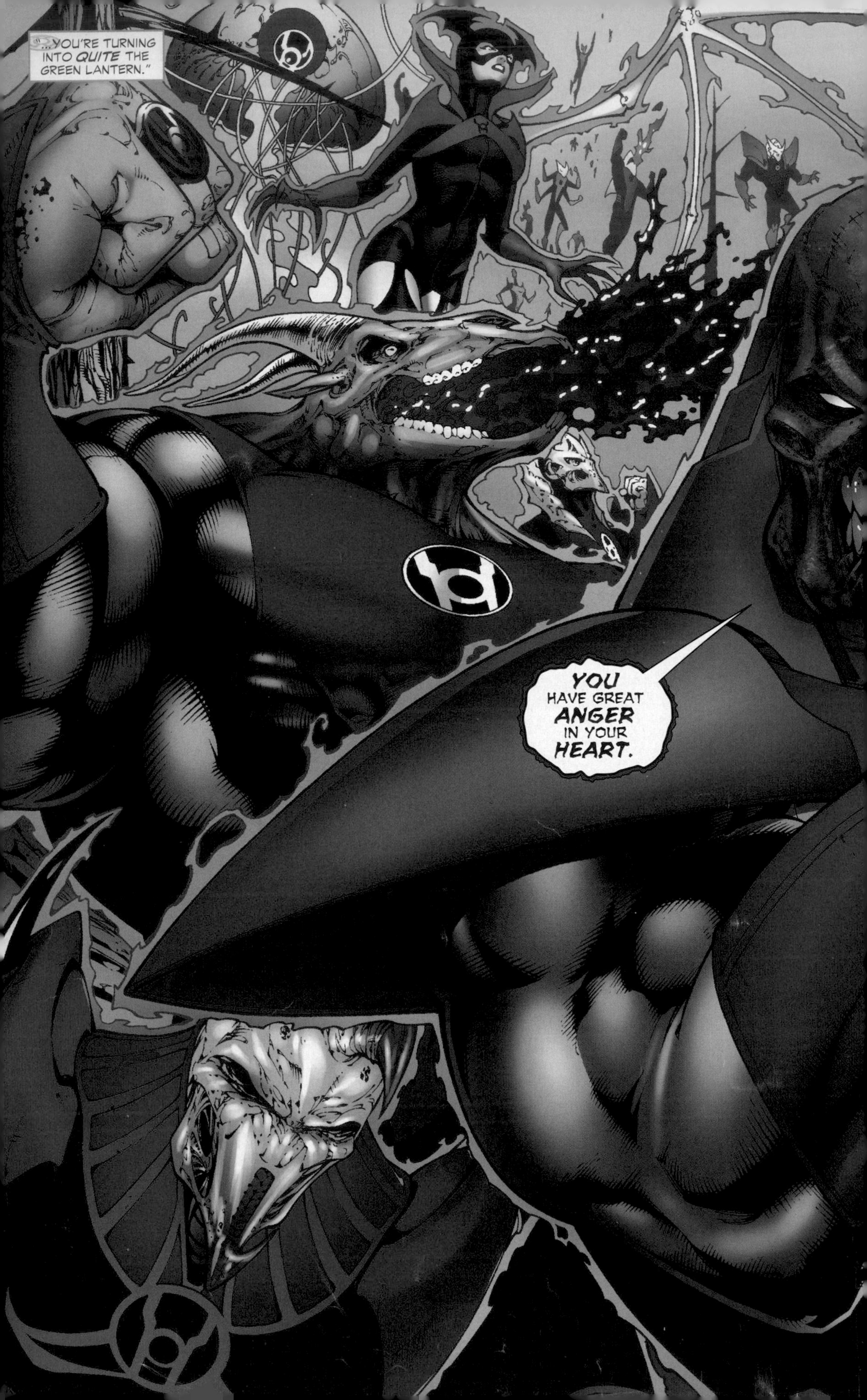

"...YOU'RE TURNING INTO QUITE THE GREEN LANTERN."
YOU HAVE GREAT ANGER IN YOUR HEART.

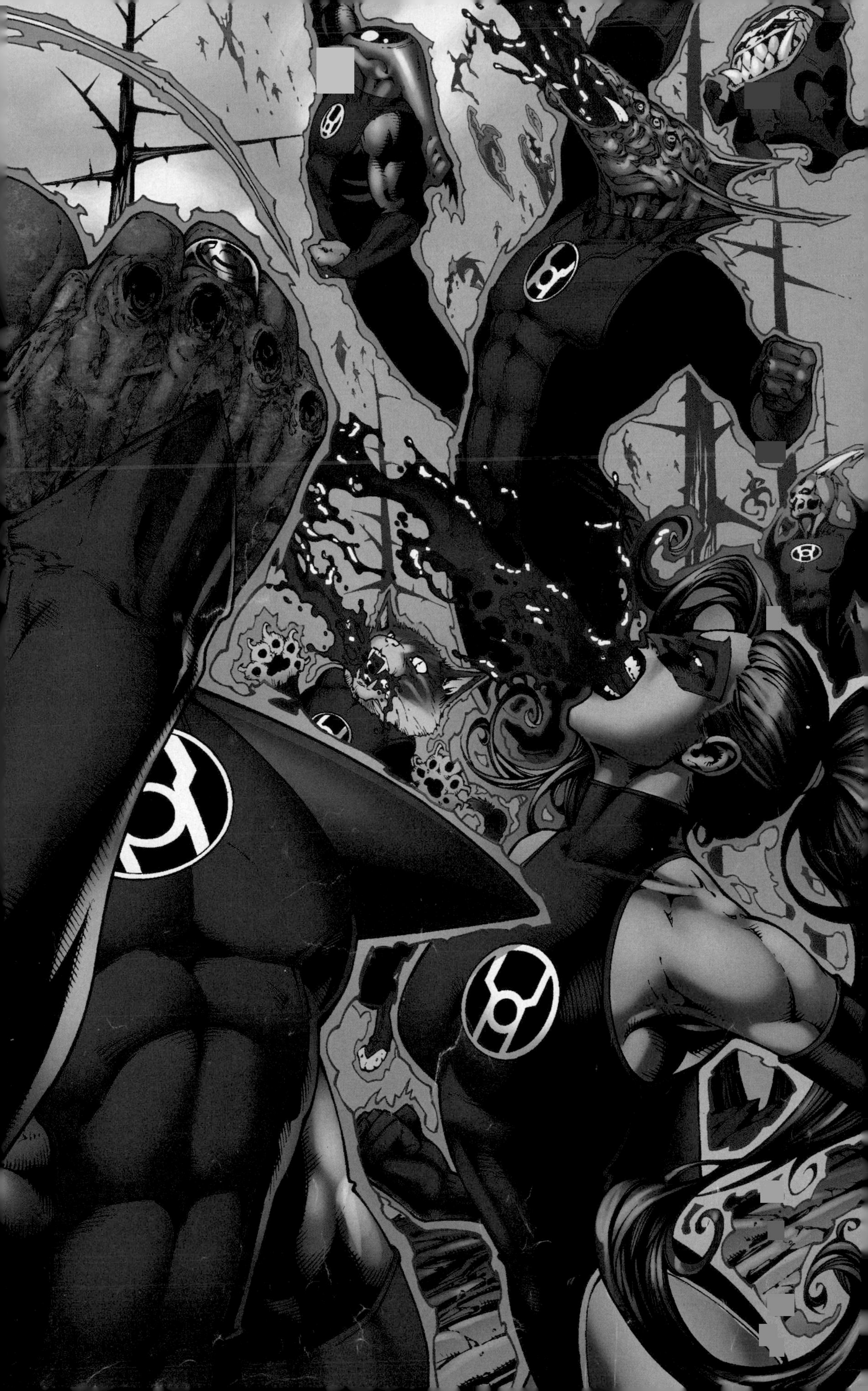

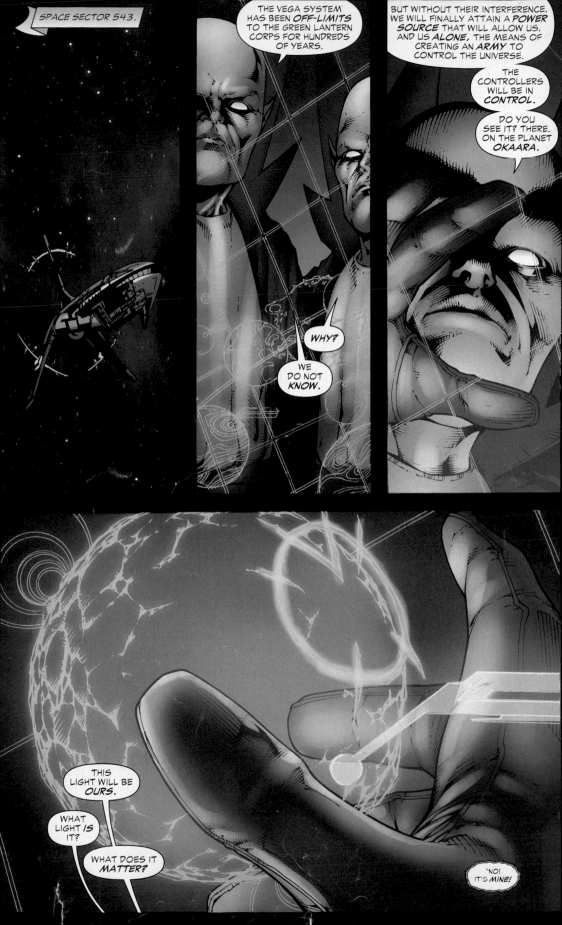

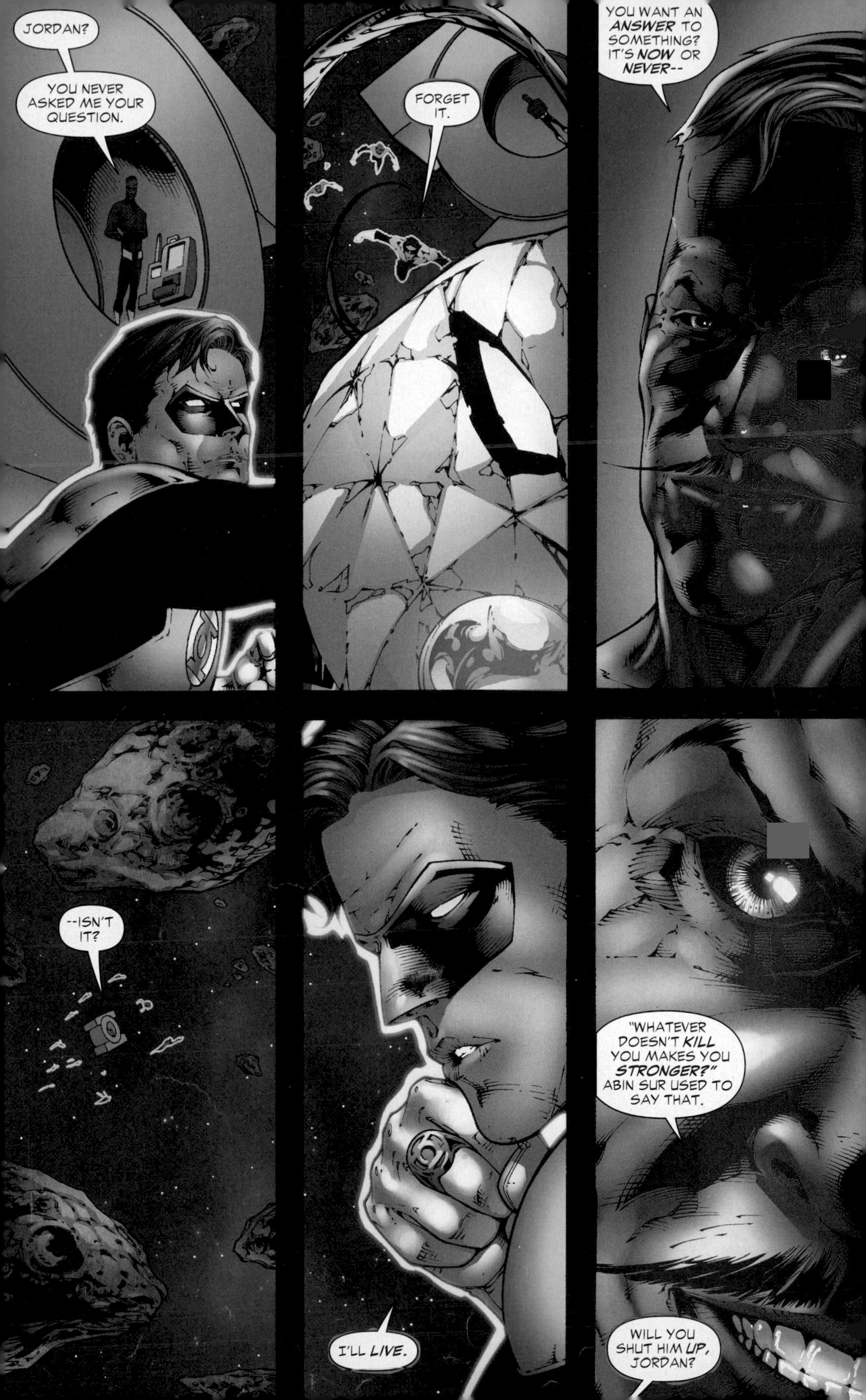
JORDAN?
YOU NEVER ASKED ME YOUR QUESTION.
FORGET IT.
YOU WANT AN ANSWER TO SOMETHING? IT'S NOW OR NEVER--
--ISN'T IT?
I'LL LIVE.
"WHATEVER DOESN'T KILL YOU MAKES YOU STRONGER?" ABIN SUR USED TO SAY THAT.
WILL YOU SHUT HIM UP, JORDAN?

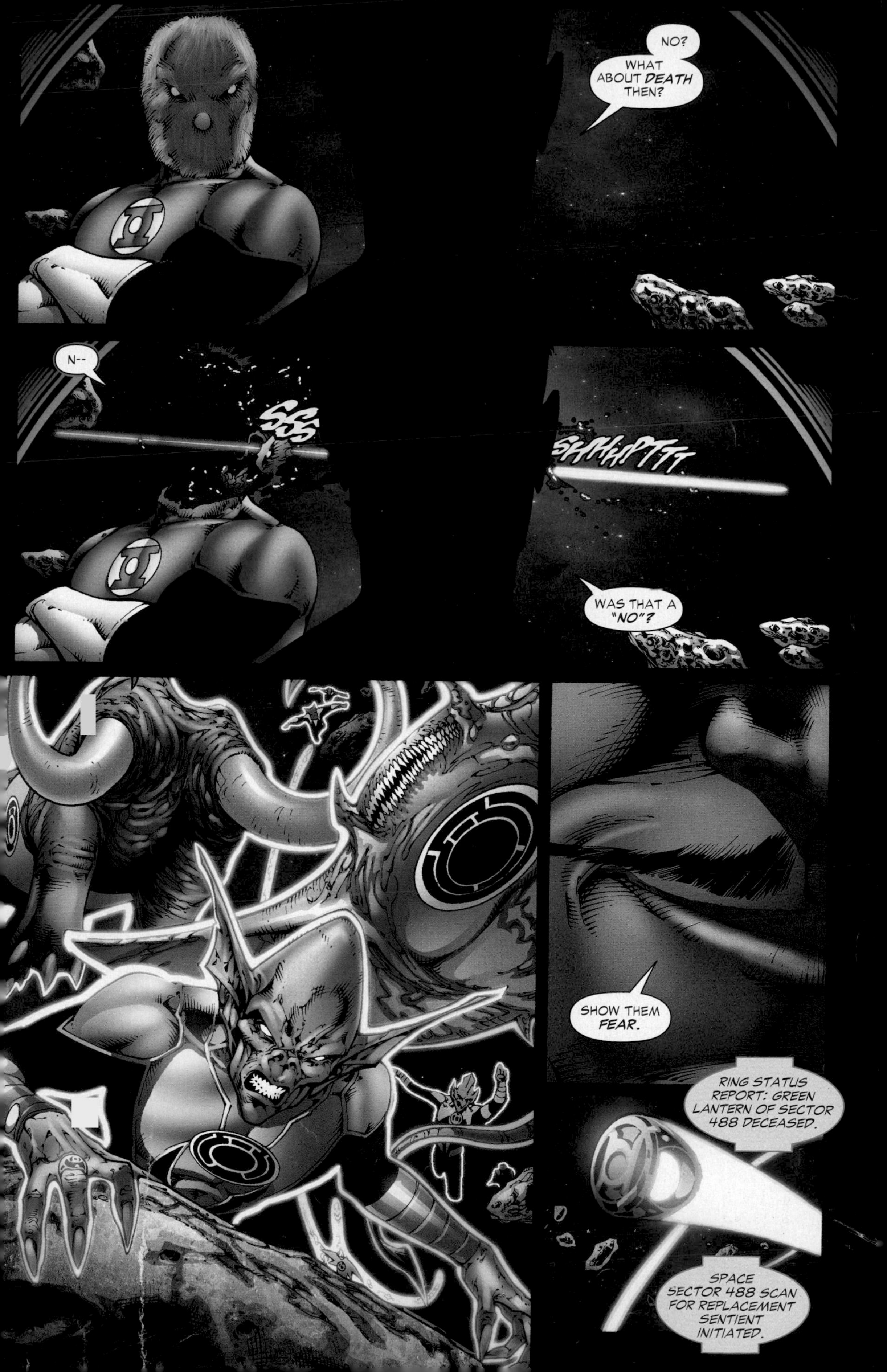

NO?
WHAT ABOUT DEATH THEN?
N--
SSS
SHHHPTTT
WAS THAT A "NO"?
SHOW THEM FEAR.
RING STATUS REPORT: GREEN LANTERN OF SECTOR 488 DECEASED.
SPACE SECTOR 488 SCAN FOR REPLACEMENT SENTIENT INITIATED.

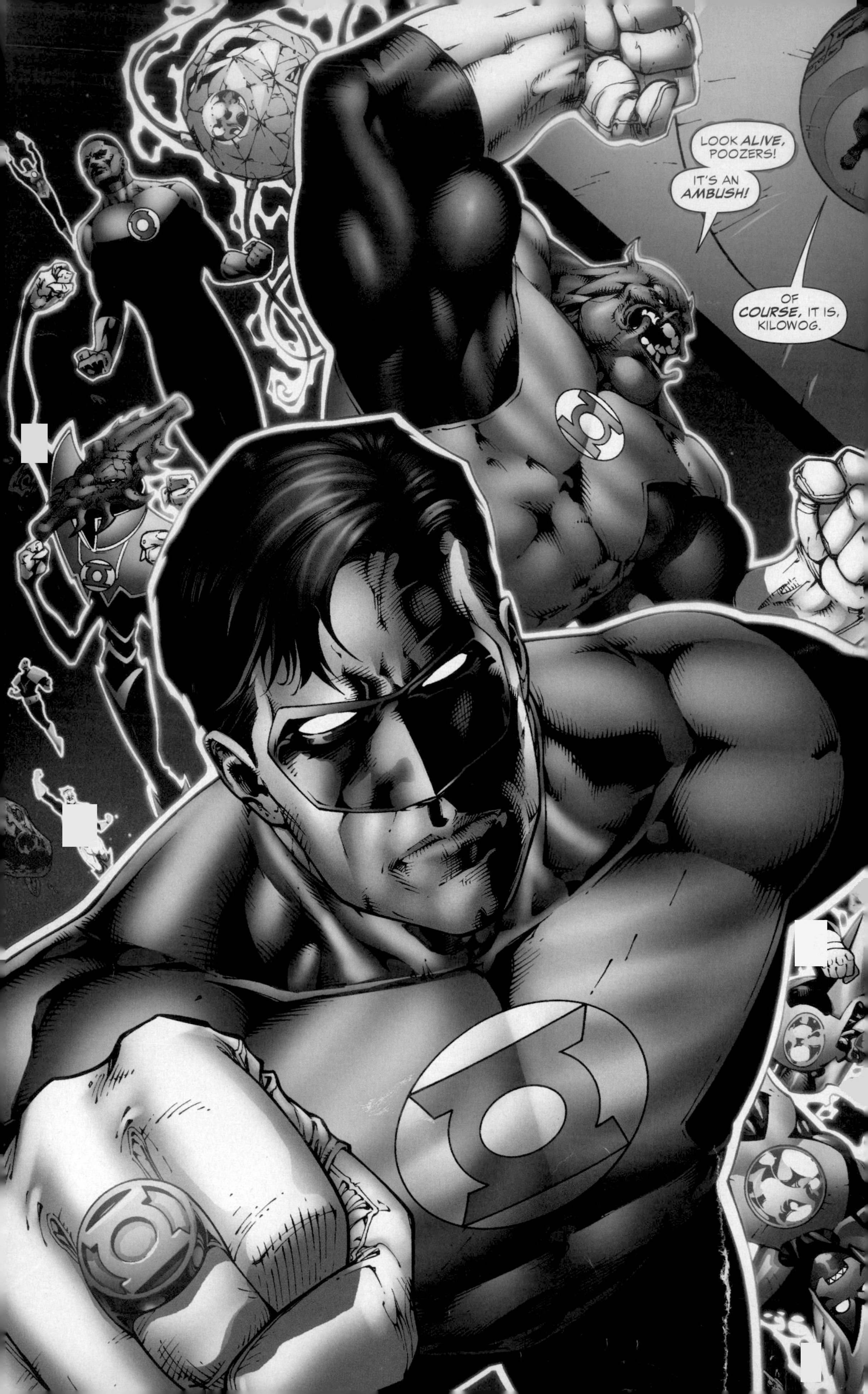
LOOK ALIVE, POOZERS!
IT'S AN AMBUSH!
OF COURSE, IT IS, KILOWOG.

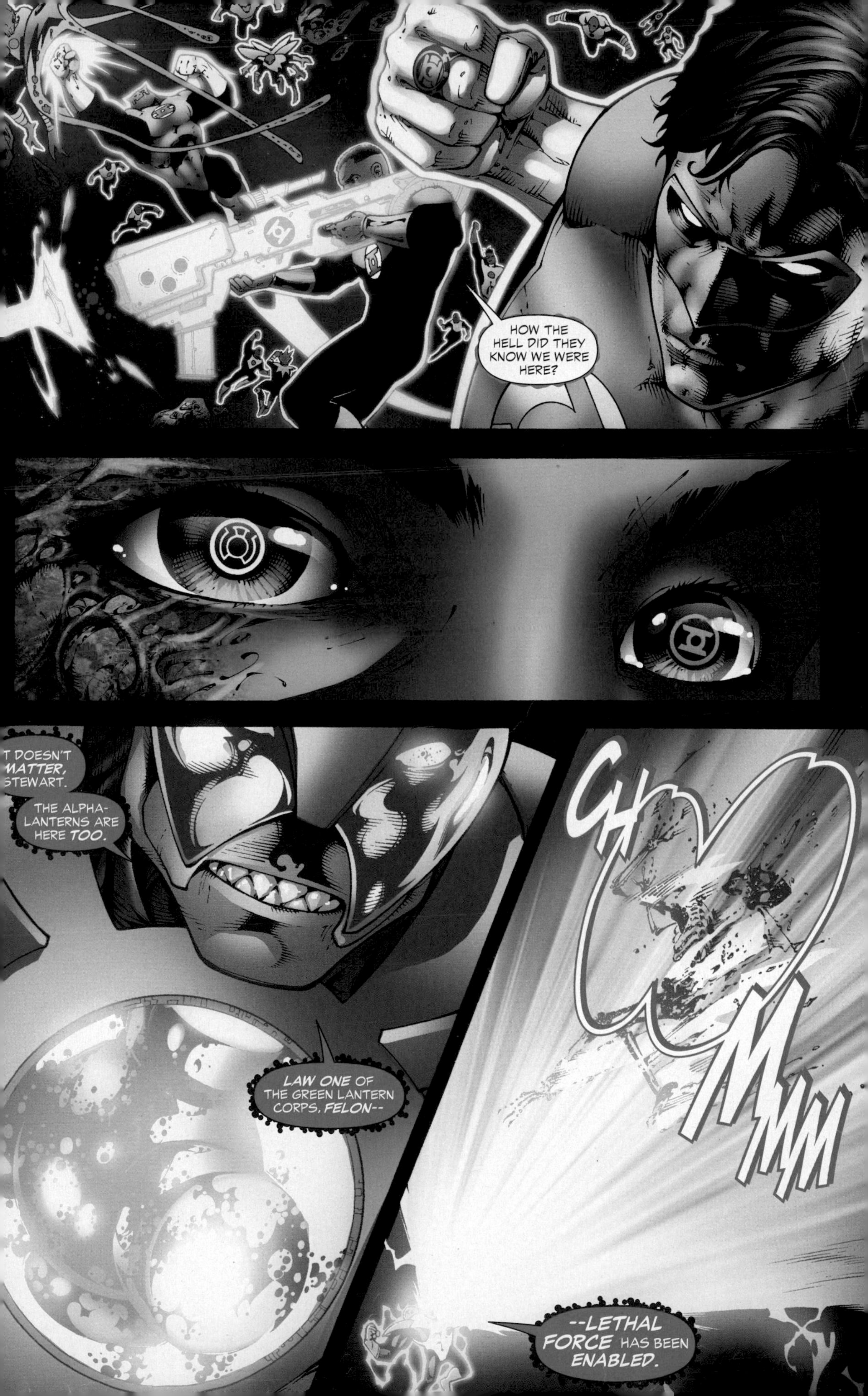
HOW THE HELL DID THEY KNOW WE WERE HERE?
T DOESN'T MATTER, STEWART.
THE ALPHA-LANTERNS ARE HERE TOO.
CHOOM
LAW ONE OF THE GREEN LANTERN CORPS, FELON--
--LETHAL FORCE HAS BEEN ENABLED.

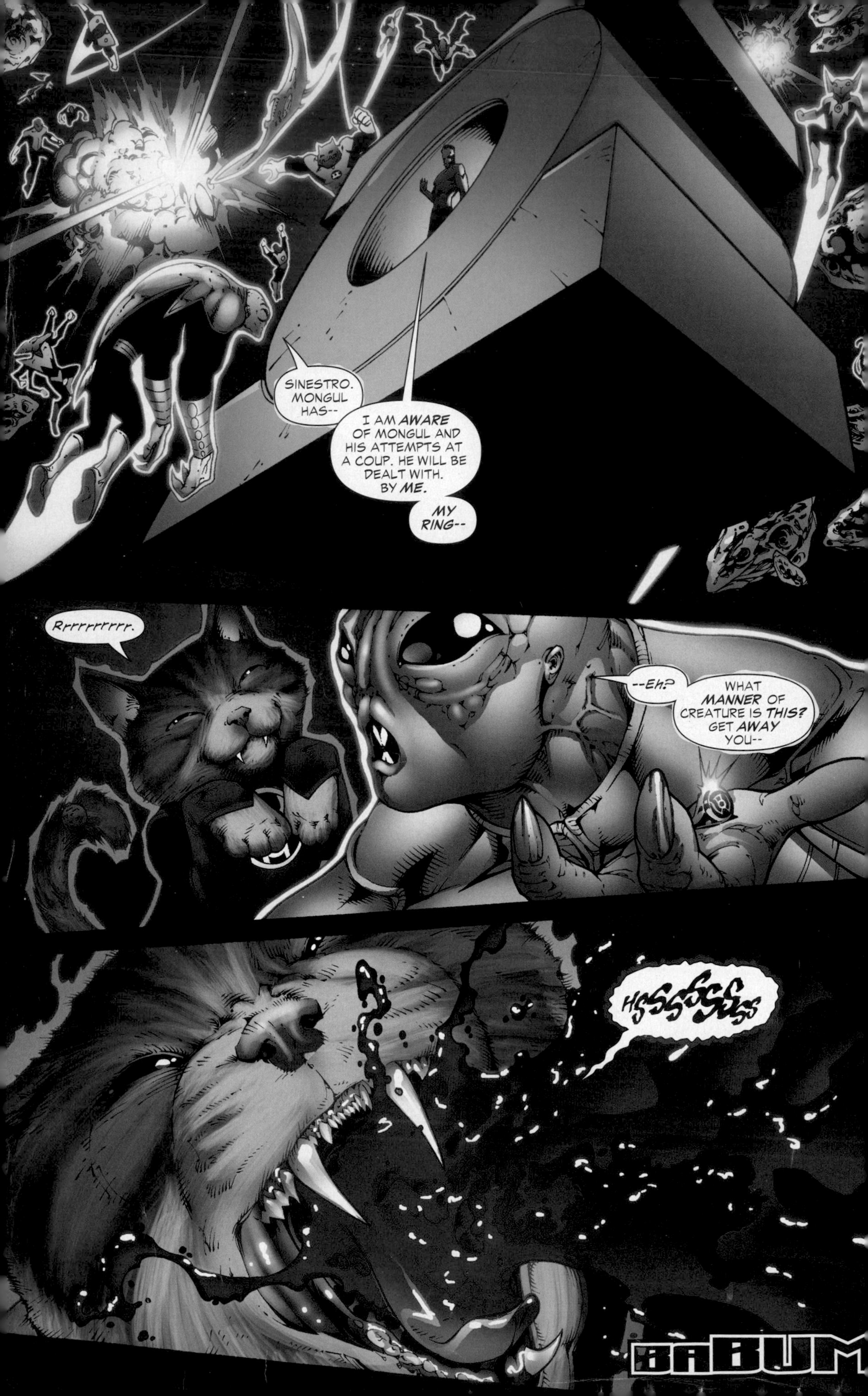
SINESTRO. MONGUL HAS--
I AM AWARE OF MONGUL AND HIS ATTEMPTS AT A COUP. HE WILL BE DEALT WITH. BY ME.
MY RING--
Rrrrrrrrrr.
--Eh?
WHAT MANNER OF CREATURE IS THIS? GET AWAY YOU--
HSSSSSSSSS
BABUM

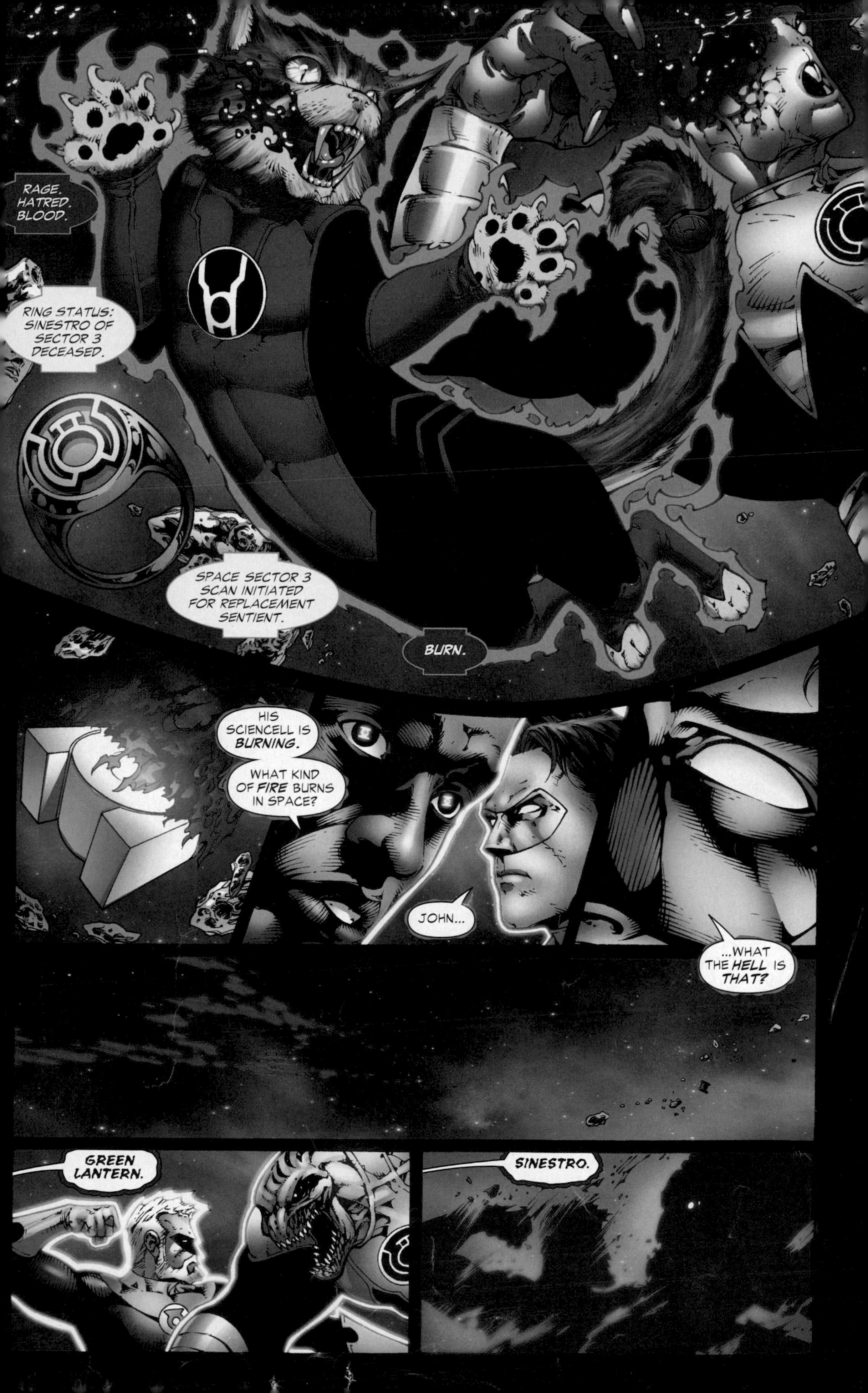
RAGE. HATRED. BLOOD.
RING STATUS: SINESTRO OF SECTOR 3 DECEASED.
SPACE SECTOR 3 SCAN INITIATED FOR REPLACEMENT SENTIENT.
BURN.
HIS SCIENCELL IS BURNING.
WHAT KIND OF FIRE BURNS IN SPACE?
JOHN...
...WHAT THE HELL IS THAT?
GREEN LANTERN.
SINESTRO.

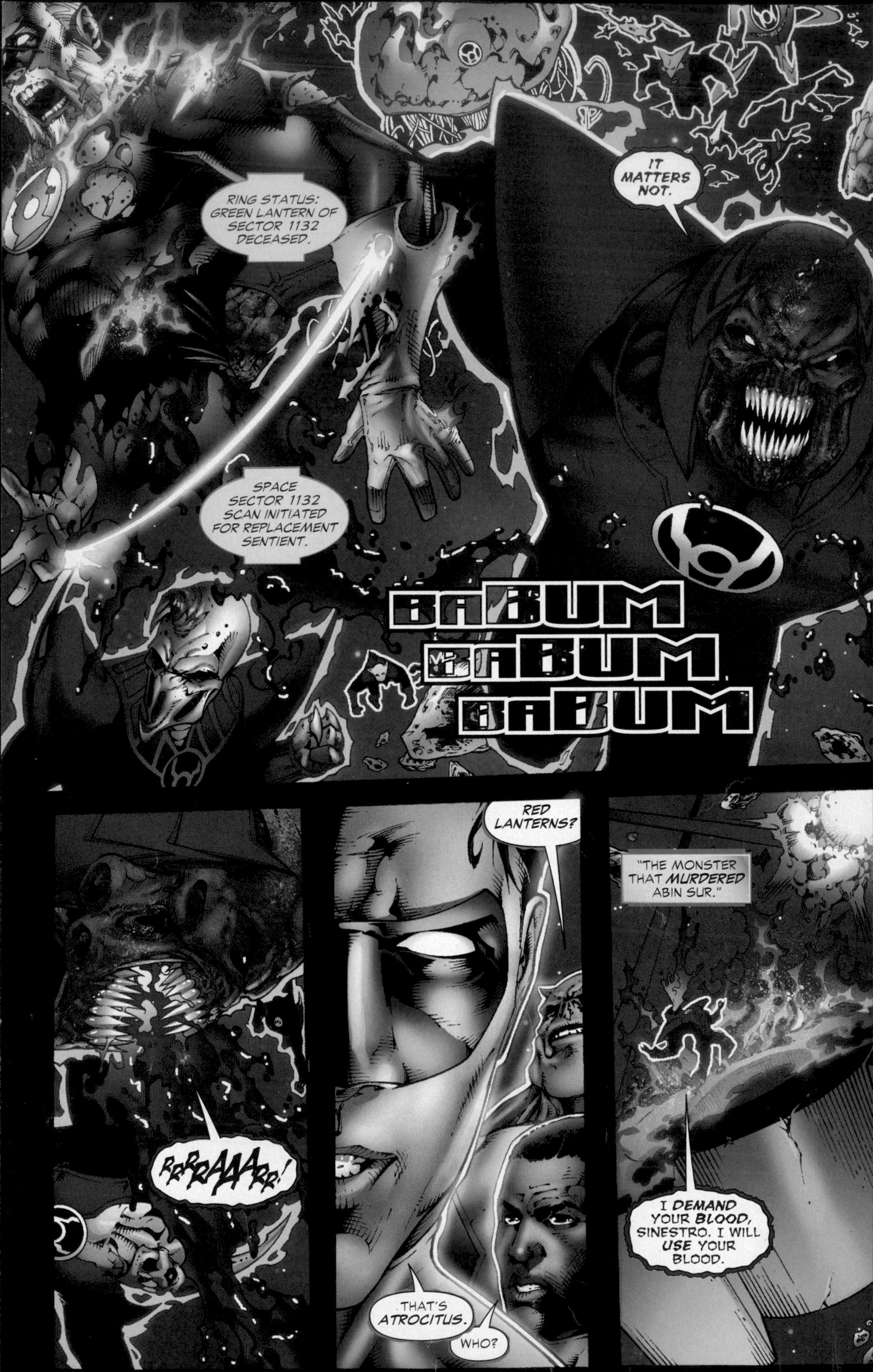
RING STATUS: GREEN LANTERN OF SECTOR 1132 DECEASED.
IT MATTERS NOT.
SPACE SECTOR 1132 SCAN INITIATED FOR REPLACEMENT SENTIENT.
BABUM BABUM BABUM
RERRAAARR!
RED LANTERNS?
THAT'S ATROCITUS.
WHO?
"THE MONSTER THAT MURDERED ABIN SUR."
I DEMAND YOUR BLOOD, SINESTRO. I WILL USE YOUR BLOOD.

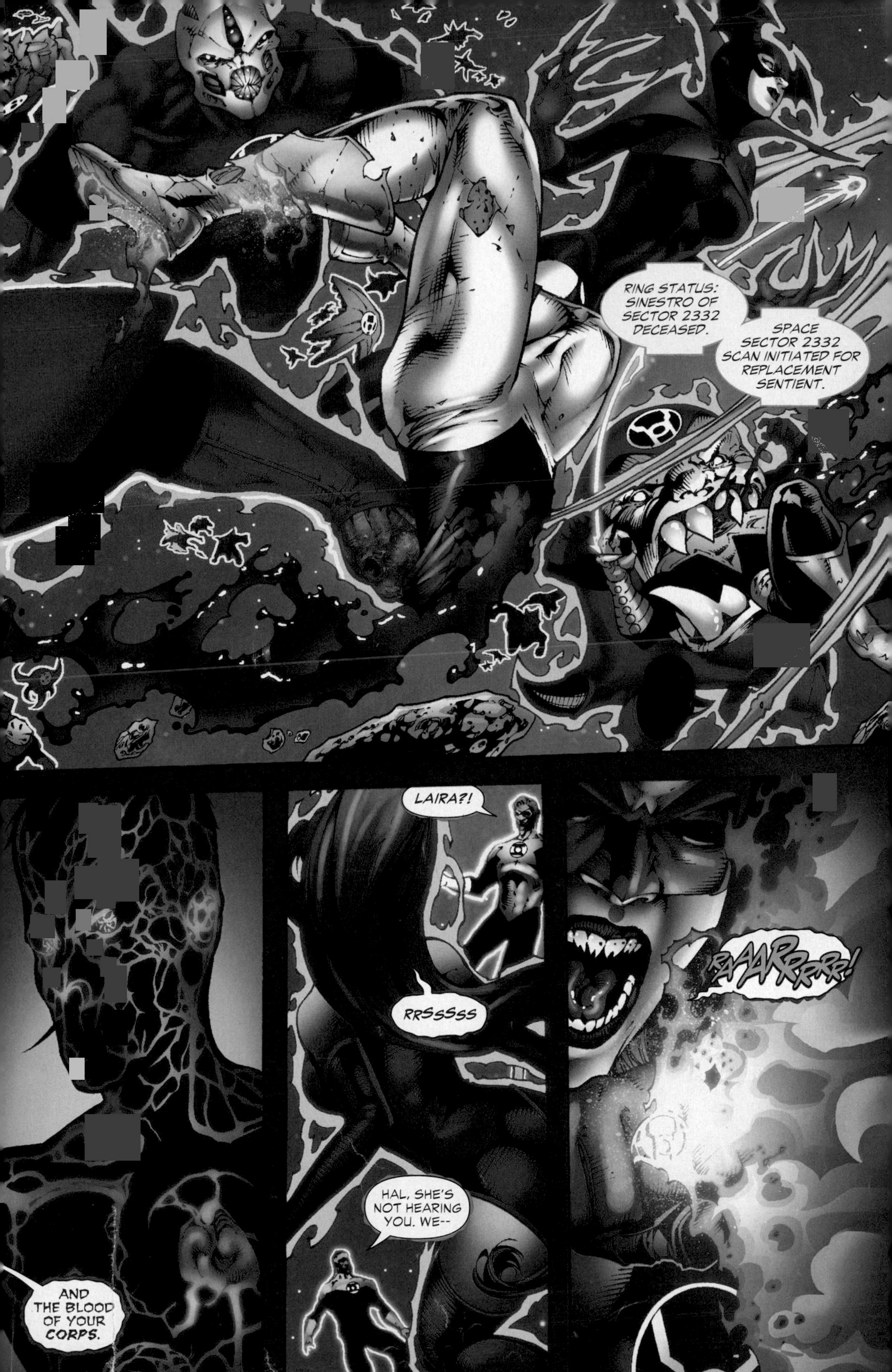
RING STATUS: SINESTRO OF SECTOR 2332 DECEASED.
SPACE SECTOR 2332 SCAN INITIATED FOR REPLACEMENT SENTIENT.
AND THE BLOOD OF YOUR CORPS.
LAIRA?!
RRSSSSS
HAL, SHE'S NOT HEARING YOU. WE--
RAAARRRRR!

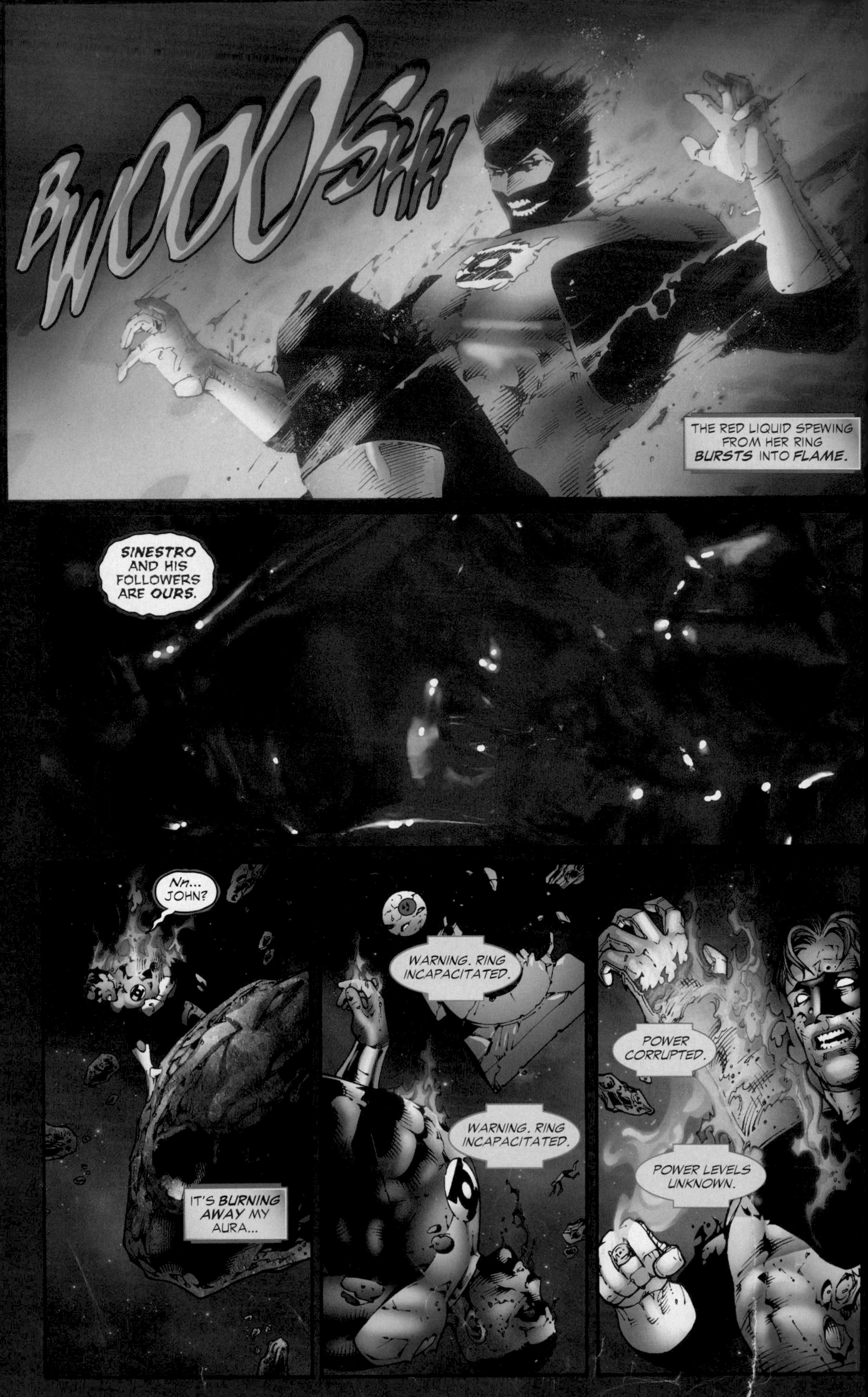
BWOOOSHH
THE RED LIQUID SPEWING FROM HER RING BURSTS INTO FLAME.
SINESTRO AND HIS FOLLOWERS ARE OURS.
Nn... JOHN?
IT'S BURNING AWAY MY AURA...
WARNING. RING INCAPACITATED.
WARNING. RING INCAPACITATED.
POWER CORRUPTED.
POWER LEVELS UNKNOWN.

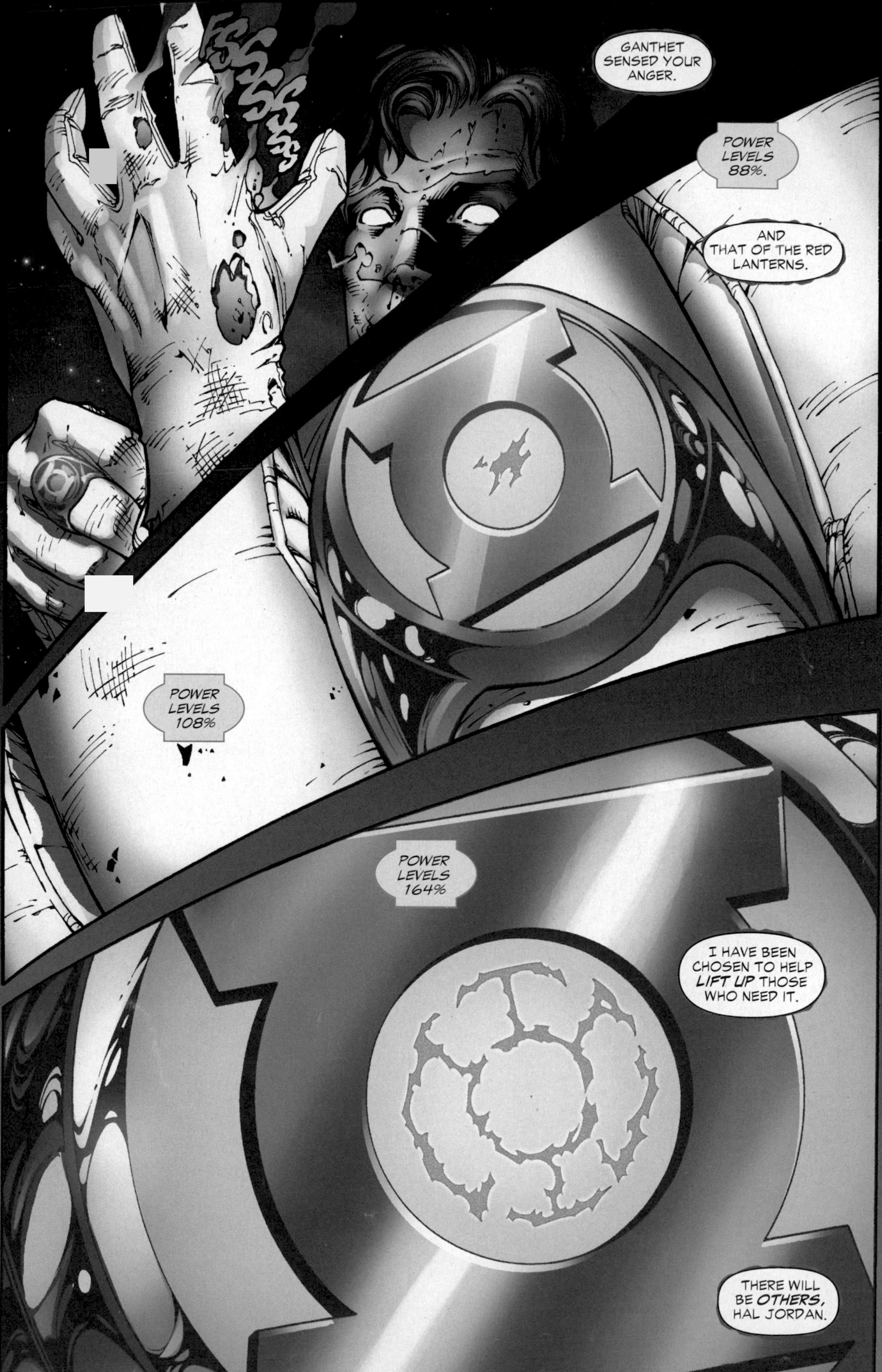
GANTHET SENSED YOUR ANGER.
POWER LEVELS 88%.
AND THAT OF THE RED LANTERNS.
POWER LEVELS 108%
POWER LEVELS 164%
I HAVE BEEN CHOSEN TO HELP *LIFT UP* THOSE WHO NEED IT.
THERE WILL BE *OTHERS,* HAL JORDAN.

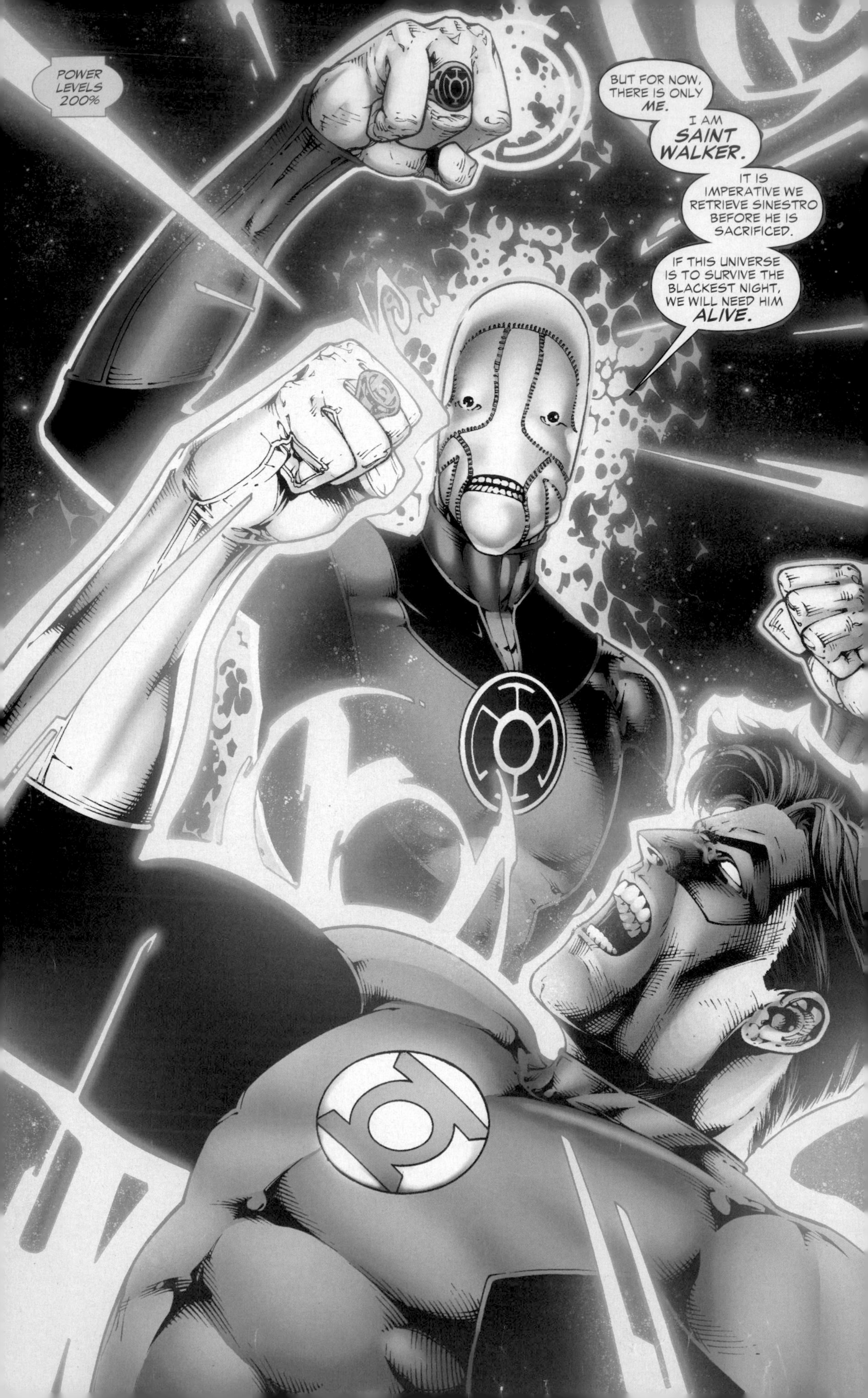
POWER LEVELS 200%
BUT FOR NOW, THERE IS ONLY ME.
I AM SAINT WALKER.
IT IS IMPERATIVE WE RETRIEVE SINESTRO BEFORE HE IS SACRIFICED.
IF THIS UNIVERSE IS TO SURVIVE THE BLACKEST NIGHT, WE WILL NEED HIM ALIVE.

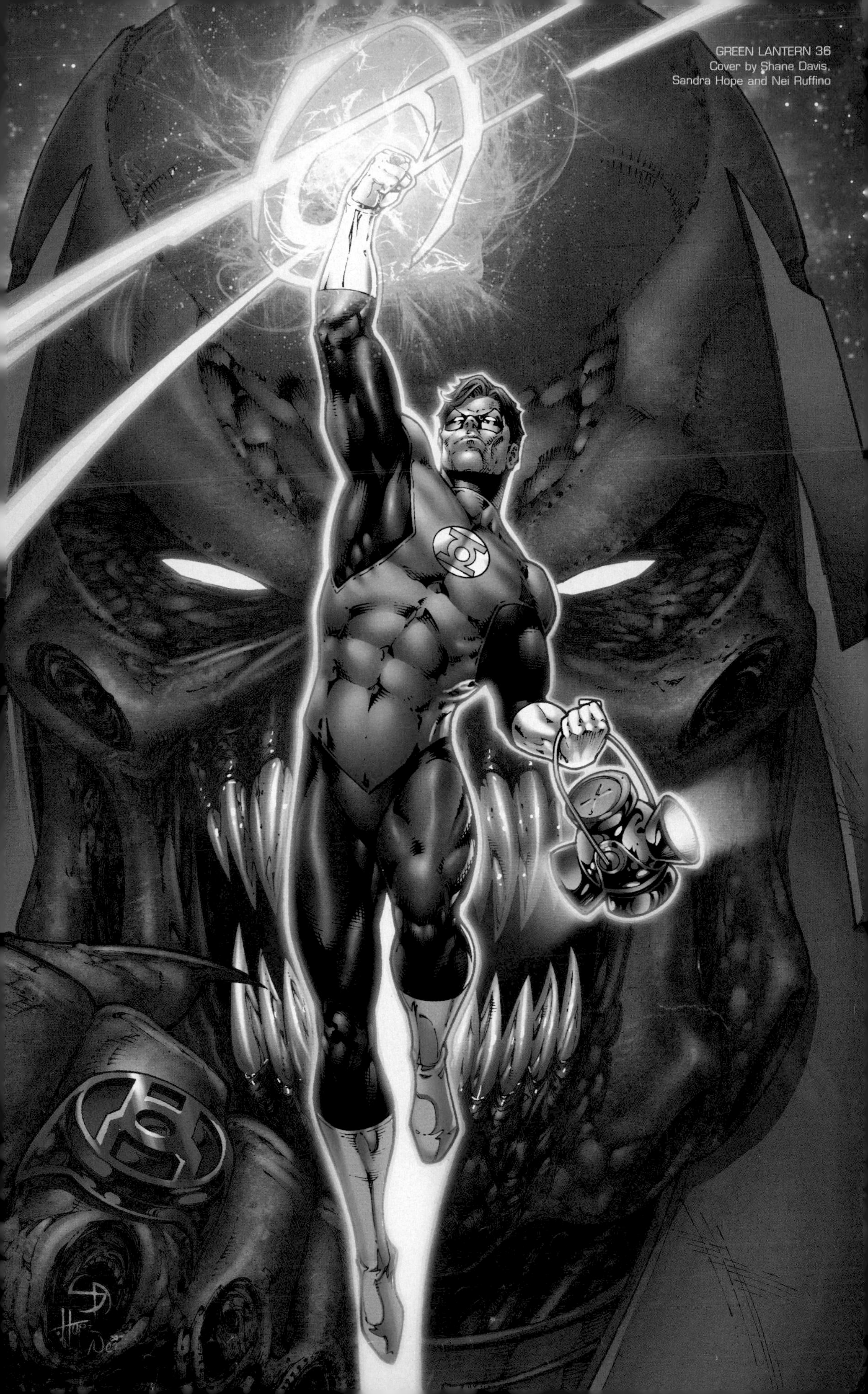

GREEN LANTERN 36
Cover by Shane Davis,
Sandra Hope and Nei Ruffino

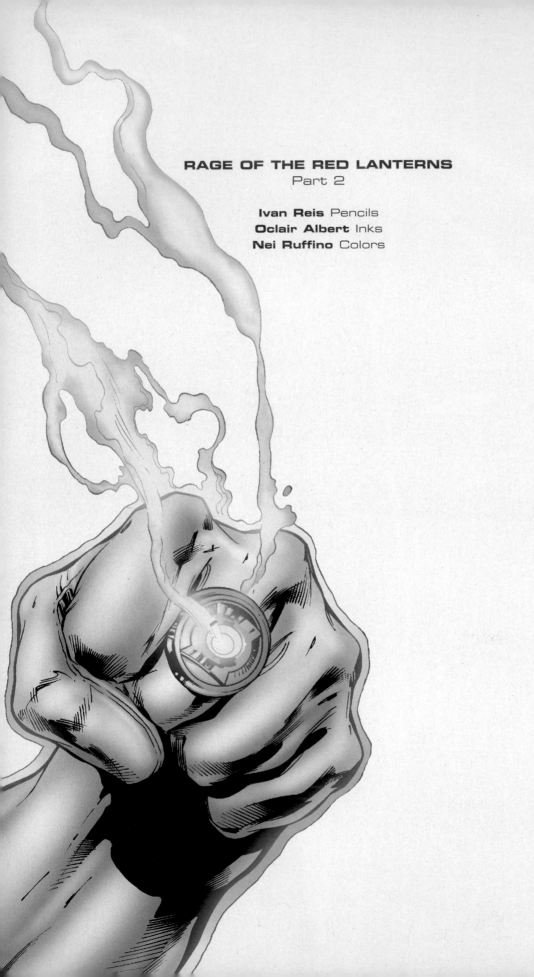

RAGE OF THE RED LANTERNS
Part 2

Ivan Reis Pencils
Oclair Albert Inks
Nei Ruffino Colors

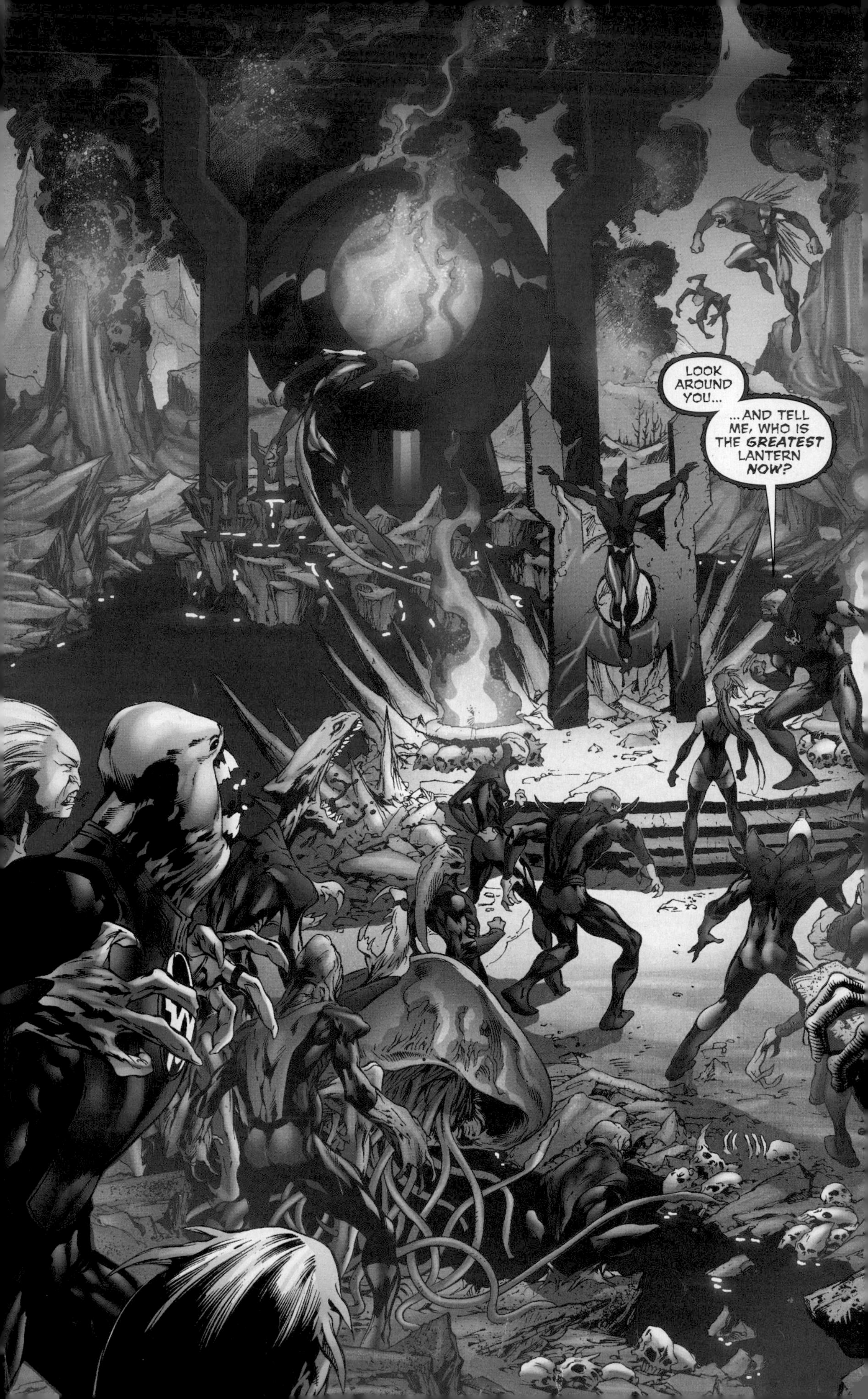
LOOK AROUND YOU...
...AND TELL ME, WHO IS THE GREATEST LANTERN NOW?

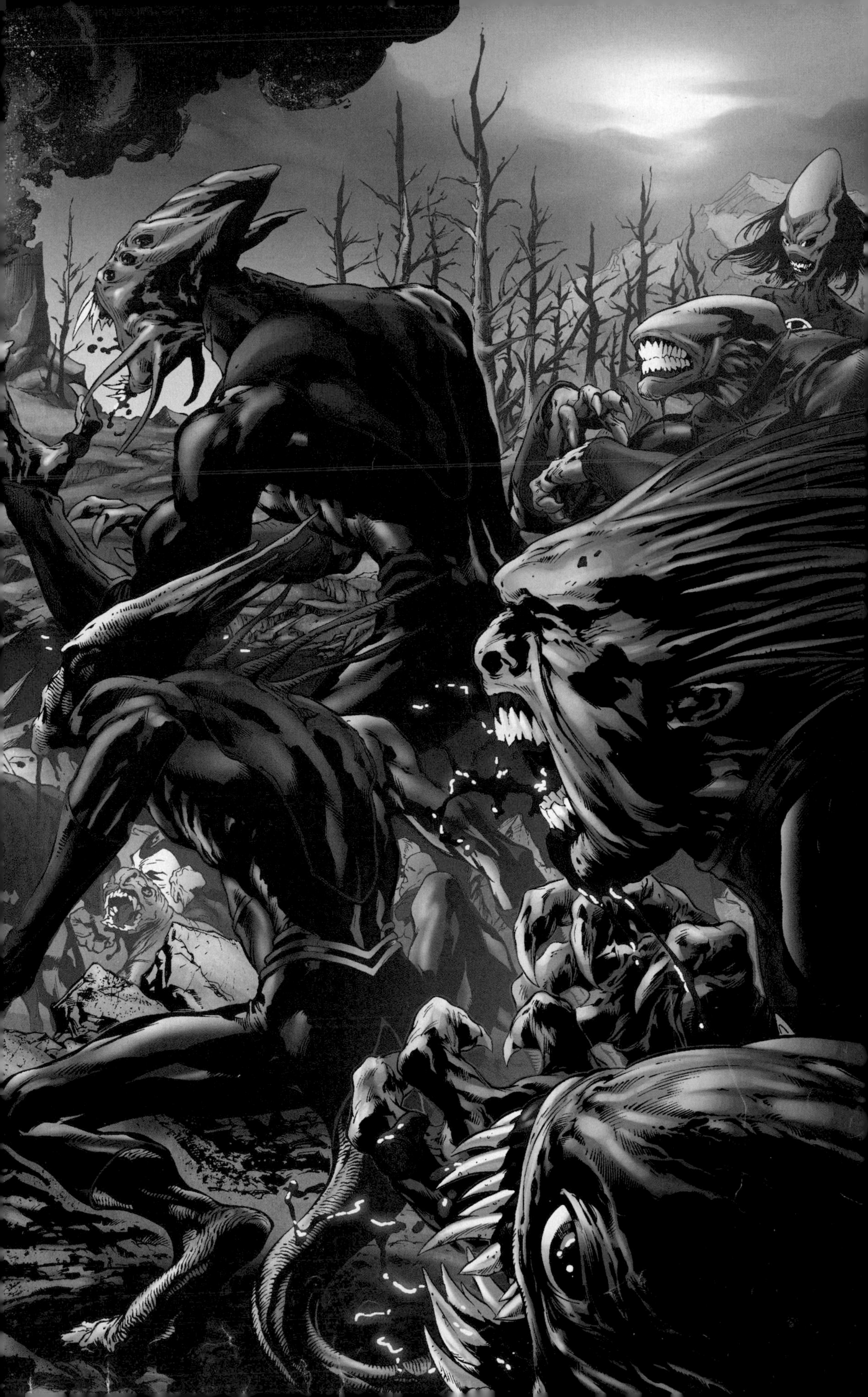

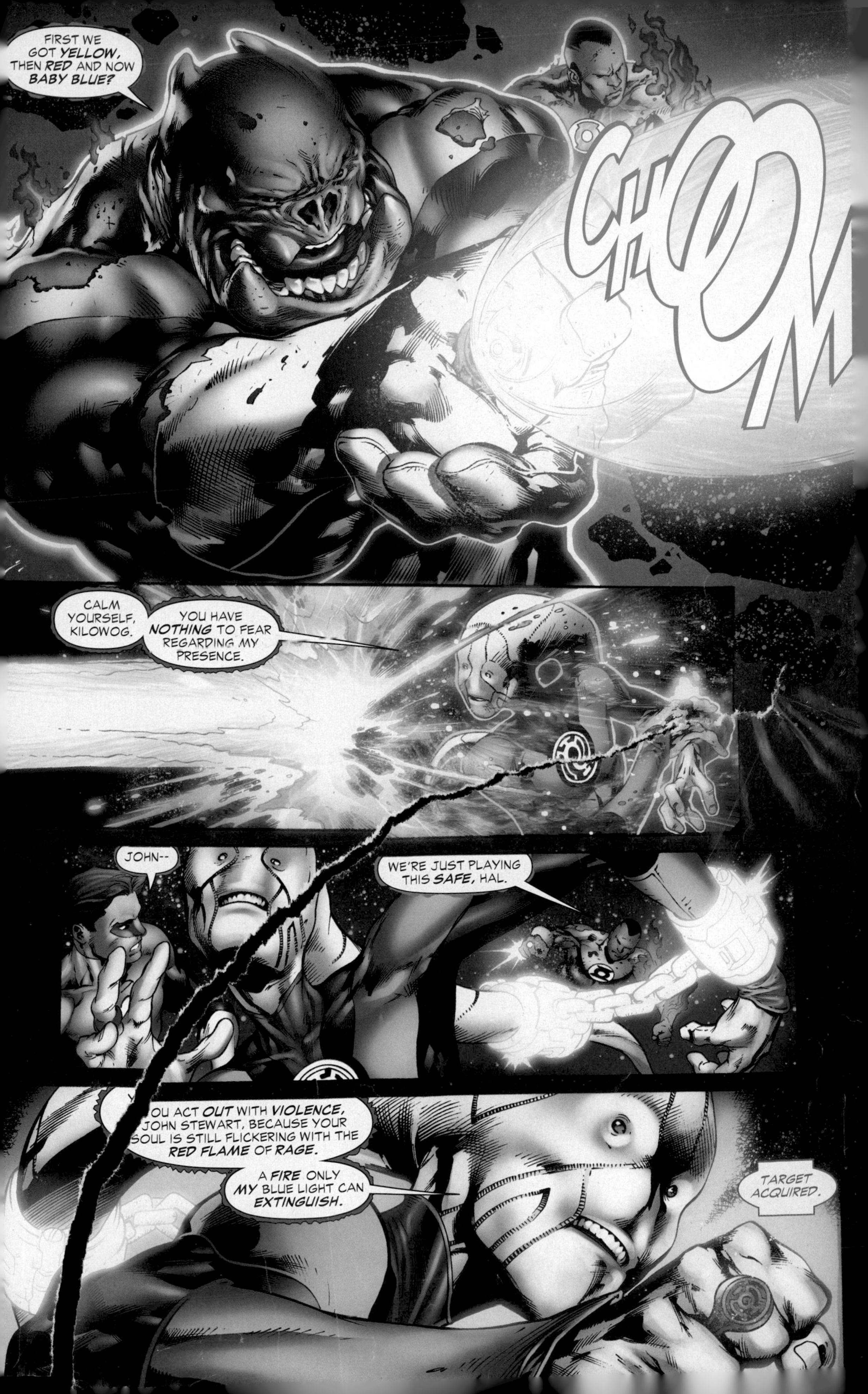
FIRST WE GOT YELLOW, THEN RED AND NOW BABY BLUE?
CHOOM
CALM YOURSELF, KILOWOG.
YOU HAVE NOTHING TO FEAR REGARDING MY PRESENCE.
JOHN--
WE'RE JUST PLAYING THIS SAFE, HAL.
OU ACT OUT WITH VIOLENCE, JOHN STEWART, BECAUSE YOUR SOUL IS STILL FLICKERING WITH THE RED FLAME OF RAGE.
A FIRE ONLY MY BLUE LIGHT CAN EXTINGUISH.
TARGET ACQUIRED.

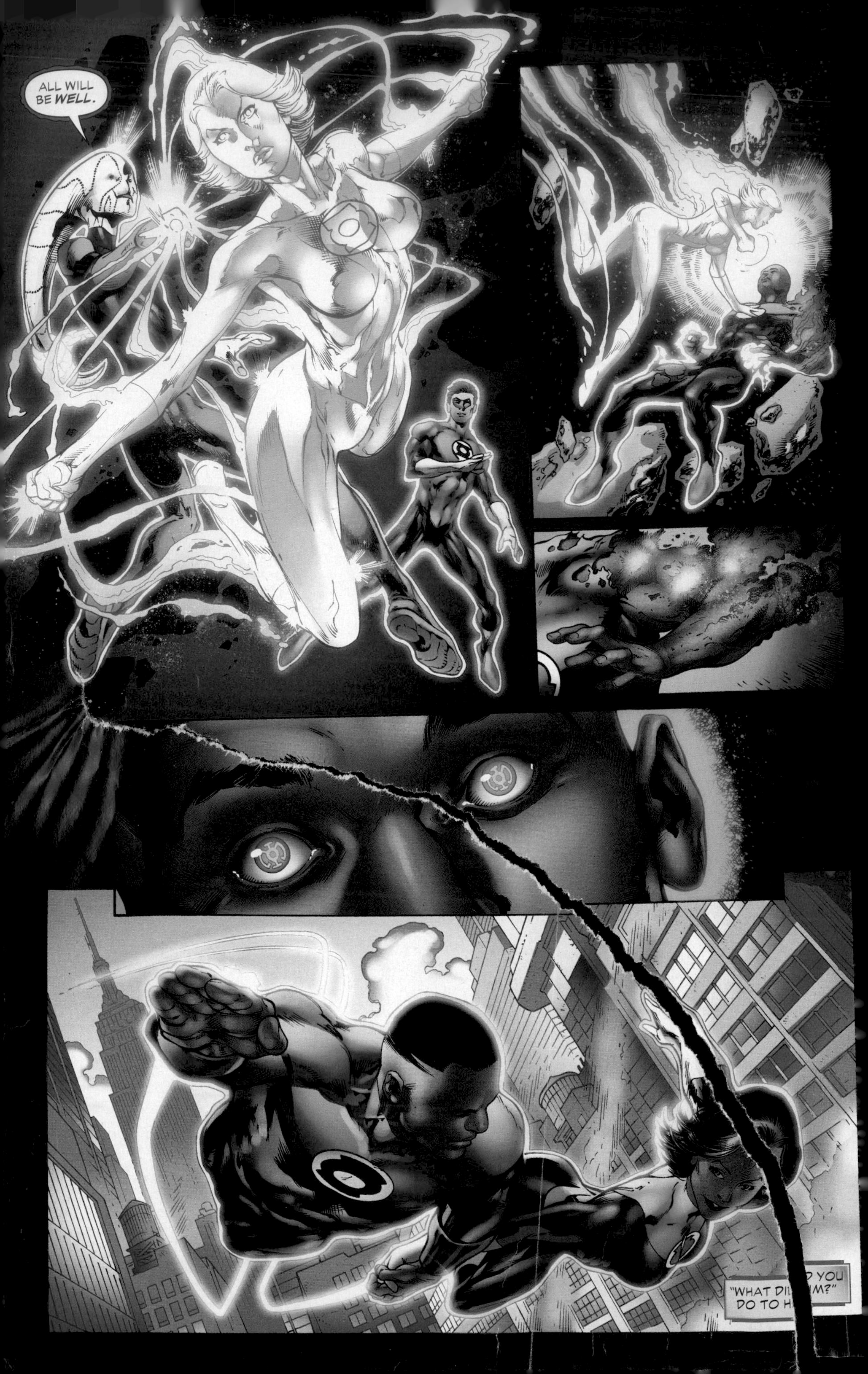
ALL WILL BE WELL.
"WHAT DI D YOU DO TO H M?"

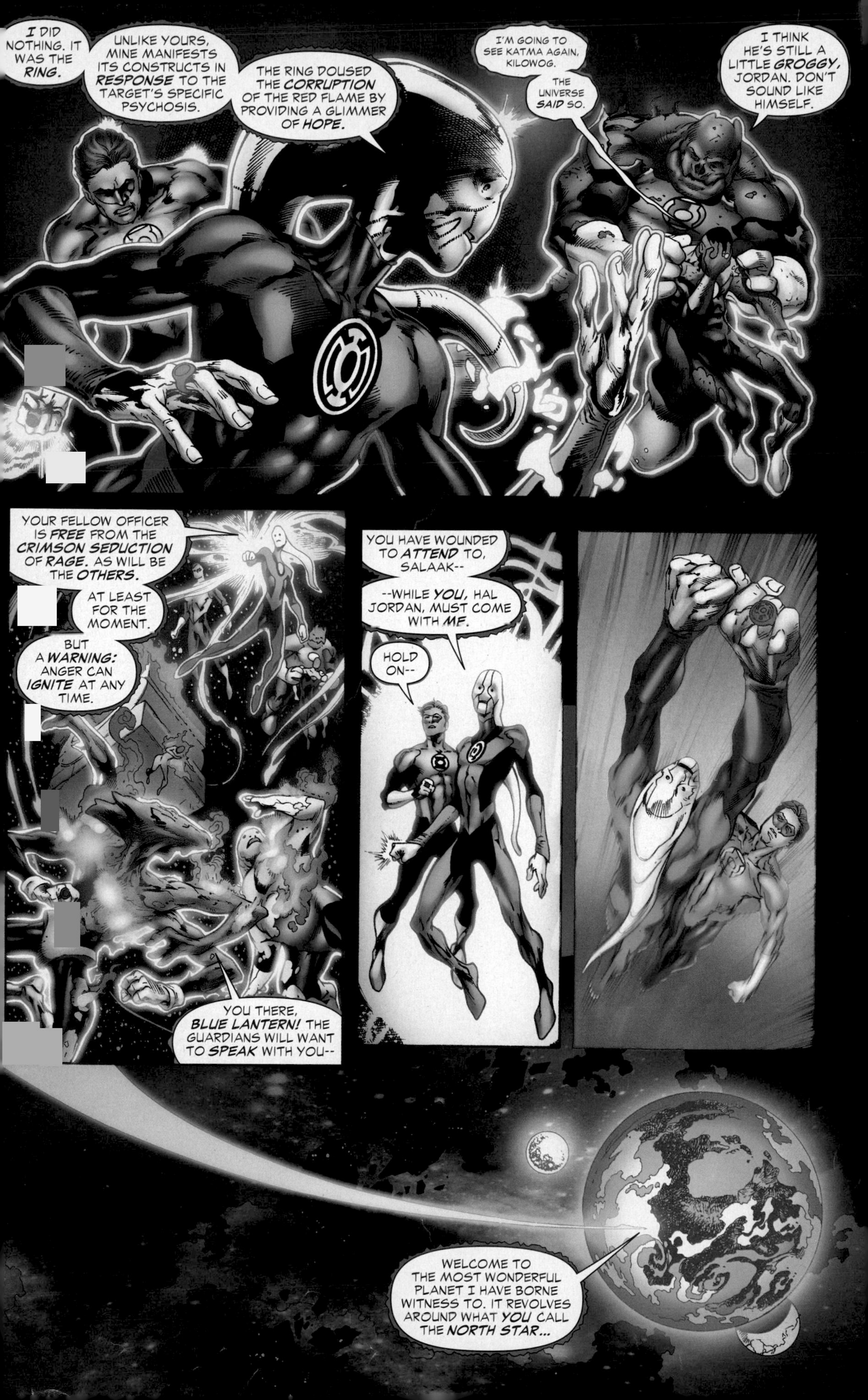
I DID NOTHING. IT WAS THE RING.
UNLIKE YOURS, MINE MANIFESTS ITS CONSTRUCTS IN RESPONSE TO THE TARGET'S SPECIFIC PSYCHOSIS.
THE RING DOUSED THE CORRUPTION OF THE RED FLAME BY PROVIDING A GLIMMER OF HOPE.
I'M GOING TO SEE KATMA AGAIN, KILOWOG.
THE UNIVERSE SAID SO.
I THINK HE'S STILL A LITTLE GROGGY, JORDAN. DON'T SOUND LIKE HIMSELF.
YOUR FELLOW OFFICER IS FREE FROM THE CRIMSON SEDUCTION OF RAGE. AS WILL BE THE OTHERS.
AT LEAST FOR THE MOMENT.
BUT A WARNING: ANGER CAN IGNITE AT ANY TIME.
YOU THERE, BLUE LANTERN! THE GUARDIANS WILL WANT TO SPEAK WITH YOU--
YOU HAVE WOUNDED TO ATTEND TO, SALAAK--
--WHILE YOU, HAL JORDAN, MUST COME WITH ME.
HOLD ON--
WELCOME TO THE MOST WONDERFUL PLANET I HAVE BORNE WITNESS TO. IT REVOLVES AROUND WHAT YOU CALL THE NORTH STAR...

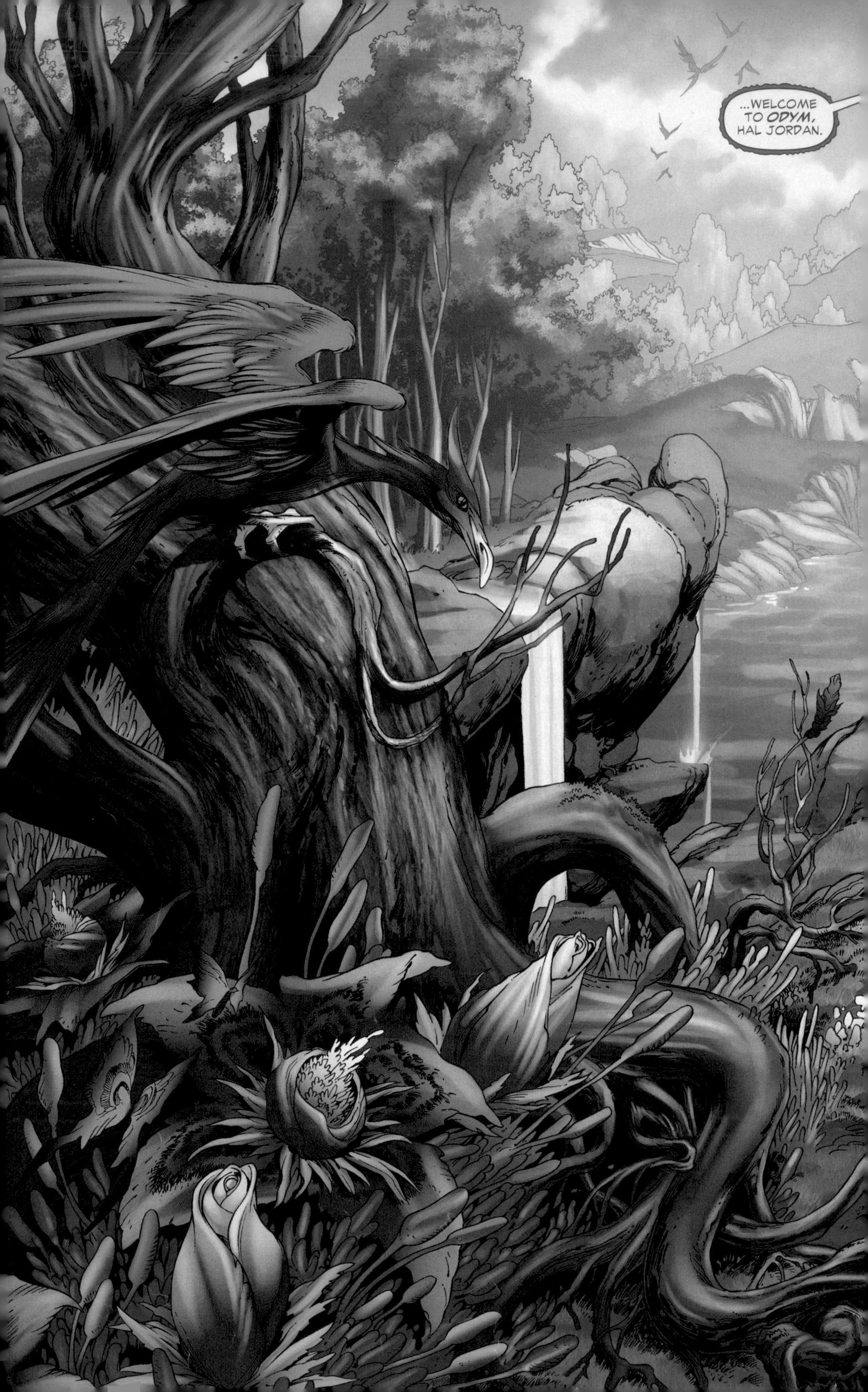
...WELCOME TO ODYM, HAL JORDAN.

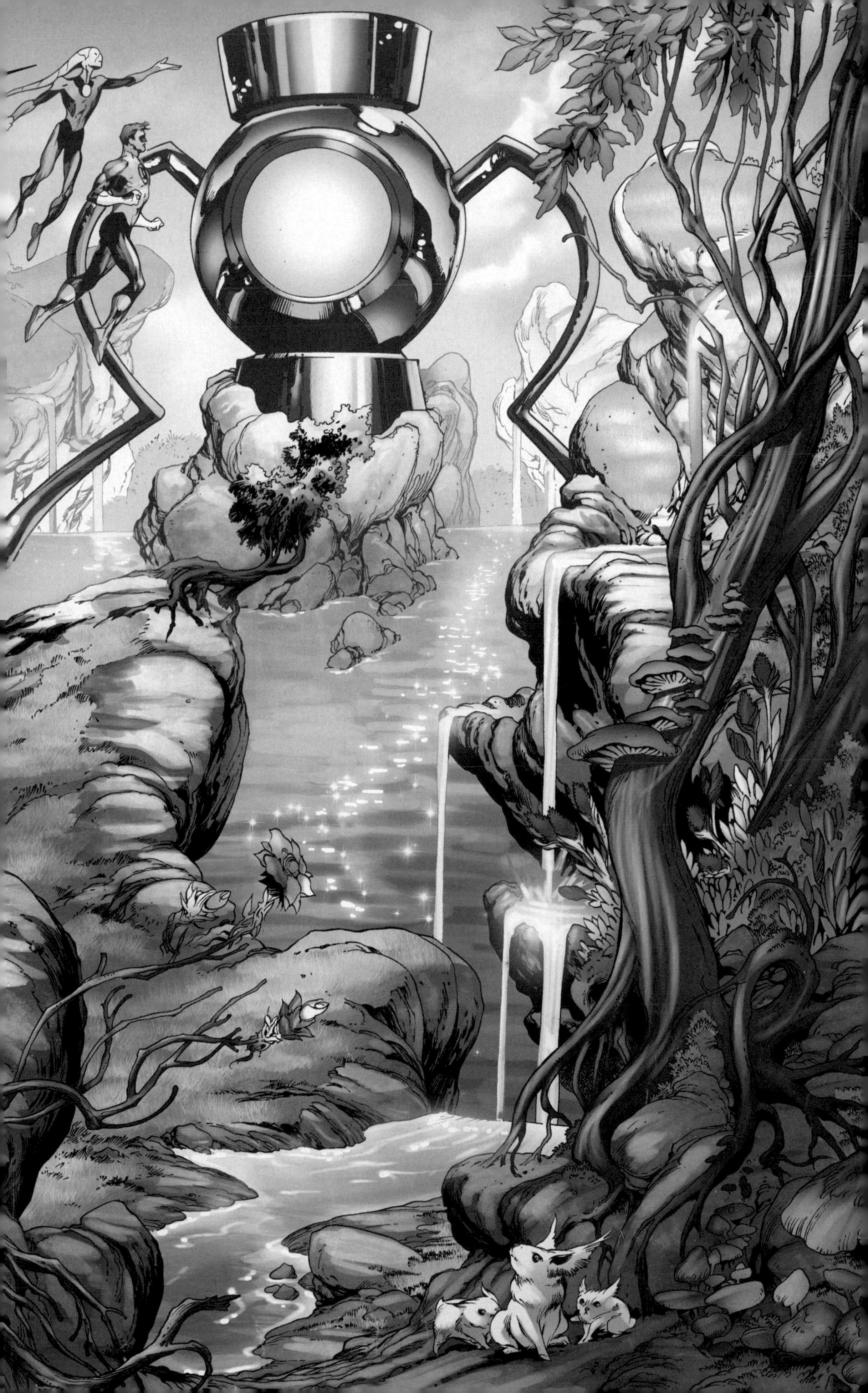

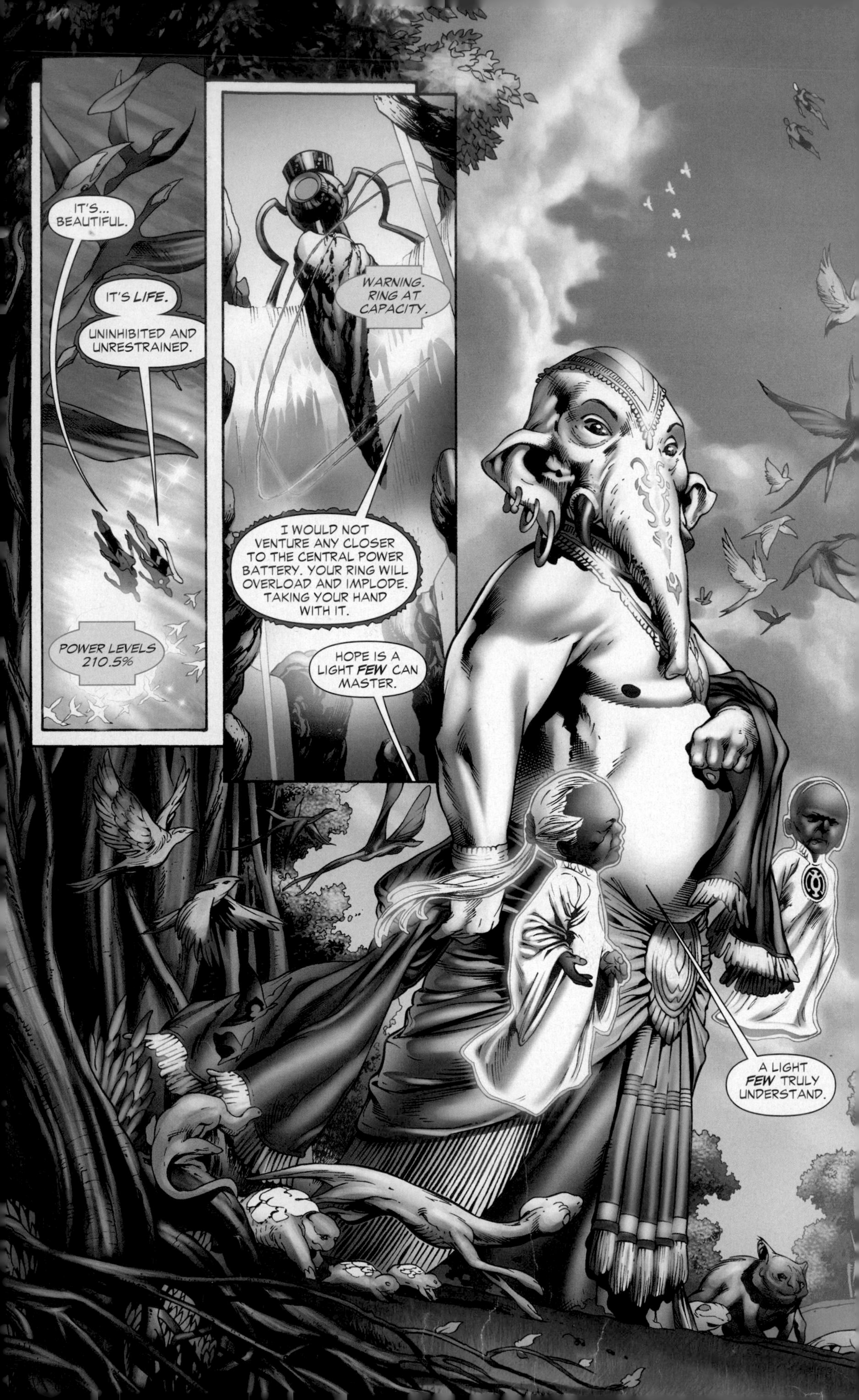
IT'S... BEAUTIFUL.
IT'S LIFE.
UNINHIBITED AND UNRESTRAINED.
POWER LEVELS 210.5%
WARNING. RING AT CAPACITY.
I WOULD NOT VENTURE ANY CLOSER TO THE CENTRAL POWER BATTERY. YOUR RING WILL OVERLOAD AND IMPLODE. TAKING YOUR HAND WITH IT.
HOPE IS A LIGHT FEW CAN MASTER.
A LIGHT FEW TRULY UNDERSTAND.

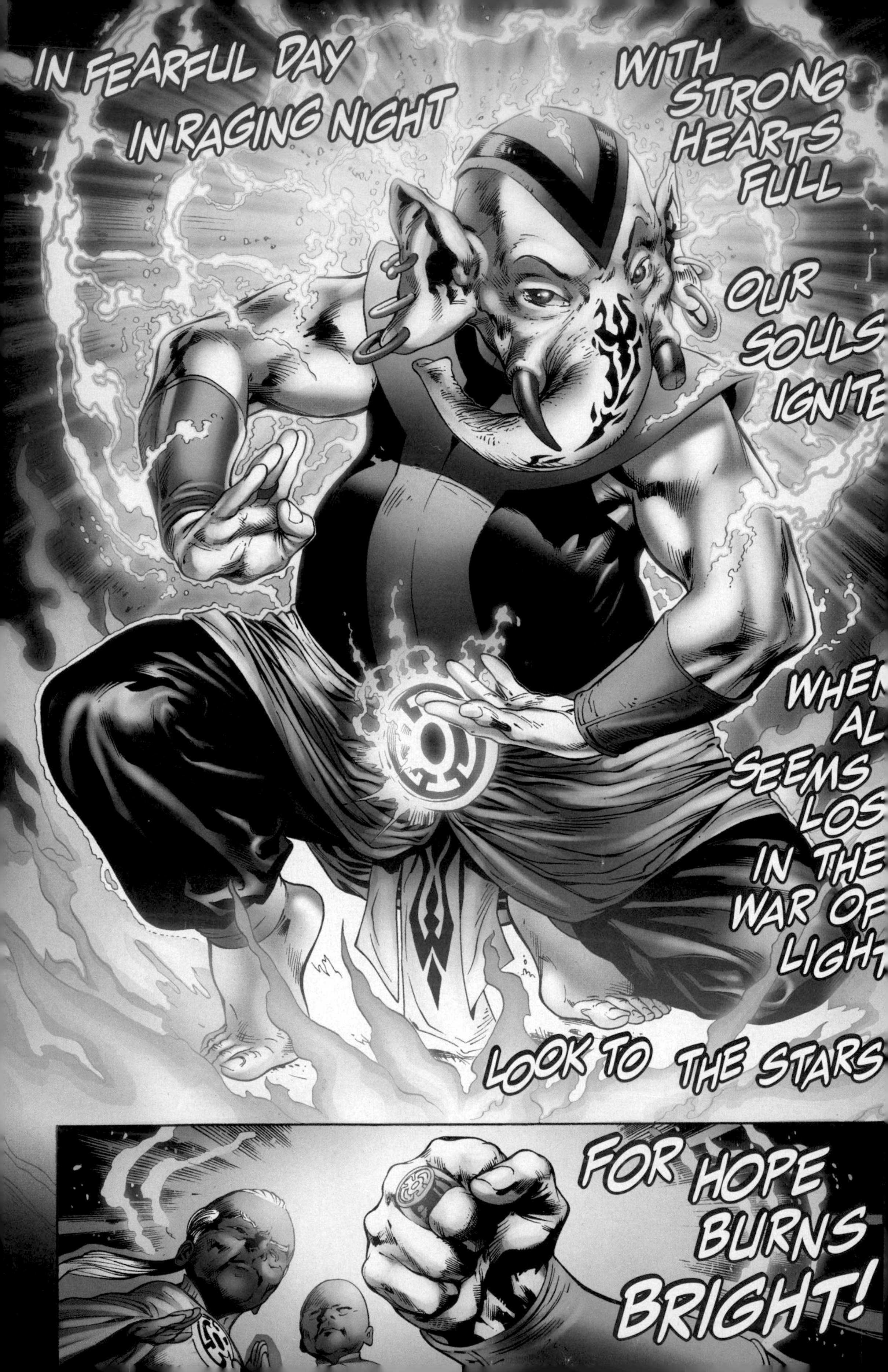
IN FEARFUL DAY
IN RAGING NIGHT
WITH STRONG HEARTS FULL
OUR SOULS IGNITE
WHEN ALL SEEMS LOST IN THE WAR OF LIGHT
LOOK TO THE STARS
FOR HOPE BURNS BRIGHT!

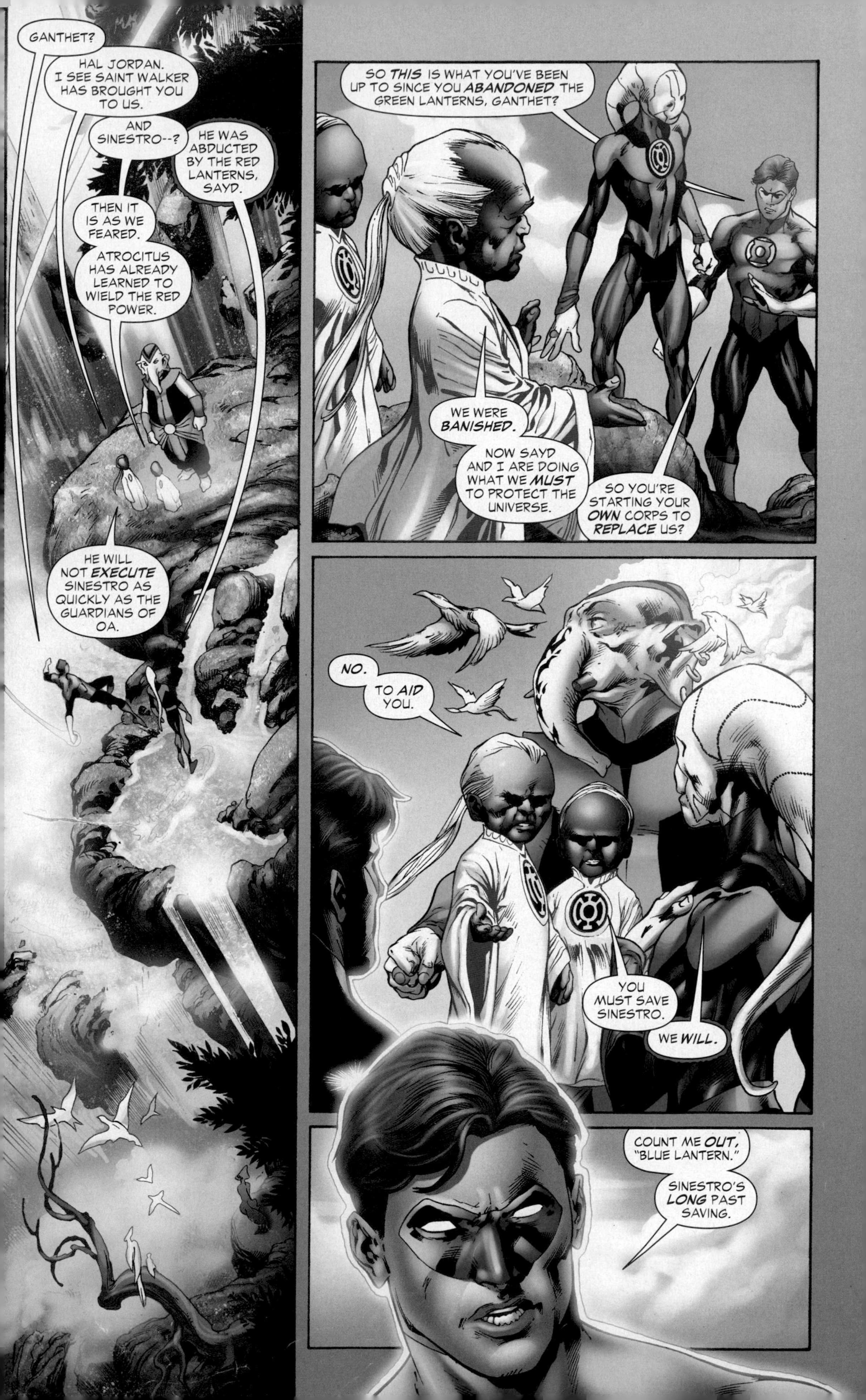
GANTHET?
HAL JORDAN. I SEE SAINT WALKER HAS BROUGHT YOU TO US.
AND SINESTRO--?
HE WAS ABDUCTED BY THE RED LANTERNS, SAYD.
THEN IT IS AS WE FEARED.
ATROCITUS HAS ALREADY LEARNED TO WIELD THE RED POWER.
HE WILL NOT EXECUTE SINESTRO AS QUICKLY AS THE GUARDIANS OF OA.
SO THIS IS WHAT YOU'VE BEEN UP TO SINCE YOU ABANDONED THE GREEN LANTERNS, GANTHET?
WE WERE BANISHED.
NOW SAYD AND I ARE DOING WHAT WE MUST TO PROTECT THE UNIVERSE.
SO YOU'RE STARTING YOUR OWN CORPS TO REPLACE US?
NO.
TO AID YOU.
YOU MUST SAVE SINESTRO.
WE WILL.
COUNT ME OUT, "BLUE LANTERN."
SINESTRO'S LONG PAST SAVING.

SOME SAID THAT OF *YOU*.

I DON'T EXPECT SINESTRO TO *EVER* UNDERSTAND HOW TRULY *SADISTIC* AND *IMPERIOUS* HE HAS BECOME.

NOR DO I PURPORT THAT THE POWER WE WIELD COULD EVER *CHANGE* THAT.

I'M NOT GOING TO "*HOPE*" FOR HIM TO "*SEE* THE *LIGHT*" OR WHATEVER YOU AND YOUR CORPS ARE SELLING.

SINESTRO MADE *EVERY* BAD AND MURDEROUS CHOICE IN HIS LIFE.

BUT PLEASE *TRUST* ME, HAL JORDAN.

I HAVE BEEN THERE TO *GUIDE* YOU SINCE SINESTRO'S *FALL*. AND I HAVE ALWAYS BEEN *HONEST*, IF NOT CLEAR.

I KNOW YOU DO NOT *TRUST* THE GUARDIANS, BUT I BELIEVE YOU STILL TRUST *ME*.

I'M ASKING YOU TO KEEP TRUSTING ME AND JOIN THESE TWO. THESE *BLUE LANTERNS*.

HELP THEM BRING SINESTRO TO *US*.

HE IS FAR MORE IMPORTANT TO THIS THAN EVEN *HE* REALIZES.

AND SO ARE *YOU*.

LIKE I HAVEN'T HEARD *THAT* BEFORE.

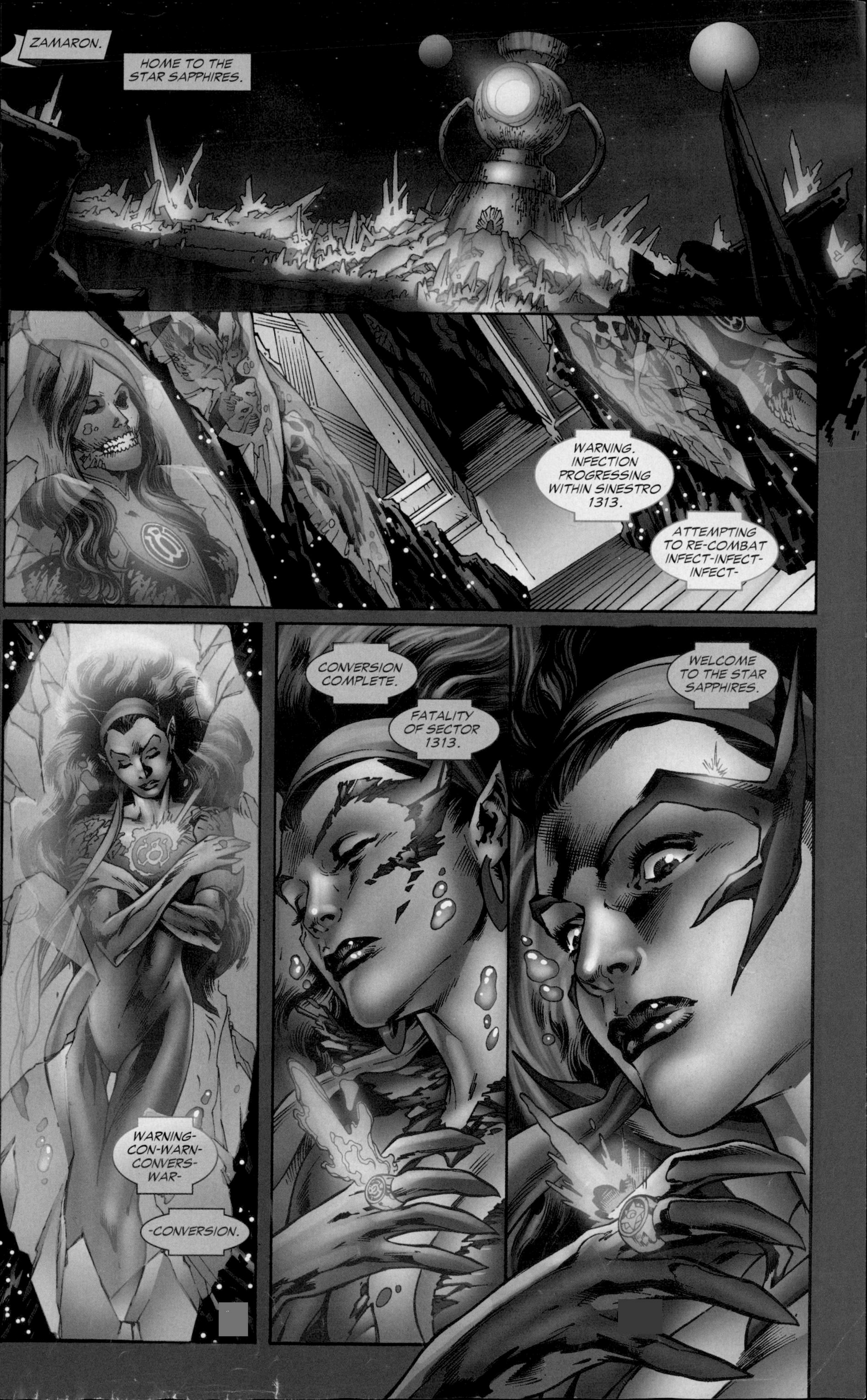
ZAMARON.
HOME TO THE STAR SAPPHIRES.
WARNING. INFECTION PROGRESSING WITHIN SINESTRO 1313.
ATTEMPTING TO RE-COMBAT INFECT-INFECT-INFECT-
WARNING-CON-WARN-CONVERS-WAR-
-CONVERSION.
CONVERSION COMPLETE.
FATALITY OF SECTOR 1313.
WELCOME TO THE STAR SAPPHIRES.

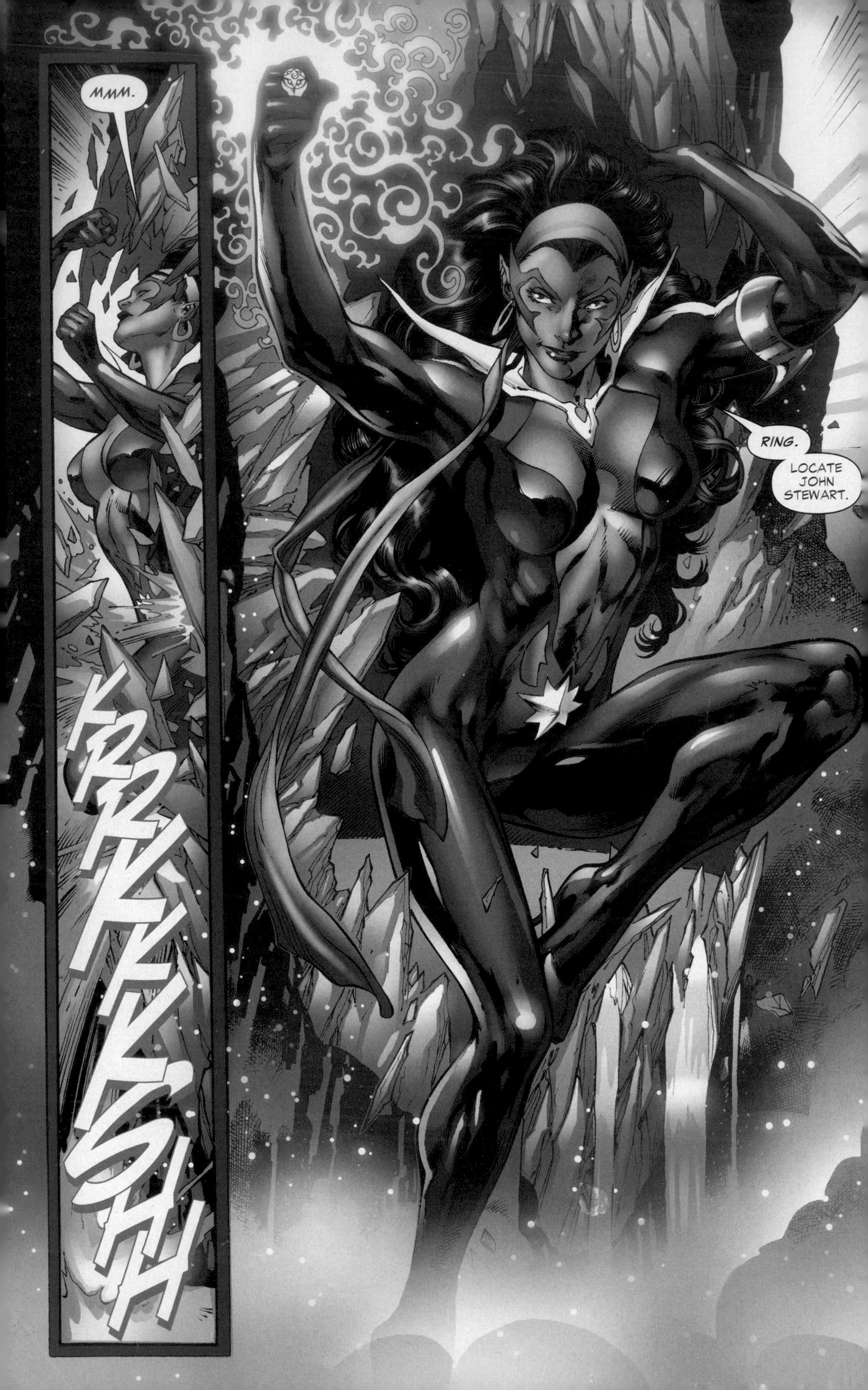
MMM.
RING.
LOCATE JOHN STEWART.
KRZKKKSHH

GREEN LANTERN 37 Cover by Shane Davis, Sandra Hope and Nei Ruffino

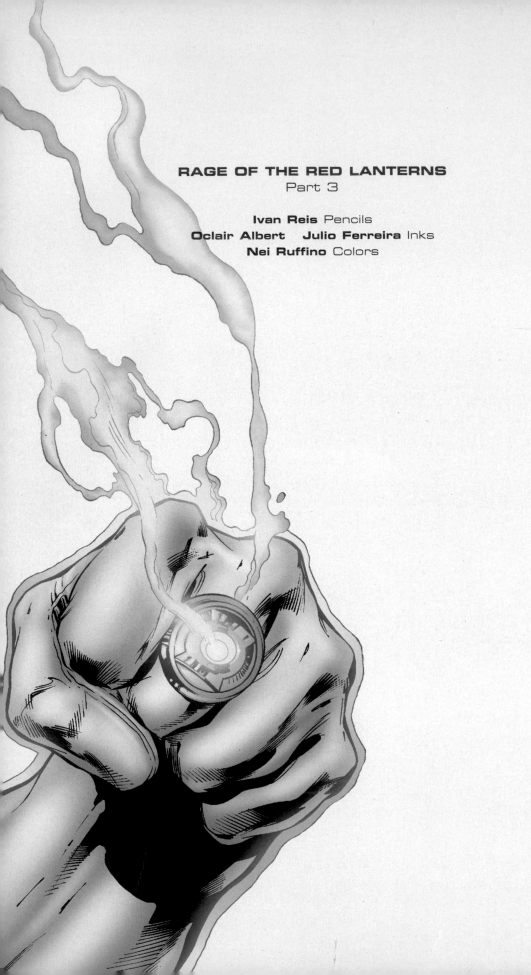

RAGE OF THE RED LANTERNS
Part 3

Ivan Reis Pencils
Oclair Albert   **Julio Ferreira** Inks
Nei Ruffino Colors

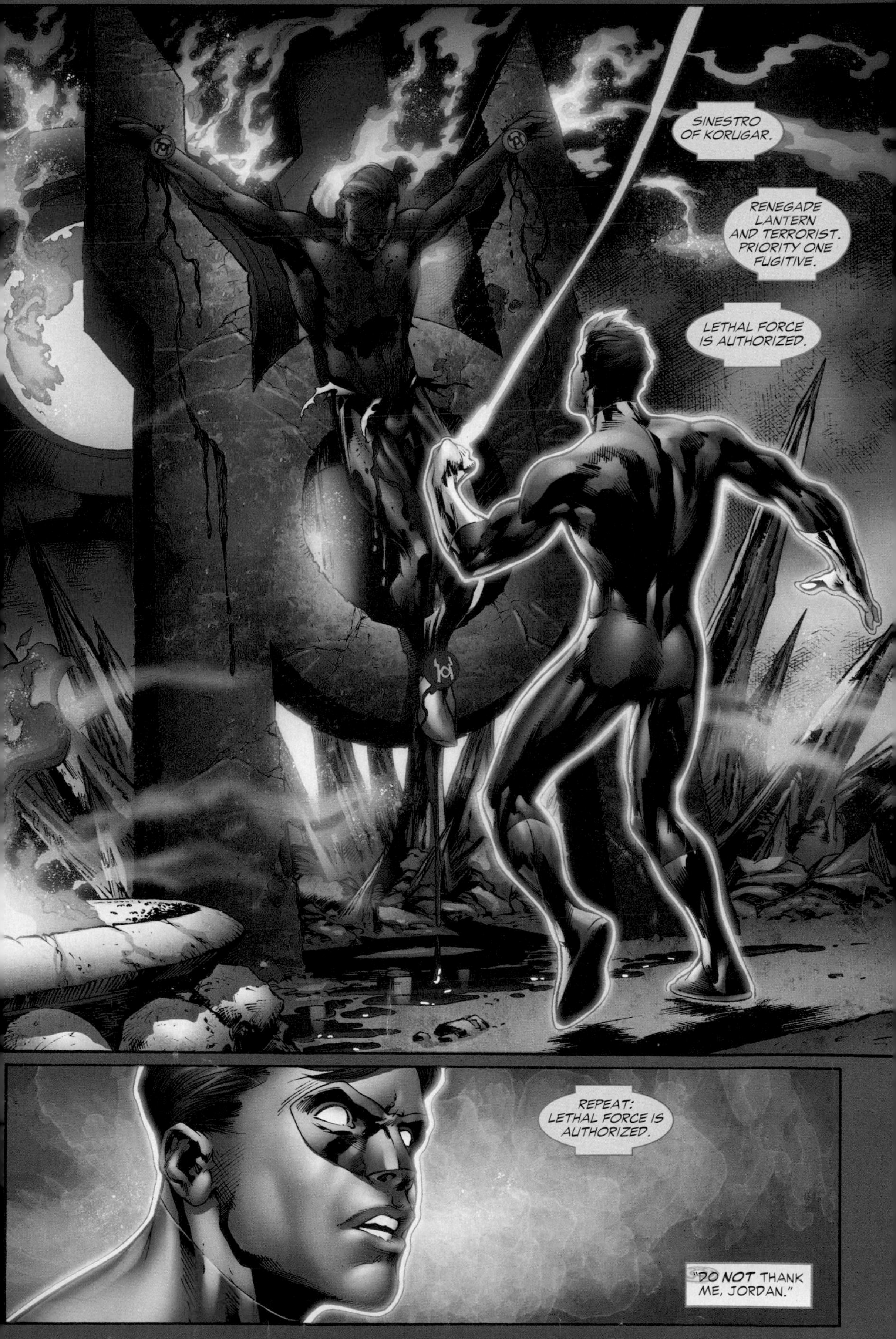
SINESTRO OF KORUGAR.
RENEGADE LANTERN AND TERRORIST. PRIORITY ONE FUGITIVE.
LETHAL FORCE IS AUTHORIZED.
REPEAT: LETHAL FORCE IS AUTHORIZED.
"DO NOT THANK ME, JORDAN."

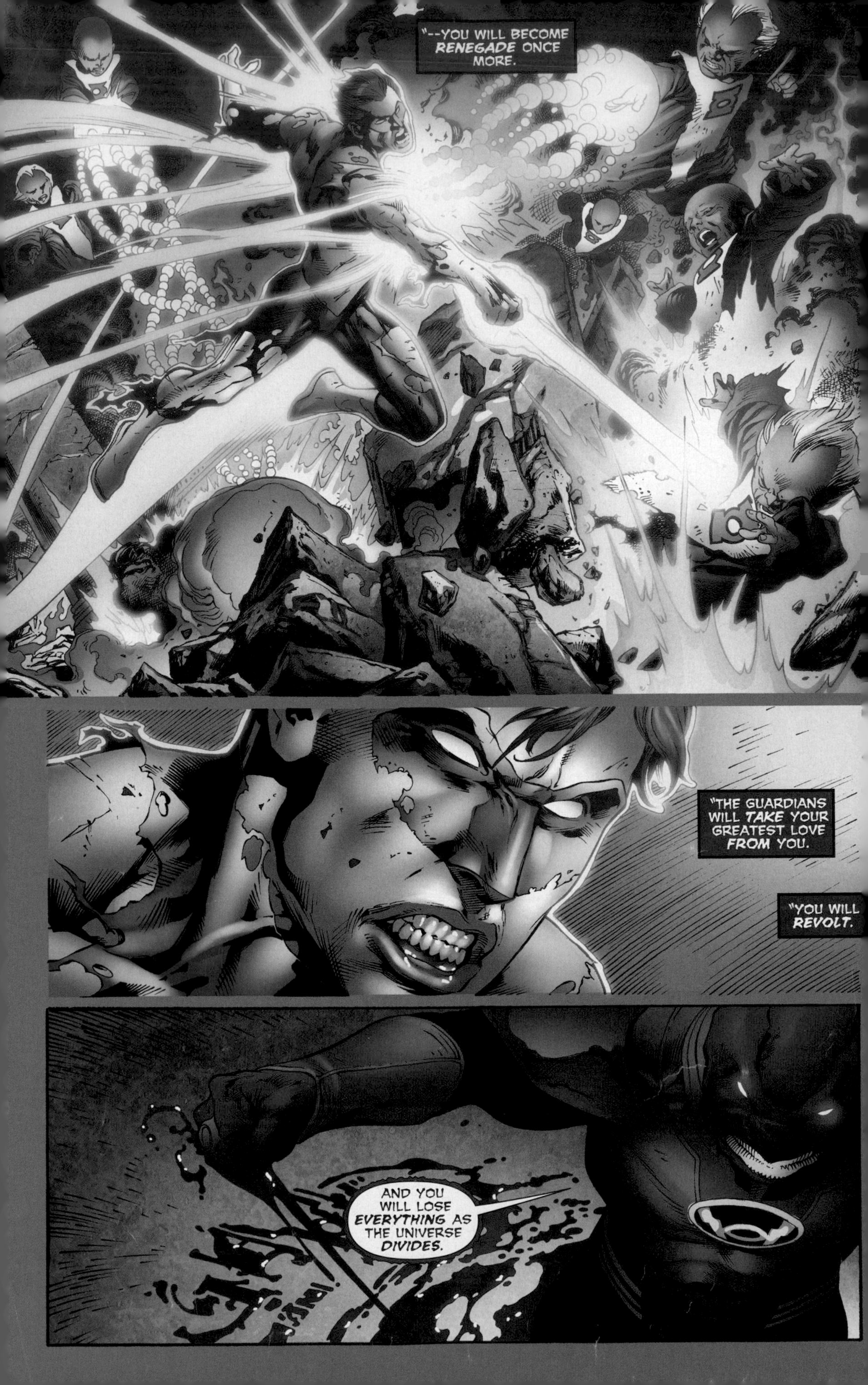
"--YOU WILL BECOME RENEGADE ONCE MORE.
"THE GUARDIANS WILL TAKE YOUR GREATEST LOVE FROM YOU.
"YOU WILL REVOLT.
AND YOU WILL LOSE EVERYTHING AS THE UNIVERSE DIVIDES.

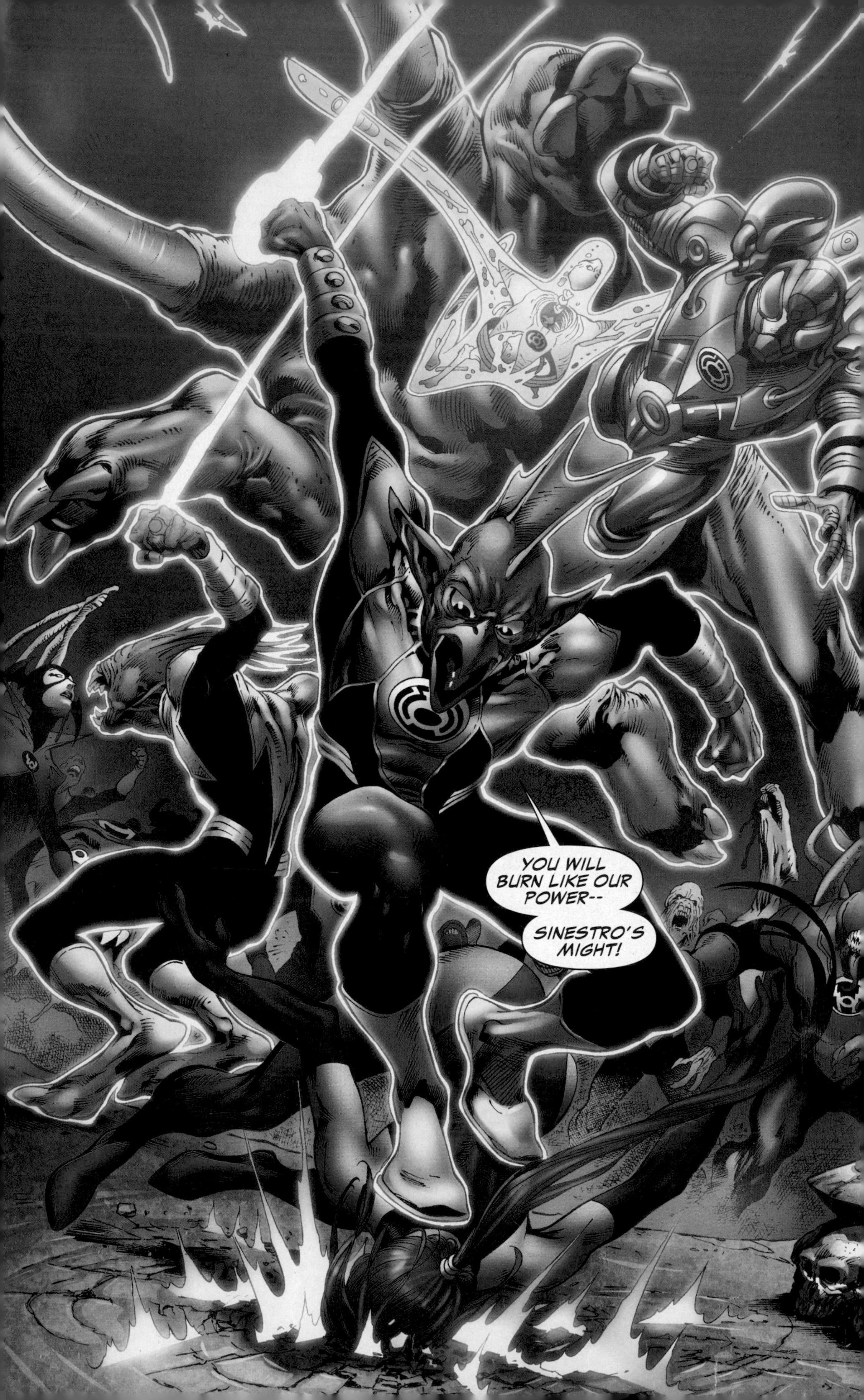
YOU WILL BURN LIKE OUR POWER--
SINESTRO'S MIGHT!

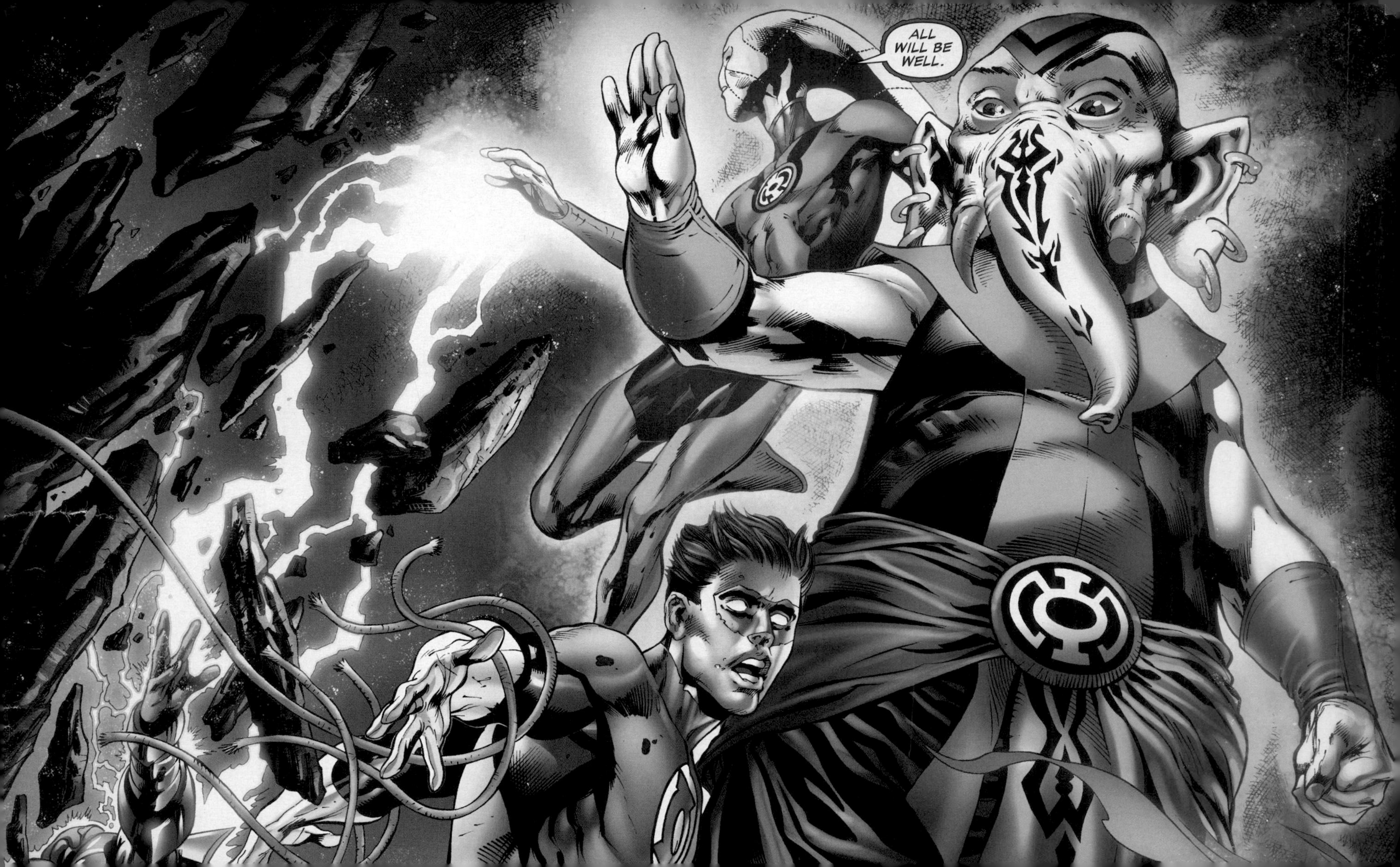
ALL WILL BE WELL.

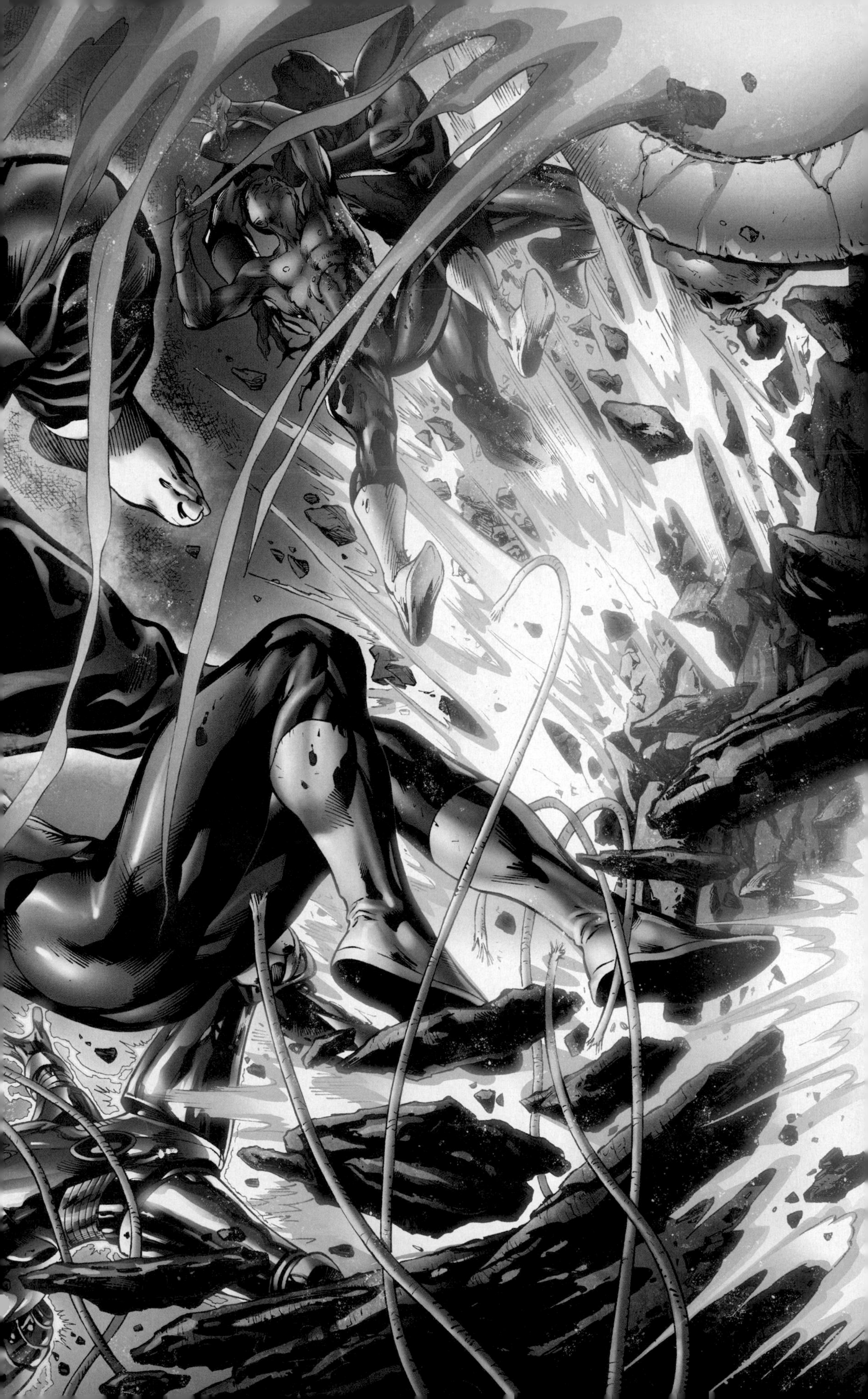

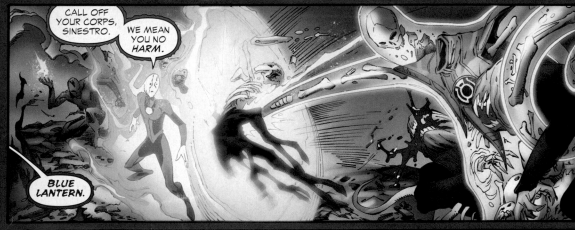

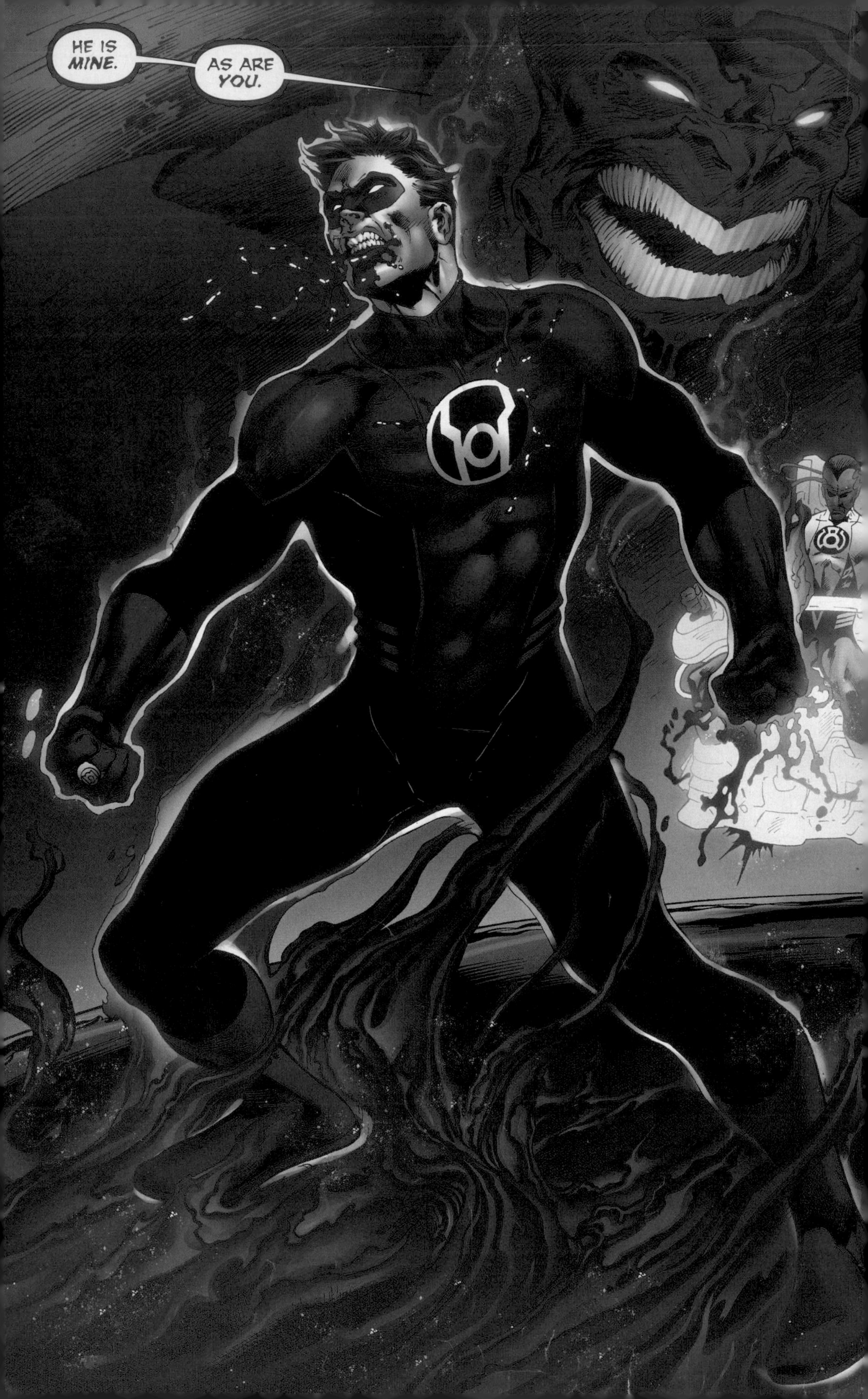
HE IS MINE.
AS ARE YOU.

GREEN LANTERN 38 Cover by Shane Davis, Sandra Hope and Nei Ruffino

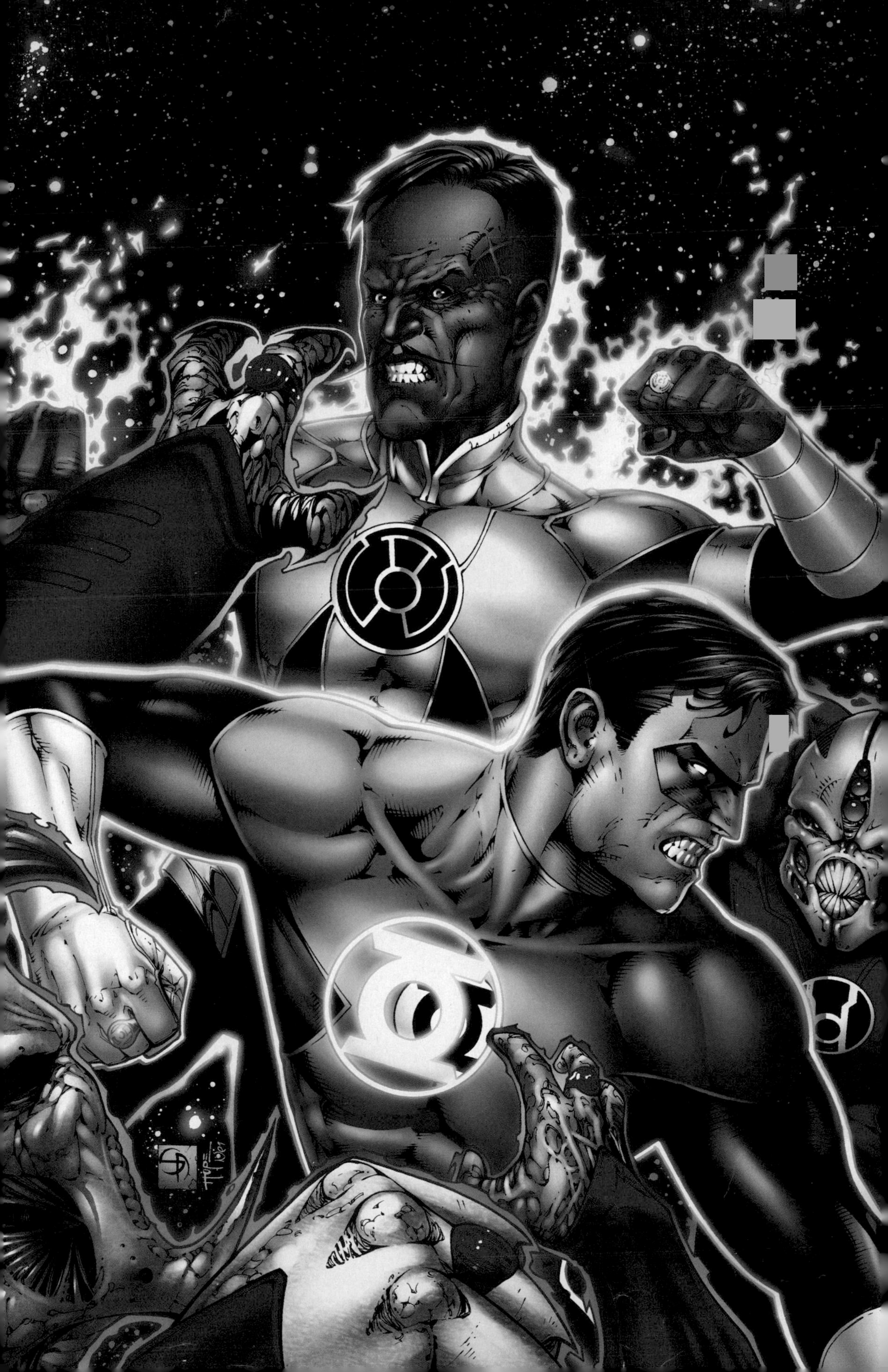

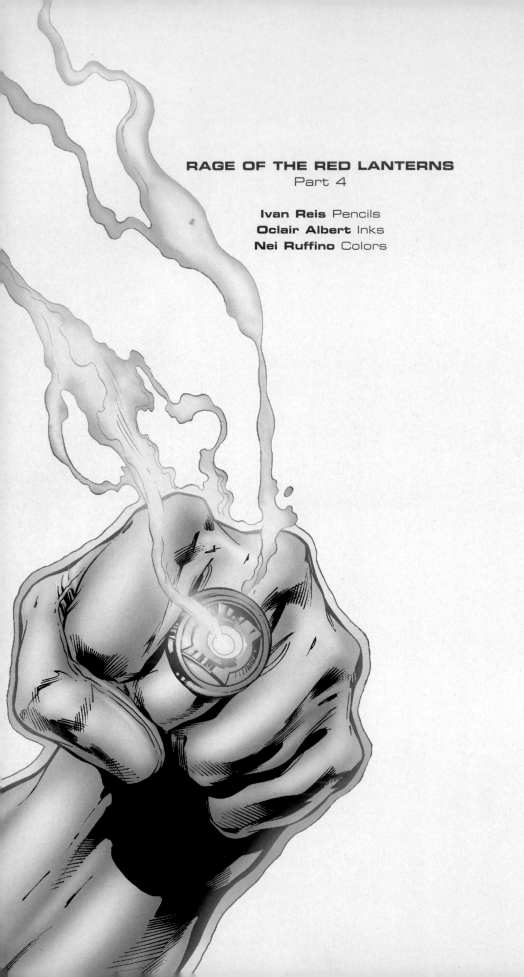

RAGE OF THE RED LANTERNS
Part 4

Ivan Reis Pencils
Oclair Albert Inks
Nei Ruffino Colors

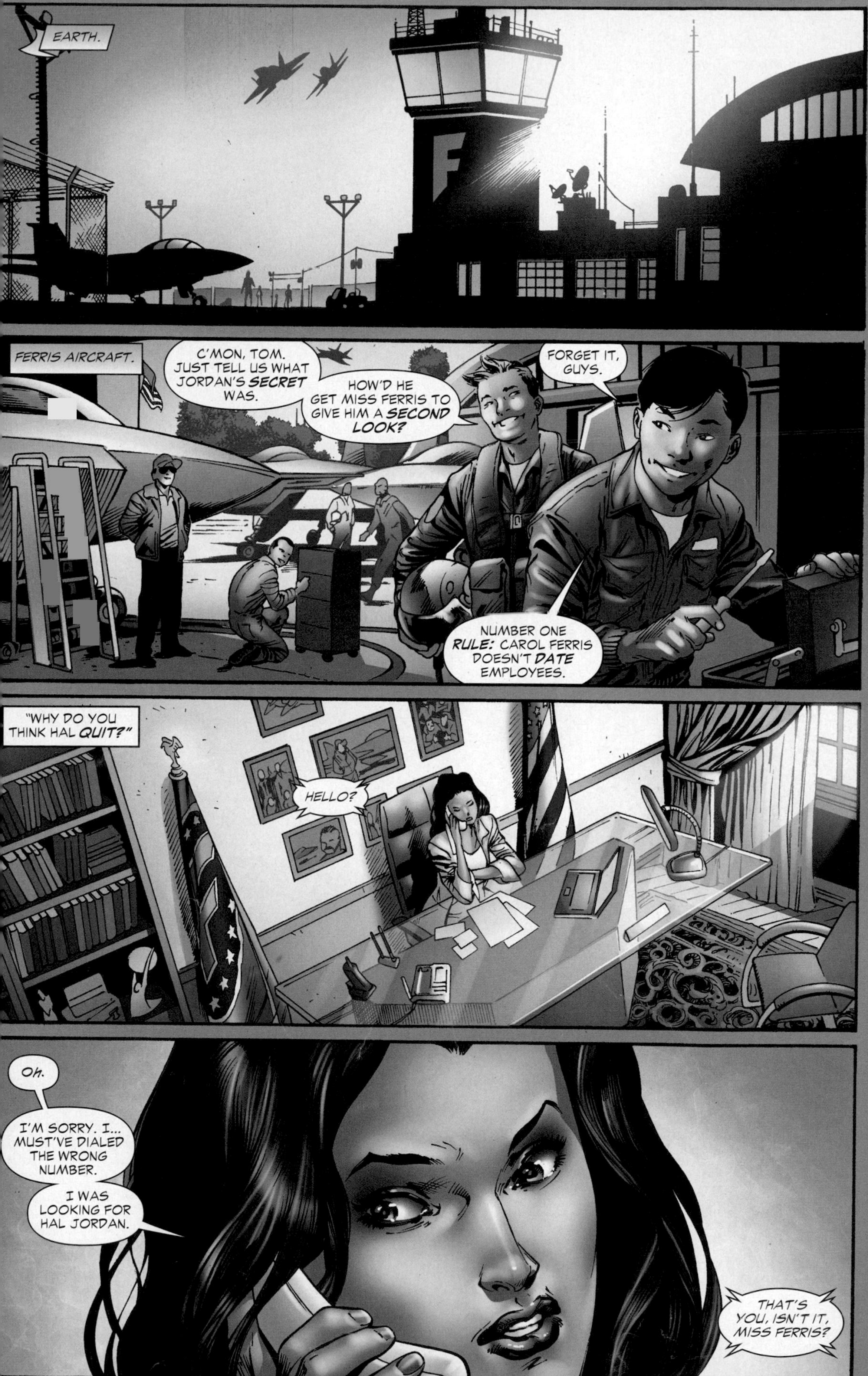

EARTH.
FERRIS AIRCRAFT.
C'MON, TOM. JUST TELL US WHAT JORDAN'S SECRET WAS.
HOW'D HE GET MISS FERRIS TO GIVE HIM A SECOND LOOK?
FORGET IT, GUYS.
NUMBER ONE RULE: CAROL FERRIS DOESN'T DATE EMPLOYEES.
"WHY DO YOU THINK HAL QUIT?"
HELLO?
Oh.
I'M SORRY. I... MUST'VE DIALED THE WRONG NUMBER.
I WAS LOOKING FOR HAL JORDAN.
THAT'S YOU, ISN'T IT, MISS FERRIS?

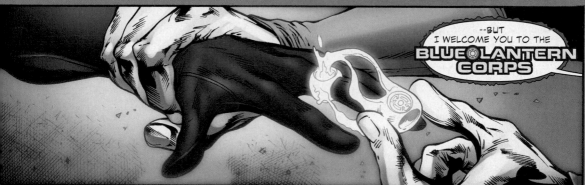

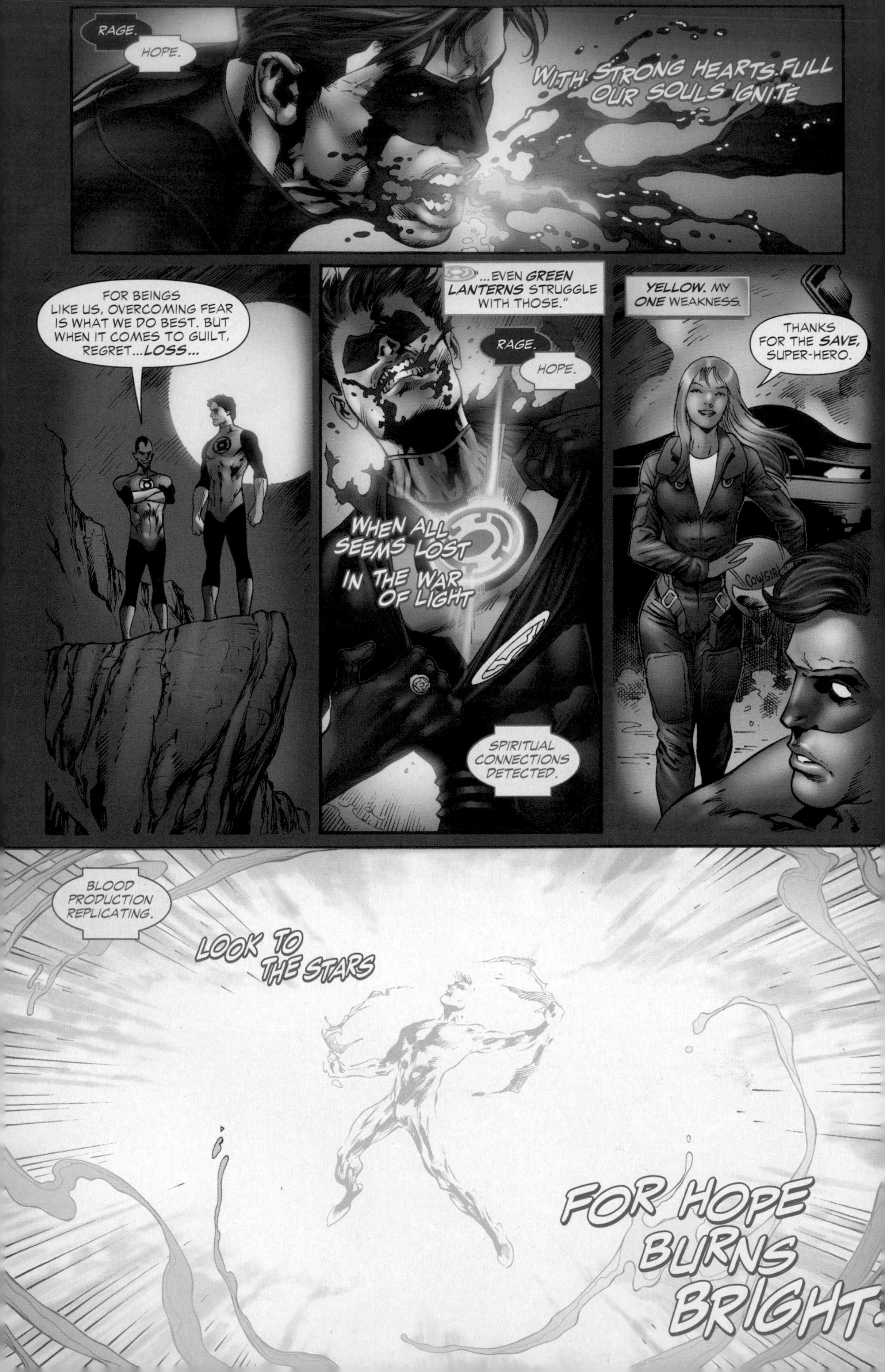
RAGE.
HOPE.
WITH STRONG HEARTS FULL OUR SOULS IGNITE
FOR BEINGS LIKE US, OVERCOMING FEAR IS WHAT WE DO BEST. BUT WHEN IT COMES TO GUILT, REGRET...LOSS...
"...EVEN GREEN LANTERNS STRUGGLE WITH THOSE."
RAGE.
HOPE.
WHEN ALL SEEMS LOST IN THE WAR OF LIGHT
SPIRITUAL CONNECTIONS DETECTED.
YELLOW. MY ONE WEAKNESS.
THANKS FOR THE SAVE, SUPER-HERO.
COWGIRL
BLOOD PRODUCTION REPLICATING.
LOOK TO THE STARS
FOR HOPE BURNS BRIGHT!

WARNING. POWER LEACHING IN PROGRESS.

POWER LEVELS 87%.

POWER LEVELS 69%.

OUR. RINGS. ARE. DRAINING.

PREPARE FOR ANTIMATTER UNIVERSE TRANSPORT.

YOU WANT MY *RAGE*, ATROCITUS?

ABIN SUR.

HOPE.

FOREVER HOPE.

KRRIKKLL

KRAAKK

THE BLUE RING... IT *DESTROYED* THE RED?

IMPOSSIBLE.

ATROCITUS!

HE IS *WOUNDED* AND *RETREATING*. AS IS SINESTRO.

WE *MUST* PURSUE THEM--

WALKER!

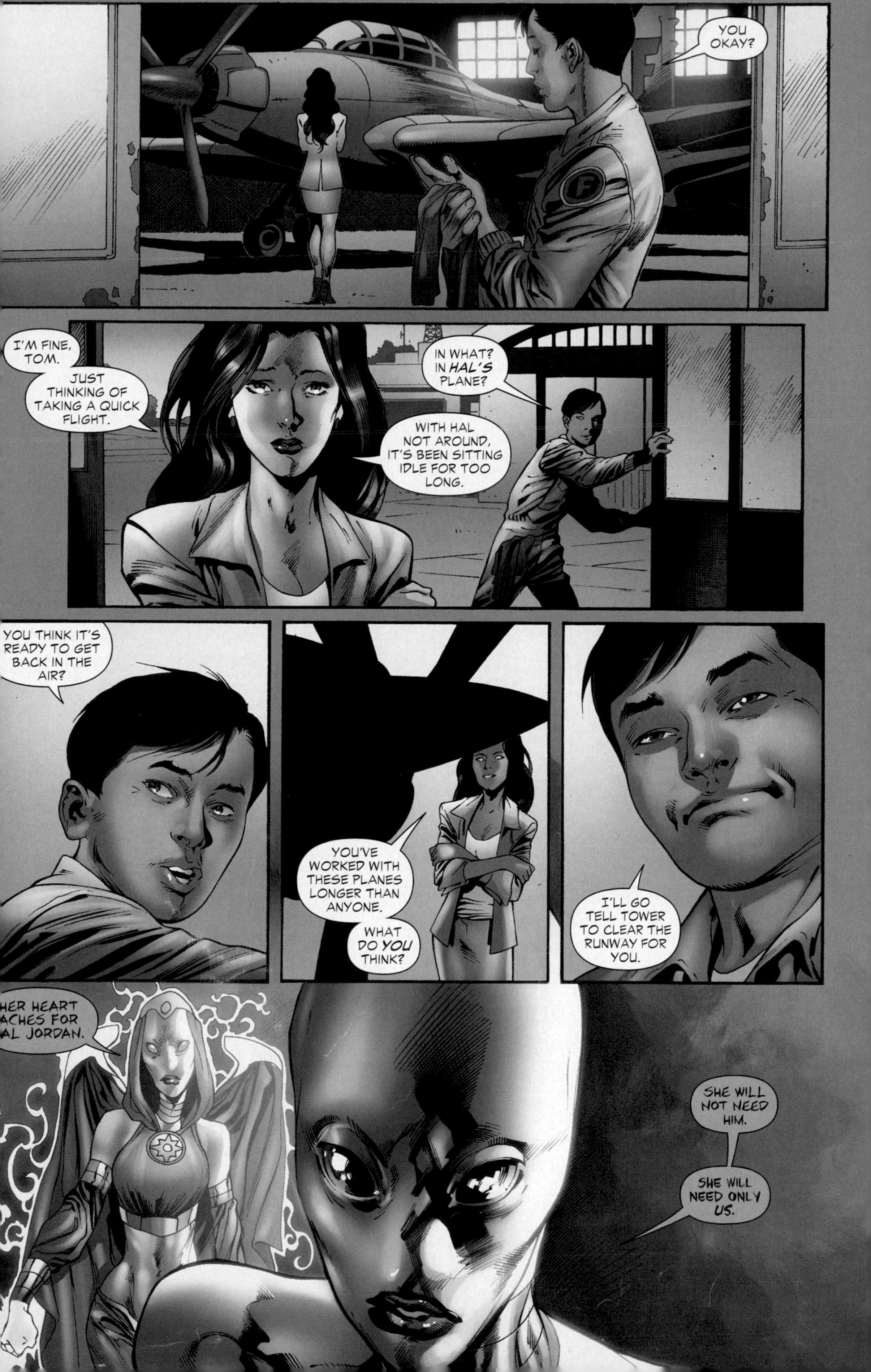
YOU OKAY?
I'M FINE, TOM.
JUST THINKING OF TAKING A QUICK FLIGHT.
IN WHAT? IN HAL'S PLANE?
WITH HAL NOT AROUND, IT'S BEEN SITTING IDLE FOR TOO LONG.
YOU THINK IT'S READY TO GET BACK IN THE AIR?
YOU'VE WORKED WITH THESE PLANES LONGER THAN ANYONE.
WHAT DO YOU THINK?
I'LL GO TELL TOWER TO CLEAR THE RUNWAY FOR YOU.
HER HEART ACHES FOR AL JORDAN.
SHE WILL NOT NEED HIM.
SHE WILL NEED ONLY US.

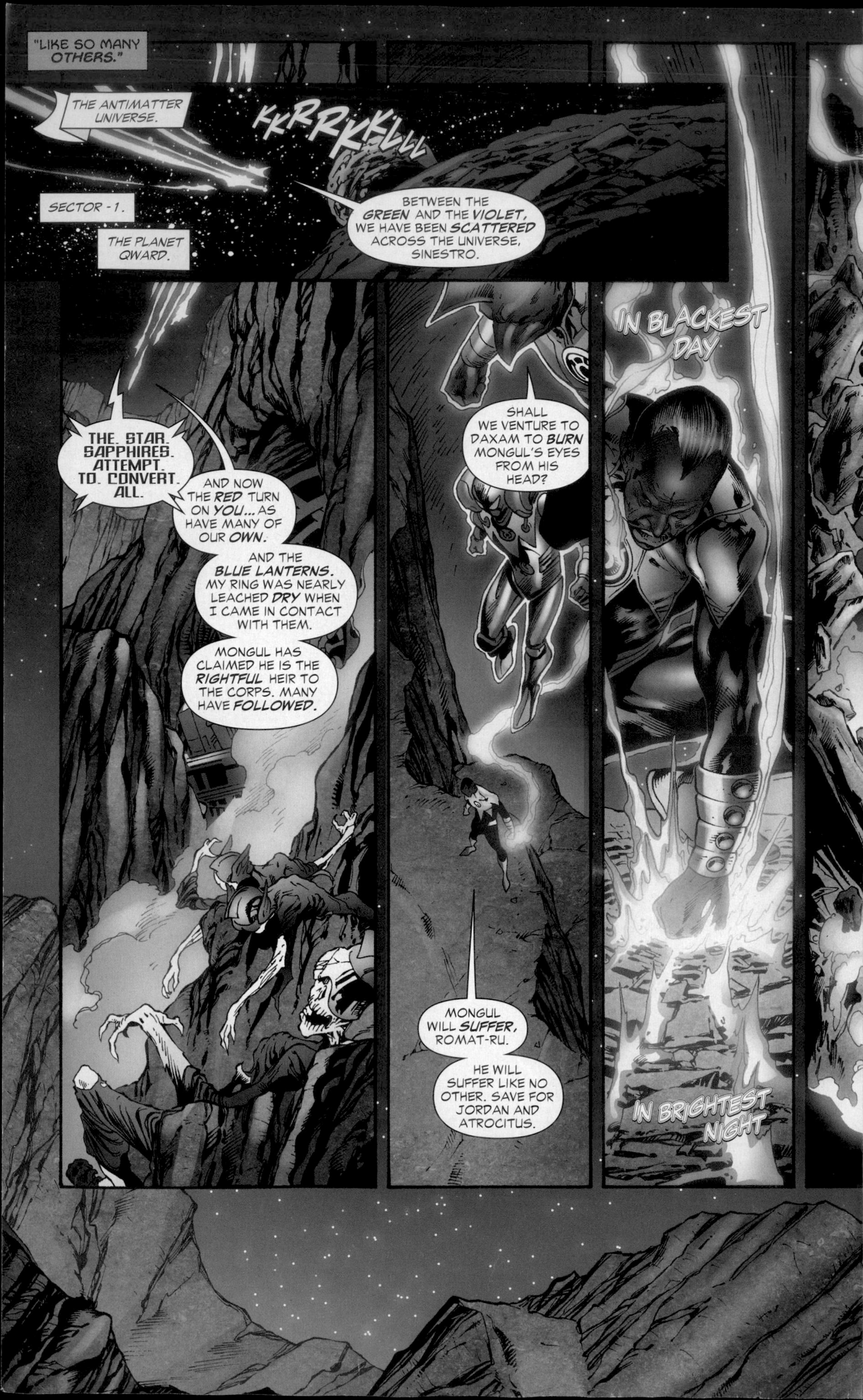

"LIKE SO MANY OTHERS."
THE ANTIMATTER UNIVERSE.
KKRRKKLLLL
SECTOR -1.
THE PLANET QWARD.
BETWEEN THE GREEN AND THE VIOLET, WE HAVE BEEN SCATTERED ACROSS THE UNIVERSE, SINESTRO.
THE. STAR. SAPPHIRES. ATTEMPT. TO. CONVERT. ALL.
AND NOW THE RED TURN ON YOU... AS HAVE MANY OF OUR OWN.
AND THE BLUE LANTERNS. MY RING WAS NEARLY LEACHED DRY WHEN I CAME IN CONTACT WITH THEM.
MONGUL HAS CLAIMED HE IS THE RIGHTFUL HEIR TO THE CORPS. MANY HAVE FOLLOWED.
SHALL WE VENTURE TO DAXAM TO BURN MONGUL'S EYES FROM HIS HEAD?
MONGUL WILL SUFFER, ROMAT-RU.
HE WILL SUFFER LIKE NO OTHER. SAVE FOR JORDAN AND ATROCITUS.
IN BLACKEST DAY
IN BRIGHTEST NIGHT

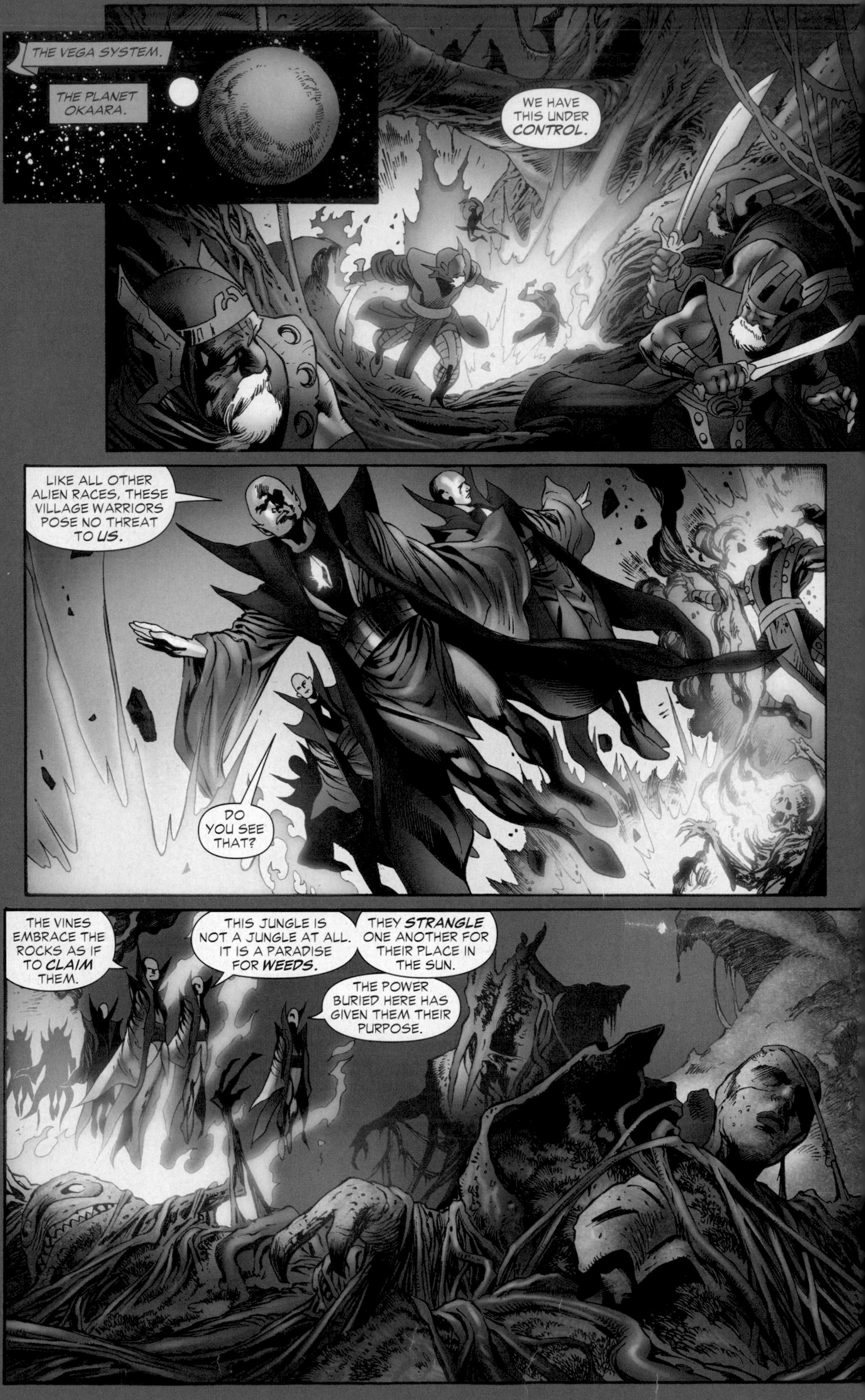
THE VEGA SYSTEM.
THE PLANET OKAARA.
WE HAVE THIS UNDER CONTROL.
LIKE ALL OTHER ALIEN RACES, THESE VILLAGE WARRIORS POSE NO THREAT TO US.
DO YOU SEE THAT?
THE VINES EMBRACE THE ROCKS AS IF TO CLAIM THEM.
THIS JUNGLE IS NOT A JUNGLE AT ALL. IT IS A PARADISE FOR WEEDS.
THEY STRANGLE ONE ANOTHER FOR THEIR PLACE IN THE SUN.
THE POWER BURIED HERE HAS GIVEN THEM THEIR PURPOSE.